The Road To Mastery

A Guidebook for Lifelong Learning

Brian L. Davis

Original Works Limited's
WISDOM WORKS SERIES

published by

WASTELAND PRESS

Wasteland Press

Louisville, KY USA
www.wastelandpress.net

The Road To Mastery
A Guidebook for Lifelong Learning
by Brian L. Davis

First Printing: March 2005

Cover Artwork
by Marston A. Jaquis

Book Design
by Brian L. Davis

ISBN: 1-933265-31-0

Printed in the U.S.A.

Library of Congress Cataloging-in-Publication Data:
Davis, Brian L., 1952–
The Road To Mastery:
a guidebook for lifelong learning/ Brian L. Davis

Acknowledgments

I am deeply grateful to the many people who contributed to the completion of this book. Your influence has grown to include all those who read this work, and to any others who may be inspired to use the ideas offered here. Thank you for believing in me.

Bill Williams, Ph.D. for planting the seed of the five levels.

George Leonard,
Michael Murphy and
Dan Millman for inspiring me to write about Mastery.

Bev Davis,
Randy Johnson,
Cindy Ewing,
Cheryl Hiltibran,
Jim Davis, Ph.D.,
Ray Yazdani,
Lynnda Upton,
Carolyn Varvel,
Johanna Gallers, Ph.D.,
Rick & Sue Davis,
Bryan Butler and
Michael Sedan for your insights, support and encouragement.

Stan and the crew at Stella's Coffee Haus in Denver for providing a wonderful place to write that encourages community.

Marty Jaquis for your artistic talents and valued friendship.

Larry Carter, Ph.D.,
Rebecca Morris and
Janet Gelernter for your critical writing advice, terrific editing skills, and continued loyal friendship.

Tim Veeley for your excellent publishing and support services.

Contents

Contacts

Please address any correspondence to the publisher at:
www.wastelandpress.net

or to the author at:
www.originalworkslimited.com

or: **www.theroadtomastery.com**

We would love to hear from you.

Please share your views of this book with us,
so we may learn from your experience.

Thank you.

> *Happiness is not in the mere possession of money;*
> *it lies in the joy of achievement,*
> *in the thrill of creative effort.*
> — *Franklin D. Roosevelt (1882 – 1945)*

Introduction:
THE FIVE LEVELS OF MASTERY

You may have heard people refer to themselves as master plumbers, or master violinists, or master teachers, or martial arts masters. Perhaps you have a Masters degree in some subject area, or a certificate or license as a master of your field. There are even books with titles that offer to teach you how to master the art of conversation, or the secrets of effective management, or the nuances of your golf game. Clearly the term *Master* in these contexts means something more than a casual acquaintance with an area of knowledge or skill. But does reading a book about mastering management skills mean the same as having a Masters degree in Management? And does having that degree qualify you as someone who has truly mastered the art of managing a business?

Probably not, and that is part of the dilemma. To make any kind of progress it helps to know where you stand, so you can then move forward toward your destination. The confusing array of meanings attached to the term *Master* doesn't help the situation, since it cannot be relied upon to determine where you are, how far you've come, or how much further there is to go. *The Road to Mastery* was written to serve as a simple and effective guide to the overall process of advancing your skills and knowledge in any area. As it turns out, there are recognizable steps or levels involved in mastery development that are common to every type of endeavor. Although the *content* of each field of study varies tremendously, the *process* of advancement in each area is surprisingly similar.

The five levels of mastery outlined here refer to *shifts* in the way the learner approaches his or her chosen discipline. There are shifts in the use of attention, shifts in thinking processes or learning methods, shifts in emphasis, and even shifts in consciousness. These shifts usually happen simply, easily, silently, and beneath your awareness. They are part of the natural progression of learning. Yet sometimes problems arise, and the smooth progress of your emerging mastery can come to a grinding halt.

The art of recognizing these subtle shifts, where and when they occur, and how to successfully negotiate them, is what this book is all about. *The Road to Mastery* provides a preview of the "learning terrain," a guide to your own personal mastery journey, and a host of tips to see you through those difficult times when your learning and enthusiasm for the whole endeavor breaks down.

The five levels of mastery outlined below describe the entire spectrum of learning, from the earliest introduction to a given topic to the highest levels of knowledge and performance that characterize mastery of the discipline. In this way, you get a map of the landscape, complete with mountain peaks, plateaus and valley floors *(the highs, middles and lows of the learning experience)*, cities and towns *(the places where people tend to stop and settle down, satisfied with their place in the world)*, the twists and turns of the road, *(the shifts in the way people experience their journey)*, and the detours and hazards that litter the roadway *(those problems and pitfalls that every traveler must avoid, surmount or endure)*.

To help you through the detours and hazards, sections of several chapters and all of Chapter 12 provide a "repair kit" to assist you in locating and recovering from the setbacks and disappointments that most people encounter. That way you can continue with your journey as far as you wish to go. Each level of the mastery process poses unique challenges that call for varying skills and different approaches to the tasks that await you. You may even find your attitude and temperament changing as you go along.

But don't worry! Most of these shifts occur spontaneously and naturally, and you'll find your personality changing along with your accumulated expertise. And that will be a good thing! As you move higher up the mastery scale, your confidence and effectiveness increase in every area of your life as you implement the dedication you've shown toward your discipline to other aspects of living. Your consciousness also broadens and deepens, bringing new levels of awareness and satisfaction to everyday life. And as you become more capable, you'll also find other exciting opportunities beckoning to you.

Overall, not a bad outcome! And all because you decided to take up some new interest and pursue it with vigor.

The first chapter, **The Road to Mastery,** begins with a look at the nature of mastery as a process, more than as a state of achievement. When viewed at its most expansive level, mastery becomes a journey of personal development and self-evolvement. Cultivating certain character traits that make the most of this process will assist you in getting as far as possible.

The second chapter, **Choosing a Destination,** deals with the topic of selecting a field to study that will be inherently rewarding to you. There are five exercises here that can help you discover your calling and feel confident in your choice. Most people think of success in terms of a single area of interest. But what if you have multiple interests, and want to excel in more than one area? Expanding your mastery journey to include several disciplines seems like a tall order, but the five key approaches included here make it all achievable.

Chapter three, **Charting Your Course,** takes you on a metaphorical journey through the landscape of learning on the way to mastery. Climb the mountains, cross the plateaus, descend into the valleys and visit the towns along the way. Learning and mastering the guitar is used as an example to illustrate the journey.

Know Your Traveling Companions (chapter four) examines the various personalities of those who travel the road to mastery, and the underlying motives they bring with them on their journey. Certain approaches take you farther than others, and you can easily see the benefits and limitations that accompany each set of intentions. Which personality is yours? What are the common characteristics that distinguish a mastery traveler from the rest of the wanderers? Since personalities aren't static, you can develop the characteristics you desire, and move beyond your current limitations to a level of achievement that truly resonates with you.

Adopting a Learning Strategy (chapter five) introduces the most popular learning arrangements and outlines their advantages and disadvantages. Selecting a strategy for learning that is appropriate for both you and your field of interest is an important step that will have far-reaching implications for your success and satisfaction with the whole mastery process.

Chapter six, **Getting Started,** deals with perhaps the most difficult part of the process—taking the first step. There is a certain amount of *inertia* to overcome at this point, and both *inspiration* and *determination* are needed to get moving and begin exploring the vast new territory that awaits you. Continuing attention to the renewal of these energies will keep you refueled and refreshed during the long voyage ahead.

As soon as you begin your journey you are now operating at **Level 1: The Novice** (chapter seven). Here is where you learn the basics of your field. Depending on the complexity of your discipline, it can take a long time to traverse this stage (which is never really complete). The time and effort you put into study and practice at this level will serve you well later on in the process.

As you internalize the basic knowledge and skills of your discipline, you move easily into **Level 2: The Adept** (chapter eight). This is where you begin to fit the bits and pieces of your earlier learning into a larger picture, combining the ingredients to produce whole, complete, successful outcomes. As you improve your ability to distinguish the important features of your learning from the lesser aspects, you begin to craft better and better results.

Once you can successfully produce some good results, it's time to demonstrate your capabilities through some sort of test, performance or competition in an arena where the results you create "count" for something. Once others are counting on you to produce results, you move into **Level 3: The Pro** (chapter nine).

You begin this process as a *Rookie,* knowing what to do, but not having a lot of "real world" experience to back it up. Since the stakes are now higher, your study quickly takes on a new urgency. You now need to develop higher quality, consistency and reliability in your results. So you dive in and start gaining more experience.

Your search for repeatable successes takes on the precision of scientific research, and refines your criteria for what constitutes acceptable results. The continued practice of the full range of knowledge and skills accumulated so far soon leads to the easy confidence and reliable performance of the *Journeyman*. Adjustments come as you search for ways to maximize your results using minimal time, effort and resources.

Going beyond the comfort of easy, repeatable results requires renewed efforts. By expanding the scope of your knowledge and applying your successful techniques in a variety of circumstances, you can advance to become an *Expert* in your field. Drawing on an extensive body of experience gained by performing under difficult circumstances, the expert learns to diagnose and solve problems in his or her field. The expert becomes the "go to" person when the chips are down.

Once you can easily and consistently produce successful results, you may be one of the few who naturally move ahead to **Level 4: The Virtuoso** (chapter ten). A subtle, but powerful shift begins at the Virtuoso level, where your knowledge and performance comes so smoothly and easily that it becomes an integrated part of who you are. As a result, you begin to interpret your discipline in your own way, specializing in some unique aspect of your field, and adding a measure of artistry to the proficiency you have already attained.

The final step to **Level 5: Master** (chapter eleven) comes when your fluidity with your material and the performance of your tasks moves beyond the artistic to the masterful, enabling you to spontaneously create new advances in your field with little apparent effort.

To master the game of tennis, for example, implies that you *rule the game.* Instead of playing within the typical limitations of other tennis players, you have somehow surpassed the game itself, and are now above it, able to steer the outcome of most any match and bend the game to your will in a powerful, yet seemingly effortless manner.

Developing such mastery is a tall order. From this brief description you can see that the level of **Master** does not come easily, and is largely populated by the champions, leaders and geniuses of each discipline.

Yet *The Road to Mastery* is available to everyone, and those with sufficient talent, energy, patience and persistence can scale the highest peaks of any endeavor, joining the great performers in their field, and achieving what most people only dream about. Your inspiration and determination light the way.

Chapter twelve, **Unpacking Your Repair Kit,** prepares you for the eventuality of something going wrong along the way. It examines the *Problems* and *Debugs* for those difficulties you are likely to encounter on your journey. The term "debug" is a common computer programmer's expression for finding and fixing any errors (or "bugs") in the software code. For our purposes here, "debugs" refers to a collection of suggested remedies for problems you may encounter. Each problem that's identified comes with a corresponding set of debugs that can help you steer past that pothole and back onto the smooth road of successful progress.

The final chapter (thirteen), **Beyond the Summit,** takes a look back over the entire mastery process from a higher perspective, and examines the shift in *purpose* that accompanies the advancement into each level. Additional insights into the mastery process are offered from the viewpoint of the teacher, as well as the learner.

At the very end of the book there is a set of two charts that summarize the processes involved in advancing through the five levels. Once you've completed reading the book, these charts can serve as a simple and valuable reference tool to consult when you need some guidance along the way.

To illustrate the concepts and principles inherent in the five levels of mastery, five different subject areas were chosen to serve as examples of the process. They span a wide range of interests, skills and talents that in different combinations touch most every avenue of human endeavor. Each area comprises both a broad topic and a specific interest area within it. They are:

Music:	playing the piano
Athletics:	basketball
Visual Arts:	drawing and painting
Trades:	the chef's world — culinary arts
Business:	management

Examining both broad topics and specific interest areas within them makes the universal nature of the mastery process more apparent. At the same time it provides examples that you can use as a model for your own interest areas. For instance, if you are taking up soccer, you can utilize the very similar process of mastering basketball as a guide to your progress. You may also find it better to draw from several examples to fit your field of interest. In becoming a woodworker or fine cabinetmaker, for instance, you might combine aspects of the artist, manager and chef examples.

The Road to Mastery was written to provide the "big picture" for all those who want to maximize progress in their chosen field. It could be considered a companion volume to any "how-to" book, course or program. While the how-to volume provides instruction in the specific knowledge and skills of your field (the *content* of your learning), this book offers an insider's guide to the whole realm of learning and accomplishment in any field (the *process* involved). The full value of the instruction you receive will only become available if you can manage your own learning process and maintain the dedicated enthusiasm of the true mastery traveler. That's where this book can help. Armed with tantalizing insight into the learning process, inspiration to light the way, and a complete set of tools and exercises, you'll be ready for the intense personal demands of your own adventures in mastery.

Woven into the mastery process is another, perhaps deeper and more valuable theme. By taking the initiative to develop some level of expertise in an area of your choosing, you expose yourself to all the most meaningful challenges that life has to offer. Traveling the road to mastery demands that you exceed your own self-imposed limitations and strive to do more than you think you can. It's an exhilarating journey that brings out the best and worst of your character, along with a deliciously rich smorgasbord of experiences that will leave you with some of the most memorable moments of your life.

If you want to live an exciting and rewarding life, travel the mastery road. There is nothing more meaningful or satisfying than the exploration of the breadth and depth of your own capabilities. Since learning is a lifelong adventure, you can use this guidebook to help you develop your full potential, in both the subject area of your choosing, and in the larger context of how this applies to the rest of your life.

Along the way in your reading you may find a number of popular sayings or expressions. Some might even call them clichés. Such phrases are used deliberately, to demonstrate that even the most mundane expressions of common sense hold a surprising amount of truth that we often ignore. While there may be "nothing new under the sun," the mastery process itself develops increasingly subtle layers of knowledge and skill that may not be obvious to the casual observer. As your mastery grows, so will your appreciation of the extraordinary intelligence and exquisite beauty hidden within the most ordinary activities and things.

This book was deliberately written as a short, compact volume that is easy to read, simple to understand, and applicable to a broad range of people and situations. As a result, the book you hold is lean, yet fully packed. So examine the ideas presented here, try them on, and use them to create your own success stories. I would dearly love to hear of your adventures in mastery (at whatever level you ascend to), and how you achieved them. Perhaps a future volume will be entitled, *Tales of Successful Journeys on The Road to Mastery.*

I hope that you find this book to be as insightful to read as I have found it to write. I am grateful and honored to contribute to your life in some small way. Enjoy your journey...

Brian L. Davis

> *Two roads diverged in a wood, and I, I took the road less traveled by, and that has made all the difference.*
> — **Robert Frost (1874 – 1963)**

Chapter 1:

The Road to Mastery
WHERE DOES IT LEAD?

In ancient times it was said that "all roads lead to Rome." Since the Romans built most of the roads in Europe, this was not a big surprise. Yet it is interesting to note that Rome is located in a valley at the mouth of the Tiber River, which empties into the Mediterranean Sea. Most of the roads, like the rivers and streams, lead downhill to Rome and the sea.

Downhill, of course, is the easy route. Gravity takes you there with little effort. And as you travel downhill, the smaller streams and roads merge to form rivers and highways. All along the way the roads become broader and smoother. The rivers become wider and deeper. More and more companions join you on the downhill journey. It is comforting to be among so many who are heading in the same direction.

Yet that very comfort comes from experiencing life from a common frame of reference, a similar place on the road. Repeated experiences, shared with others, create the foundation of ordinary, commonplace reality. As long as you remain in the valley of your common experiences, life is safe, normal and predictable. Some would say *boring.*

The road to mastery travels in the other direction. It leads to the hills, the peaks of experience, the soaring vistas above the crowd below. The road to mastery is the "road less traveled." Relatively few people venture in this direction for very long. The reason is simple—it's all uphill! All this climbing takes work, and lots of it.

To climb these mountains, you must be bold, courageous, energetic, imaginative, and fearless. And in addition to all the work involved, there are also hidden dangers. The soaring heights are accompanied by plunging depths. The peaks of experience are matched by the possibility of disappointment and despair. Wrong turns, dead ends, potholes and more await the mastery traveler. Clearly, the road to mastery is not for the faint of heart. It requires the heart of a warrior and the soul of an explorer, since your ultimate destination lies ahead, through unfamiliar territory. The road to mastery may be treacherous, but it is never boring.

What is this thing called mastery, and how is it attained? It is tempting to think of mastery as a place to long for, or a feat of accomplishment, or simply the province of those with exceptional talents and genius. Though the term Master is used here to designate a level of performance that is reserved for the highest achievers, it is more important to look at the means of arriving at the level of mastery than the specific knowledge and skills embodied by the master. In each case of master and subject area to be mastered, there is a unique combination of factors that lead to an expansion of what is known about the field, and the quality of performance used to express it. *Masters lead their colleagues into new territory.*

Yet the road to mastery is more than any of these ideas. It is a process, a becoming, a transformation. The essence of mastery may be likened to the story of the alchemists of the Middle Ages who strived to turn lead into gold. Despite the popular misconceptions involving greed and rampant materialism, those pioneering alchemists had a different purpose in mind. They were involved in a secretive process of purification, refinement and experimentation that was both personal and chemical. The process was designed to lead the alchemist to enlightenment. The goal of converting base metal into gold was both a physical and symbolic act that embodied the alchemist's transformation from an ordinary person to an enlightened master, possessing wizard-like powers and capabilities.

Similarly, mastery is a journey, more than a destination. It's an adventure lasting a lifetime, a voyage of discovery, a self-evolvement. The act of mastering a particular discipline becomes the vehicle for this evolution, a way of measuring and testing oneself along the way. Regardless of the level of success achieved, following the road to mastery is the way to a life well lived.

In striving to become better and better in your chosen field, you will struggle, make mistakes, learn from them and continue on, often in the face of difficulty and disappointment. To do this takes courage, dedication, resolve, trust, love and sacrifice. Traveling the road to mastery brings out the best of human nature and ability. Only on the road to mastery can you encounter such hardships, and by conquering them, reap such rich rewards of accomplishment.

Our modern media-driven society regularly trumpets the exploits of celebrity masters—the superstars of sports, the geniuses of science and literature, the most polished or flamboyant of artists, actors and musical performers, and the most daring and successful leaders, inventors and entrepreneurs. Ironically, this obsession with celebrities tends to discourage the rest of us from becoming masters. The gulf between the knowledge and abilities of the celebrity masters and our own budding interests seems so vast that no amount of work, or practice, or raw talent could bridge that yawning gap.

So you ask yourself, *"Why bother?"* Common sense tells us that there is only so much room at the top, and every field already has its stars, celebrities and spokespeople. "How could I possibly attain that sort of stature? The cards seem stacked against me as a newcomer. Besides, if I fail to reach star status, what is the point of all the work it takes to learn a new field? Maybe I just don't have the talent, the resources or the guts to compete with the best in the game." It all seems so hopeless that most people never bother to work toward mastery at all.

Well, the book you hold paints a completely different picture of this dismal scenario. First of all, contrary to popular belief, *there is more room at the top of your field than anywhere else!* How can this be? Look at it this way. For every major league baseball star, there are dozens of minor league players making a living at the game with modest success. And for every minor leaguer, there are hundreds more people who play organized hardball or softball in their towns, and thousands more who play occasionally at the company picnic or hit and catch with their kids.

Where is the opportunity greatest? *At the top*, where fewer people compete. The players at the highest levels of any field are the ones who make the greatest contributions, reap the biggest rewards, and find the most fulfillment.

Every field is hungry for new stars, because it is the stars who are doing new and different things in their fields, and performing at the highest levels. In fact, people *become* stars by doing something new, different or better. And newcomers have a distinct advantage in coming up with new ideas and superior performances. Because newcomers do not have the weight of tradition that comes with performing the "old" way hundreds or thousands of times, they are more flexible and daring in deriving "new and improved" methods that result in advances in their fields. Advantage: newcomer.

"What if I don't have the talent to succeed? What good will it do me to work hard and still be only a mediocre performer?"

Let's respond to these questions with another question. *What is the alternative?* If you don't put your heart and soul into developing your potential in a particular field, how will you know if you're any good at it? Look at the worst-case scenario:

The worst thing that can happen is that you discover something you have no talent for, or simply don't like. Then you will at least know enough to put your time and energy into something else. Sometimes knowing what doesn't work is just as valuable as knowing what works well.

Traveling the road to mastery embodies a challenge to learn and experiment and do your best at every stage of development. In the process you learn about yourself. You learn your strengths and weaknesses, your capabilities and your limits. You also learn how to overcome those limitations, and go as far as your natural talents and drive can take you.

This can be immensely gratifying. While you may not become

a star, the knowledge you gain from pushing yourself to the limit can only serve you well in your next endeavor. In the process you also build self-respect. That self-respect is developed each time you are willing to push yourself a little farther. You'll also gain a new perspective on life that is priceless. Here's a personal example:

When I was a young boy in grade school, I heard that I could "go out for a sport" in seventh grade. Since I was naturally athletic and a fast runner, I thought that this was a terrific idea. I'd try out for the basketball team. The only problem was, I didn't know anything about playing basketball, and my parents were of little help, since they didn't play either. So I convinced my dad to put up a hoop in the driveway and I played all summer long, shooting and dribbling every chance I had. When the tryouts for seventh grade basketball came, I did poorly, with little sense of the game and shaky skills. I just barely made the third string by hustling and working hard in practice. The coaches noticed my desire, if not my talent.

I quickly recognized that I'd have to compensate for my short height, small hands and limited jumping ability in other ways. Throughout middle and high school, I became the champion of hustle, enduring more floor burns than anyone else on the team. At home I played for hours on end, working on my shooting, ball handling and offensive moves. In practice I worked my tail off learning plays and defensive strategies to become the playmaking point guard. I studied the pros and learned some neat tricks that helped me to outplay taller, stronger, and faster opponents. After years of playing basketball in high school and later on in intramural college games and as an adult, I'd reached the peak of my talents in basketball during my mid-twenties to early thirties.

Though I was a long way from being a star, I wouldn't trade my time as a basketball player for anything. There is nothing like the feeling of hitting a clutch jumper with only seconds to play, or to steal the ball and then convert the layup at the other end of the floor, or to drill the perfect pass to a teammate as he streaks to the basket. Besides the satisfying memories, I now have an intuitive understanding of many principles of physics, body movement, teamwork, attitude and strategy that I could not have obtained any other way. But the biggest prize of all was to learn about myself. I got to explore my physical and mental limits, learn about leadership, responsibility, sacrifice, and the psychology of winning. Very valuable stuff.

Little did I know it at the time, but I was traveling the road to mastery. The discipline of basketball became my tool for learning about myself and the world. Later on, I would adopt many other such tools in what has become a type of spiritual exploration. *The road to mastery became my road to self-mastery.*

Diligently learning the knowledge and skills of any field allows you to explore and expand the extent of your powers as a human being. You begin to identify with your discipline, and it becomes a part of how you define yourself. Having such solid reference points for self-identity is an essential ingredient for developing confidence and effectiveness in dealing with the world.

Being able to say, "I am an accountant," or "I am a tennis player," or "I play the saxophone," is the beginning of the process of knowing who you are. This ongoing process involves the discovery of just how much you can accomplish in each realm, and which other realms might be interesting to explore. By piecing together a patchwork of areas where you have some level of mastery, you develop a unique outlook on life that will feed your creativity, and deliver the deep satisfaction that comes from performing successfully in a variety of fields.

What does it take to become a master of my field? There are several qualities that students (and that's all of us) can cultivate to assist them in becoming masters. The degree to which you develop these character traits determines, to a large extent, how far you are able to progress along the road to mastery. The primary difference between champions and geniuses and their lesser counterparts is not so much their level of natural talent, nor their physical gifts, nor even their accomplishments, but rather their strength of character.

Examples: Albert Einstein, perhaps the most universally acknowledged of all geniuses, flunked algebra in high school.

Famous Dutch painter Vincent Van Gogh created over 1500 images in his ten-year career, yet sold only one painting during his lifetime. Physicist and chemist Marie Curie overcame tremendous economic and societal pressures to earn her two Nobel prizes. Boston Celtic great Larry Bird was neither fast nor a good jumper, yet he is considered by many to be one of the best forwards ever to play basketball. Composer Ludwig van Beethoven wrote his hauntingly beautiful Ninth Symphony after he had become completely deaf. American bicycle racer Lance Armstrong, who nearly died from testicular cancer at age 25, recovered and came back to win the Tour de France six times in a row (so far).

The champions and masters of every field have tremendous character strength. Developing the following character traits will help you scale each level of mastery. The definitions from *Random House Webster's College Dictionary*, and other comments may provide some additional insight into the value of each trait:

Confidence: (from the Latin word for **trust**) *belief in oneself and one's powers or abilities without a display of arrogance or conceit; self-confidence; self-reliance; assurance; full trust.* Self-confidence comes from repeatedly recognizing and reinforcing your own success.

Courage: (from the French word for **heart**) *the quality of mind or spirit that enables a person to face difficulty, danger, pain, etc. without fear; bravery.* Courage is the ability to get out there and perform despite your fear and uncertainty.

Desire: (from the Latin word meaning **to long for**) *a longing or craving, as for something that brings satisfaction; hunger; a strong wish for something that is, or seems to be, within reach.* Desire is best fueled by identifying a realistic goal and deeply visualizing the scene where you attain and enjoy that goal.

Detachment: (from the French word meaning **to separate**) *aloofness, disinterest; not involved or concerned.* In this sense, detachment from the outcome of your efforts makes it easier to make mistakes and then learn from them.

Discipline: (from the Latin word for **disciple**) *1. activity,* *exercise or regimen that develops or improves a skill; training. 2. a branch of instruction or learning.* 3. The ability to make a choice and stick with that choice in the face of other temptations. 4. A set of exercises performed at regular intervals over a period of time.

Gratitude: (from the Latin word meaning **pleasing**) *the quality or feeling of being warmly or deeply appreciative of kindness or benefits received.* If you come to see each experience (whether successful or not) as a gift, then being grateful welcomes ever more experiences that you can learn from.

Mindfulness: (from the old English word meaning **image, model or remembrance**) *the quality of being attentive or aware; to perceive or notice; to care about or feel concern.* Being extra attentive and perceptive speeds learning and rewards you with deeper and richer experiences.

Patience: (from the middle English word meaning **to suffer**) *quiet, steady perseverance; diligence; the ability to suppress restlessness or annoyance with delay.* Progress does not always come as quickly as you would like, so be patient with yourself and the process of learning. It will all come in due time.

Perseverance: (from the middle English word meaning **tenacity or persistence**) *the determined continuance in a state or course of action, in spite of difficulties, obstacles or discouragement.* Perseverance is perhaps the most valuable of all of these characteristics, one of the undisputed keys to success.

Playfulness: (from the old English word meaning **to dance or rejoice**) *the quality of being full of play or fun; pleasantly humorous or jesting.* Playfulness arises from being detached from the outcome of your actions. Being mindful of your actions creates a great sense of care and precision with your performances. If you can let go of your concern about the results you create, a playful quality will emerge in your performances that adds an energetic, smooth flow that will surprise and delight you. Life is not serious.

Cultivate these qualities as you proceed with your learning, and your experiences will become much more rewarding, while your personal sense of mastery will grow and expand effortlessly.

> *The self is not something ready-made, but something in continuous formation through choice of action.*
> — *John Dewey (1859 – 1952)*

Chapter 2:

Choosing a Destination
WHAT FIELD SHOULD YOU PURSUE?

Before setting off on a new trip, experienced travelers start by picking a destination, then finding an accurate map of the area. Next comes the purchase of a good guidebook (or the services of an actual guide), and a visit to the store to outfit themselves with all the equipment and supplies needed for the trip. Studying the map and guide book will help you plan your route, making sure you hit all the really interesting spots while avoiding the dumps, dives and the dreary, desolate roads.

So, where do you want to go? You may have heard this question many times before. Most often it's in the form of "what do you want to do with your life?" or "what do you do for fun?" or "what do you want to be when you grow up?" Many people balk at this question. It stumps them because they feel trapped into making a life-altering decision on the spot. Yet, chances are that you've put a great deal of thought into this topic.

The problem is that you may well be undecided—torn between choosing one of several possible careers, hobbies, sports, arts, instruments or crafts. If you have little experience with the areas you are considering, you simply cannot make a valid decision. You don't have enough information! You can either dive in and try your hand at any of the choices that present themselves and see which one works for you, or if the decision involves a great deal of time and money (like a career decision), then you may want more information before you start.

So relax. First of all, whatever decision you make, it's not all that wrenching. If you choose incorrectly, you can always choose again. The big fear is that if you fail, your life will come tumbling down around you. Of course, that's possible if you let it happen. But it certainly doesn't have to be that way.

Part of the process of traveling the road to mastery is to adopt the attitude of the explorer. The explorer knows that he will encounter many wrong turns and setbacks in his travels. *But he doesn't care!* That's part of the fun of it. Because even on the most disastrous route, he knows that he will experience amazing new adventures and stumble upon unexpected treasures along the way, if he just keeps his eyes, mind and heart open to all the possibilities. It is that unexpected quality—the surprises—that makes each journey an adventure worth savoring.

Now if it really doesn't matter what you choose, how do you make a decision? The answer to that question is easier than it looks. Just go by *feel.* At some deeper level you already *know* which one to choose. The task is to get in touch with the part of you that already knows. What you are looking for are feelings of *inspiration, excitement, passion, mystery and simple enjoyment.* If you do not have those feelings operating while performing in your chosen field, you simply will not have what it takes to go very far. The reason is that those feelings mentioned above are your *fuel.* Without them you will soon run out of steam and either give up, or become bored, irritable or resentful.

This is what happened to most of those people who are unhappy with their work. They made the wrong choice, and did not recognize the warning signs telling them that they should look elsewhere for work satisfaction. At some point they felt *stuck.* They were stuck with taking the wrong job in the first place (because they "had to") or stuck in that job because they didn't see a way out of it.

[Getting out of *stuck* states is a lengthy topic that is well beyond the scope of this book. If you are *stuck,* consult Paul Scheele's book and audiotape course *Natural Brilliance.*]

Don't let this happen to you. Here are a series of exercises you can use to tap into your latent decision-making powers. Give them a workout and see what happens. What you are looking for in all cases are feelings of *inspiration, excitement, passion, mystery and simple enjoyment.* As an example, let's say you are trying to decide between four careers that appeal to you: becoming a photographer, medical doctor, rock climber, or computer graphics specialist. (Don't laugh! You'd be surprised how many people have such widely varying interests that call to them.)

CAREER DECISION EXERCISES

1. Find some people who are already doing each of the jobs you are interested in, and are happy with their profession. Talk with them about their experiences. Follow them around and get a feel for the everyday tasks that they perform, and how you would feel if you were the one in this position. Take notes. Ignore your internal commentary about how you don't have the knowledge or skills to do this or that task. Look for the feelings mentioned above.

2. Make a list of all your responses to the following statement: **I am happiest when I am doing** _____. Fill in the blank with as many responses as you can. Do not censor yourself in the process. It doesn't matter how silly or inappropriate they may seem. Continue until you have at least 20 responses.

3. Repeat the process above using this new statement. Again, list as many responses as you can (at least 20), without censoring yourself. **If I knew I couldn't fail, I would do** _____.

4. Examine the results of these first three exercises.
   a. Were there any red flags from the first exercise? For instance, maybe you were always interested in medicine, but you found the experience of spending all your time in a hospital with desperately ill people to be depressing. Are there alternate ways to be a doctor that do not involve hospital care? Make adjustments to your career choices to fit your findings and your temperament.

   b. Did aspects of your career interests from the first exercise appear in the next two exercises? If not, then perhaps your initial choices were not all that exciting to you. **c.** Do any of your responses in the second or third exercise bring up some exciting possibilities that you hadn't considered? Add the new interesting responses to your short list of possibilities. Let's say you remember that you always wanted to be a fireman as a kid, so you add that to your list of photographer, doctor, rock climber and computer graphics specialist.

d. If you still have several possibilities that seem equally exciting to you, see if you can combine the most desirable aspects of each into a new or existing profession.

In our example, perhaps you could be part of an emergency rescue team flying into remote places where you would have to use your climbing skills, or as an EMT that accompanied firemen on their calls. You might even do research or reporting by photographing the accidents you are called to handle and then use your computer skills to touch up the photos, catalogue the results and enhance your research or reporting. Be creative with this process and see what you can come up with. Involve friends, family and mentors. Most everyone will enjoy contributing to your puzzle. Often, those close to you will recognize aspects of your personality, interests and capabilities that may elude you.

5. Spend some quiet time alone with no distractions. Close your eyes. Take each of your remaining career possibilities, and one by one, imagine yourself in the middle of doing your work. In your mind's eye, picture yourself doing the most exciting parts of your work. Feel the feelings that go with the experience. Feel the excitement, the fun, the fear, the challenge, and the demanding nature of your work. Feel yourself being up to the task, diving in to perform perfectly under pressure. Register your feelings on your own personal emotional response meter for each of your choices.

After doing these exercises, you will surely be able to tell which one scores highest, and then your choice will be easy. Even if you still have several choices that beckon to you, there's nothing that says you can't do more than one!

THE DILEMMA OF THE MULTI-TALENTED
This previous exercise brings up a sticky little point that has proved to be troubling for many people. How can you be successful

at more than one thing at the same time?

One of the things that you may have noticed is that the vast majority of people who are the leaders, champions, and masters of their disciplines are very tightly focused on their field. Many do almost nothing else. They eat, drink, work, play and sleep with it.

Take a look at people like Bill Gates, Rupert Murdoch, Sam Walton, Richard Branson and Martha Stewart in business; or Lance Armstrong, Tiger Woods, and Venus or Serena Williams in sports. These are the 800-pound gorillas of their fields, and each is single-mindedly dedicated to dominating their fields by becoming the best there is. They do one thing and they do it very, very well.

This is the model of success that most of us grew up with, and the one promoted by almost everyone. It goes something like this:

Find something that you are really good at, and concentrate on doing that one thing until you become a master of it. This is how you become successful and happy in your life.

Sounds like great advice, and clearly the highly successful people mentioned above took that advice and ran with it. But this just doesn't work for everyone. Some people find that if they concentrate on only one thing for a lengthy period of time, they go stir-crazy! Many folks need lots of variety in their lives to feed their restless sense of curiosity about the world around them. They want to excel in lots of areas.

Fortunately, there are plenty of examples of people who excel in several fields at once. The classic example is Leonardo da Vinci, who seemed to be able to do it all. In addition to being the famous painter of the Mona Lisa, he also was a superb sculptor, inventor, scholar, medical illustrator, weapons and defense systems designer, and political advisor. But don't forget people like Ben Franklin, Thomas Edison, Steve Martin, Oprah Winfrey, and countless others who display impressive versatility.

Most of the multi-talented successful people have managed to parlay their success in one area into a similar level of success in other areas. Brilliant inventors (like Edison, Alexander Graham

Bell, and Henry Ford) became successful entrepreneurs and then shrewdly dominant business people. World-class skiers and speedskaters (like Eric Heiden, Sheila Young, Greg LeMond, and Jacques Villeneuve) became winning cyclists and Formula 1 racecar drivers. Award-winning actors (like Clint Eastwood, Rob Reiner, Forest Whittaker, George Clooney, Ed Burns, and Penny Marshall) became writers, directors or producers of hit movies or TV shows. The list of people who have become successful in multiple fields could go on and on.

How do they do it? One key seems to be the ability to find a connecting thread to weave its way through all the different fields where you want to excel. By following that connecting thread, you can see where knowledge and skills learned in one area become applicable to the next area. Transferring skills from one musical instrument to another, or one sport to another may be obvious, but some crossover possibilities may not jump out at you.

The connection between being a doctor, photographer, rock climber and computer graphics specialist (from the earlier example) sure wasn't obvious. Yet the combination of some of those skills into a new and perhaps different field may be the key to staying stimulated and increasing your overall satisfaction with work and life. *Looking for the connections* is clearly one of the keys to success in multiple areas. Applying those connections in creative ways can add another new dimension to your success.

Another key is the ability to *concentrate on one thing at a time.* If focusing on one area to the exclusion of all else is an effective approach, we can simply apply that idea to multiple areas by successively and sequentially concentrating on each area. Studying medicine diligently for several hours, then taking a break to go rock climbing in the hills can be a great way to mix up your activities and renew your energy and passion for each discipline. This works especially well when the activities use varying physical, mental and emotional contexts. That way, one activity can be the "antidote" to the other.

This ability to jump from one activity to another depends on creating some "closure" with the first activity before moving on to the next one. If the medical student does not feel complete with her studies before venturing out to go rock climbing, all she will think about is the unfinished work she has left behind, and those thoughts will not only haunt her through the rest of the day, but may distract her enough to cause a critical lapse in concentration or judgment that could cause a fall.

If she can set a small goal for her studies that can be completed in the time allotted, and represent a worthy and satisfying advancement, then when she is done, she's done! She could say to herself, "I'll study and take notes on Chapter 7 this morning, then go climb Sheet Rock in the afternoon."

This approach can work, because she has set a definite goal in each area, and allotted a definite (but not rigid) time for each to be accomplished. When the first goal is complete, then she is free to focus 100% of her attention on the second goal. And focusing 100% of your attention on the activity at hand is the key method that **all** successful people employ. This ability to easily shift attention from one area to another is crucial, and it depends upon completing each task before going on to the next.

This highlights a problem that many people face—trying to do everything at once! This only creates confusion, scattered attention, limited success and frustration. Relax. If you have pending demands or goals in each area and you feel the need to handle all of them at once, slow down. *Break up your tasks or goals into smaller pieces* that can be handled in shorter amounts of time. This third key enables you to accomplish a little in each area so that progress is evident in all of your disciplines. Don't underestimate the difference this kind of reinforcement can bring.

[Using a system like Steven Covey's "First Things First" approach from his book, *The Seven Habits of Highly Effective People,* can help make this a routine for you.]

The topic of reinforcement brings us to the fourth key to success in multiple areas. *Reward yourself!* Once you've accomplished each small goal you set (for the day, week, etc.) make sure that you take the time and effort to congratulate and reward yourself for work well done. It is a natural human tendency to be critical of yourself. Too bad there isn't that same natural tendency to acknowledge your successes. You have to create that habit on your own.

By making it important to recognize and reward your own accomplishments, you increase your confidence, your consistency and your passion to continue along the path you've chosen. These rewards don't have to be elaborate or involved. Just a pat on the back, literally or figuratively, can be surprisingly effective. In fact, if you set up the reward ahead of time, then you won't forget it. For instance, our medical student can set it up so that when she finishes studying Chapter 14, she can go for a walk in the park with a friend and take pictures.

Did you notice how this reward is set up to include another one of her interests (photography)? If you are truly excited about each of the fields you've chosen for yourself, then the mere prospect of accomplishing something in one area can be a great motivation to continue that sense of progress in another area. Sneaky, huh?

If you are clever, you can set it up so that the reward for one accomplishment is the start of another, in a sort of circular round-robin fashion. To continue with our medical student's photographic walk in the park, she can come home and download the images to her computer, having some fun tweaking and editing the images in Photoshop© to enhance their artistic merit. As one of her editing tasks, she could create close-ups of various body parts to use in a parlor game for her medical study group. The game could be to name all the organs, bones and muscles involved in each image. Coming full circle, she is back to studying medicine again!

The final key is to *be creative and have fun.* It has been shown that you actually use more of your brain when you are being spontaneous and enjoying yourself. If you are not having fun doing what you love to do, then something is terribly wrong. Usually, the slide into "no-fun" happens when you start to take things too seriously. *Remember, it is your effort that is important.* The results you create will come of themselves.

Sometimes the results are terrific, and just what you are looking for. Other times the results will fall short of the mark and need to be revised. Take it easy on yourself. You have complete control of the effort you invest. You *don't* have complete control over the results you obtain. So don't beat yourself up when you don't win all the prizes right away! Relax, be playful, and explore the possibilities in a creative way.

Of course, these five keys to success in multiple areas are equally applicable to success in a single area. Since the remainder of this book is oriented toward developing mastery in a single area, it is useful to note that you can apply all of these ideas and processes to multiple interest areas as well.

> *I did not know the exact route myself, but steered by the lay of the land...*
>
> — *Henry David Thoreau (1817 – 1862)*

Chapter 3:

Charting Your Course

TRAVERSING THE LEARNING LANDSCAPE

Now that you've chosen a field to explore, it's time to take a look at the map. What's ahead on your journey to mastery? Where do the roads go? What does the terrain look like? Where are the featured attractions and the places to avoid? Let's take a metaphorical trip along the road to mastery, and see.

The journey to mastery typically starts out on a highway in the valley, while you are busy traveling to some other destination. At this point you haven't yet decided to take up your new discipline. Then suddenly the clouds part and you catch a glimpse of an alluring mountain peak. The light hits the slopes just right, and its beauty calls out to you. At that very moment, you are struck with an overwhelming desire to climb the mountain and stand upon its peak. You can just imagine the view from up there. How much more you could see!

You can also feel the exhilaration of the climb to the top, and the satisfaction inherent in knowing that YOU scaled this peak. And as you stare, transfixed with the beauty of the mountain and the power of the idea of climbing it, you notice a little road winding up the side of the hill. This is the moment of inspiration.

You realize that there is something worth doing, that YOU could be the one to do it, and that a path exists that will take you close to your goal. All the ingredients are in place for you to embark on your journey.

In my case as a young boy contemplating the sport of

basketball, I was drawn to the beauty and power of the game as I watched the pros play on television. Yet it never really dawned on me that I could become a *real* basketball player, like those I saw on TV. It took the announcement of tryouts for the seventh-grade team to awaken that possibility. It was my moment of inspiration.

The word ***inspiration*** literally means *to breathe life into*. It is the realization that there exists something that is immensely desirable to do, and that what previously seemed impossible or unavailable is now available and beckoning to you. Inspiration breathes life into an idea so that it advances from an idle dream to a force powerful enough to move you to action. It's "an idea whose time has come."

As soon as you take action you begin the journey to mastery. Let's say that you are inspired to play the guitar. You go to a concert featuring your favorite guitarist. It turns out that he is even more amazing in person than on his CDs. One song after another, and the music gets better and better. His lush and powerful playing manages to evoke emotions in you that you didn't know existed. In the excitement, you vow to yourself that some day **you** will play the guitar like that!

Then, a few weeks later, as you are rummaging through the attic looking for some camping gear, you find an old guitar belonging to a relative, just sitting there gathering dust. *Ka-Ching!* Your path of opportunity unfolds before you.

The first thing you are likely to do is to plink around on the old instrument, just to see if you can recreate the melody of a favorite song from your guitarist idol. Perhaps you are successful. Perhaps not. These first exploratory steps are a hit and miss proposition. Teaching yourself is like traveling along one of those local roads that parallel the interstate highway. For a while, at least, the two-lane road stays parallel, and then it wanders off to some tiny village, and around all the little hills and dales. It may actually go in the same direction as the interstate, but it is almost always slower, bumpier and fraught with blind curves and hidden hazards.

If you're teaching yourself, you're "reinventing the wheel."

At some point you realize that thousands of other folks have already learned what you are now learning, and there probably exists some simple, easy-to-follow method that will teach you what you need to know. So you do some investigation and find a book, a tape or CD set, a course, a tutor, or a program of study, and now you have given over the task of teaching to someone who knows more than you do. Good move. You have now hopped over to the interstate.

On the interstate, things move along smoothly and swiftly. As a *Novice* you are learning the fundamentals of playing the guitar. In most cases there are plenty of other people around you traveling in the same direction, learning the same things that you are. It feels safe and comfortable on the highway, but kind of dull and predictable. You can just set the cruise control and go through the motions, learning chords and strumming and picking techniques.

The trouble is, there are always some folks who go blazing by at 90 miles per hour, momentarily sending waves of panic through your system as you struggle along at somewhere near the speed limit. To make matters worse, the road has plunged into the forest and you can't see much of anything except trees for mile after mile. You haven't seen a road sign since the last town, which was quite some way back. Your doubts start to haunt you. *Why am I so slow? Can't I go any faster? Why can she learn this stuff so easily, while it takes me forever? Where am I going anyway? Is this really the right road? What's the point of all these chord progressions? I still can't play a tune...*

Discouraged, most people give up along the way. Their car overheats, breaks down or runs out of gas. Some simply turn around and go back the way they came, deciding that the guitar is not for them. It's just too hard, or takes too long to see the progress they had hoped for.

But you are one of the lucky ones. You find all you need in the nearby town, and return to the highway, refueled and refreshed. At last you emerge from the forest as the road starts up the mountain. You've moved through the Novice level and are now starting to put the chords together into recognizable songs. Things are looking up, literally. You peer out over the dense forest where you've been, and see how much you've accomplished. Amazing really. But now the road is getting steeper and progress is slower. You've moved off the interstate and onto a local road, which is narrower and still thick with traffic. The simple songs present little difficulty, but the ones you are really interested in playing are much harder. Who knew?

You redouble your efforts. Now that you have the notes and chords down, there is the matter of timing. Ugh! Finally you manage to play the song the way it's supposed to be played. You've peaked! At the top of the mountain you take a moment to stop and check out the view. Wonderful. You did it! You've reached the summit of the *Adept* level.

But as you look around, you realize that the mountain you have just scaled is merely one of the foothills of the range. The REAL mountains are far ahead, and the only way to get there is to go down...

From here the road descends around the far side of the mountain and on to the plateau of the *Pro* level. There are medium-sized towns all along the route, with several roads to choose from that lead through all the mountains in the range. You've left behind the big cities of the valley and plains. Those cities are inhabited by the folks who decided to drop out of their guitar studies, or by those who never played in the first place. Once in a while the former guitarist may bring out his instrument and play a few songs at a party when people are too drunk to care. But mostly, the guitar remains in its case in the closet.

The inhabitants of the medium-sized towns on the plateau are at a higher level. They are the journeymen. They have learned a limited repertoire of songs and have practiced playing those songs many times. They play regularly, and are really quite good. Perhaps you've seen them play at local bars, coffee houses or other venues. Some make a living with their guitar. Some play their gigs as a sideline, or as a hobby. For the most part, the journeymen (and women) are happy playing the songs they know and love. They are comfortable. They have settled down.

But you are determined to become a better player. Another mountain looms ahead. The only road available is a narrow county road, still paved but kind of lumpy. Slowly, painstakingly, you ascend to the level of the expert. Your playing technique is nearly flawless, and you can deliver most any song beautifully with just a couple of practice sessions. At last you can play the songs that inspired you when you first began. In retrospect, it doesn't seem all that difficult. You can even see some of the flaws in your idol's technique, and wonder why he never corrected them.

You pass through a small town straddling a ridge near the top of the mountain. This town is where the session players live, along with the backup players of all the better bands. These are the pros, who can pound out their music without fail, anytime, anyplace, and with any kind of audience. Most live very satisfying lives, playing with some of the best musicians around. Others are moody, restless and resentful. They look around and see that they are not the stars of their bands, yet they feel that they are better players than many of the marquee names they work with. They may even be right.

On the far side of town the road begins to drop again into a deep ravine formed by a raging mountain river. Many little streams flowing from the tall mountains up ahead feed the river. The descent is dizzying and steep. Over a bridge and on to the other side of the river, you notice that the road no longer goes up the mountain, but follows the banks of the river down into the distance. Giant mountains surround the bowl of a valley you've just entered, their snowy peaks hidden in the clouds. There are no real roads leading up these mountains, only a few barely recognizable paths left by deer and elk that disappear into the forested slopes.

You take a while to choose one of the paths that looks promising, and start ahead. Progress is slow and erratic as you feel your way along though the tall trees and dense underbrush, sensing which path to take. Some of your choices end up leading nowhere and you have to retrace your steps. Gradually you are developing your own guitar style, experimenting with different techniques, styles and genres, and letting your mood, personality, and a mysterious inner voice guide you.

Suddenly you break through the forest and emerge above the tree line. Ahead is a gorgeous little lake tucked into the side of the mountain. The view to the valley below is breathtaking. The setting is so beautiful that you begin to plot out a scheme to make this very spot your home. You have reached the peak of the *Virtuoso* level, with your own unique vision, playing style and musical character. As time goes on you continue to round out your budding style, building a repertoire of songs to give life to your new guitar form. The home you build by the lake takes much of your time, and you revel in your success as a guitarist. The music you are making seems to express some deep essence of who you are, and to your delight, other people are drawn to it as well.

Then one summer day you are relaxing on the deck of your mountain home, and you look behind you and remember that there are still mountain peaks all around that you have yet to climb. What wonders could they bring? What interesting new terrain lies beyond? Once again inspired, you vow to continue your climb to the tall peaks, and it's time for new adventures.

You round up supplies for the ascent. Since there are no roads or paths to follow and the slopes are very steep, you will need to hike with climbing gear this time. The ascent is arduous and the air is thin, so you find yourself tiring easily. You are not as young as you used to be. Yet your determination is strong to forge ahead and make new discoveries. After what seems like an eternity, the final rise is crested and you stand atop the mountain's summit.

Now the view to the valley below is even more amazing than before. You can see far into the distance in all directions. Beyond this range are the other mountain ranges, valleys and plains of faraway lands. Where the horizon meets the sky, you glimpse a deeper blue that just might be the sea. Gazing out over the landscape below inspires further creativity within you. The music you are now making is as breathtaking as the view. Audiences sit stunned at your concerts before rousing into thunderous standing ovations. You have become a *Master.*

Stories are told and books are written about you and your musical gifts, as your exquisite style becomes legendary. Yet each time you play, it all seems kind of mysterious. The magical sounds that flow forth from your guitar erupt like some dormant volcano that you have managed to tap into. Though your control over the strings is impeccable, there appears to be a hidden source that, in your best moments, takes over and plays with power and grace that is dazzling. You've felt tantalizing moments of this mysterious power for a long time now, and that, more than any call of fame or glory or riches, has spurred you on.

Long after you've retired from the spotlight, you play on in the quiet solitude of the lakeside setting, teasing the magic from the strings. When you pass on, the home you made becomes a shrine to your musical contributions, attracting musical pilgrims from near and far...

> *Travel only with thy betters or thy equals; if there are none, travel alone.*
> — *The Dhammapada (The teachings of Buddha)*

Chapter 4:

Know Your Traveling Companions
EXAMINING THE LEARNING PERSONALITIES

The titles of each level of mastery (Novice, Adept, Pro, Virtuoso and Master) refer to the kind of performance characteristics you aspire to within each stage of development. Each stage has a particular set of learning goals, characteristics and processes, while spanning a range of achievement. Thus, while people in the Pro stage are all going through a similar learning process, their range of achievement varies widely. At one end is the Rookie guitarist just starting out with new gigs, who may stumble through the set. In the middle is the routine playing of the Journeyman, and at the far end of the Pro stage is the flawless perfectionism of the consummate professional—the Expert.

The mastery process described in this book is not always the sort of linear climb that the story told in the previous chapter might imply. It is quite possible to advance to the next level in some areas and lag behind in others. For instance, your strumming and picking could be coming along nicely, while learning proper chord selection is proving troublesome. Don't be too concerned by these disparities. Each person learns at his or her own speed and intensity. Pay close attention to the upcoming chapter that corresponds to the level you are working on, and look for the hints that will help you advance.

Travelers on the road to mastery bring their own attitudes and approaches to learning their new subject area. Some of those attitudes and approaches serve to limit and define their possibilities for advancement and achievement. This assortment of personalities and approaches reflect the different reasons people have for undertaking their journey in the first place.

Below are snapshots of the ten types of mastery travelers you'll encounter: *The Tourist, The Settler, The Homebody, The Guide, The Hunter, The Refugee, The Entertainer, The Explorer, The Conqueror* and *The Warrior.* Which one are you?

The Tourist travels for the purpose of being entertained. Tourists head for new destinations to "see the sights," observe the locals, experience the attractions, and gather mementos of their holiday. Their travel is strictly a visit, with no intention to involve themselves in the problems or concerns of the natives. They are there primarily to observe. It's all very temporary.

Mind you, there is nothing wrong with being a tourist. Everyone can benefit from a short excursion to new surroundings once in a while to relax and enjoy what other people and places have to offer. Perhaps the trip will stimulate new ideas, or at least provide an escape from the humdrum routines of regular life. Sometimes, the whole experience can be quite thrilling. It's a big world out there, and there's clearly much more to see and do than any one person can experience. So the tourist's attitude is like that of a diner at the buffet line. *I'll have a little of this, and a little of that...*

The tourist's approach to learning is usually quite casual. They have decided to "try out" a new area of interest, just to get the flavor of the subject. If a Tourist were learning the guitar, she would steer herself to the fun portions of playing the instrument. Since she doesn't plan to stick around for long, she will have little patience for the long hours of practice it takes to become really good at it. She would eagerly accept a bit of tutoring so she could get up to speed quickly and play a few of her favorite songs. After that, the thrill wears off quickly, and she's on to something else.

The Settler has a different purpose. When settlers travel, it's to find a place to call home. Using a combination of searching and exploring, they eagerly and purposefully stride ahead, scanning the landscape, looking for the ideal spot to build their home. They may not be sure of what they are looking for, but they will know it when they find it.

As learners, settlers begin enthusiastically, absorbing as much as they can, looking for a "fit" for themselves. The latent question is, "Can I be happy and satisfied doing this?" They are really looking for comfort. If they don't find it comfortable doing this new discipline, then they drop it and look elsewhere. If they do find it comfortable, then they adopt it and make it their own.

The journeyman guitar player might be a good example. He can play well enough to satisfy himself, his employer or the other members of the band, and those who pay to hear him play, and stays at that comfort level for as long as it is rewarding. When he gets bored with the songs he plays, he can invent variations of them, or learn some more interesting music.

The Homebody never wanted to travel in the first place. He was content to be where he was, and thinks that the whole idea of going someplace new is a threat to what he knows and loves. After all, if you are pleased with where you are, why move? It is the travelers who are always stirring up discontent by never being satisfied with what they have. The homebody doesn't want to learn anything new. Homebodies have spent considerable time arranging their lives "just so," and they don't want to hear about any new ideas or information that might rock the boat. They are content, or at least comfortable with their pain.

When traveling, homebodies quickly become the baggage of the trip. They are the ones to resist every suggestion, and use their considerable inertia to drag the group to a halt. The only reason they are on the journey at all is because "somebody made them come along."

The Homebody guitarist only wants to play the songs he knows, in the style and tempo that he prefers. Anything else is some sort of heresy. He can't understand why anyone would like to listen to or play other music in other styles. He's no fun. If the group of travelers is to survive their journey with a homebody aboard, their only hope is to either convert the homebody to one of the other personalities, or jettison the baggage that he represents.

The Guide is the opposite. She just likes the whole idea of traveling. In fact, guides like traveling so much that they want to share the experience with others. They are fascinated with every facet of the terrain. Again and again they go out and hike every trail, swim every lake and paddle every stream in the area. Soon they become experts in their field, knowing all the details of their locale. Their enthusiasm spills over to other people, and they find themselves teaching, coaching or guiding the newcomers.

Like the settlers, the guides are enthusiastic learners, but their concern soon turns to "becoming the expert," and they corner a small area of the field they are learning as their own little fiefdom. Like the settlers, they too are seeking comfort. For the guides, comfort lies in being known as the knowledgeable ones in their subjects. The urge to look further ahead and explore new frontiers dwindles. The guides end up teaching guitar lessons to the newcomers, or organizing and preserving the history of a particular guitar form.

The Hunter has ulterior motives for traveling. He wants to capture a certain aspect of what he is learning and use it for some other purpose than its primary intent. Hunters have little use for the remaining depth and breadth of the field. For instance, the hunter as guitar player might want to learn enough so that he can play that dramatic soaring riff that some famous guitarist uses as a signature piece in his concerts. The hunter wants to bag a trophy to impress his friends and associates. His skill level often reaches a very high point in that one narrow area he's interested in. But the one-dimensional aspects of his learning will show through when asked to perform in some other related area. He may struggle trying to play less difficult songs that require different techniques.

The opposite personality of the hunter is **The Refugee.** The refugee is or was *being hunted.* They are folks who are fleeing from some other situation, and are looking for a refuge in a new area of learning. Perhaps the last situation was too limiting, or too psychologically or physically taxing, or they felt persecuted by the others in their field. Now they are looking for a place where they can thrive. Using our guitar example, perhaps the budding violinist found the orchestra setting to be too confining and rigorously competitive, so she takes up the guitar, where she can use some of the skills she's learned in a more laid-back environment. In this fresh setting she may be able to relax more, and enjoy her slowly developing expertise as a guitarist.

The Entertainer is usually a fun-loving sort of person, and perhaps a bit of a show-off as well. He likes to be the center of attention, and developing an area of expertise enables him to gather a crowd who will shower him with the attention he craves. Entertainer personalities are the life of the party, and they know that if they are going to command attention from the group, they had better be good at what they do, or they'll risk scorn and ridicule.

Most entertainers are not this calculating about the learning process, though. They simply love what they are doing. Playing the guitar well is much more fun than playing poorly, so they work and play at it to raise the enjoyment level for themselves and any others who will listen. Some entertainers get to an enjoyable and satisfying level of attention and remain there, becoming more inventive only when the audience starts to turn away. Others recognize that greater expertise or some sort of "hook" to their playing will attract greater attention, and they spend their time finding a niche that will serve them well.

The Explorer's motive for traveling is the wonder of discovery. Explorers are driven by their exceptional curiosity and their unquenchable desire to scout the limits of both their field and themselves. Explorers are the most likely ones to discover new and interesting lands, returning only long enough to report about them. They live and breathe their work, and can be quite obsessive about it. For the explorer, the most important aspect of the journey is finding out what is around the next bend in the road.

The explorer guitar player can't wait to experiment with a new technique, and will happily spend hours or months perfecting it. She will study music of other countries, cultures, and historical periods as fodder for her fertile imagination. Explorers are at the forefront of *fusion* and *world* music forms that span genres and techniques and create new combinations. The major difficulty for explorers is to *finish what they start*. Their natural curiosity often has them chasing after new horizons before they have fully absorbed what they are currently learning. The danger that they face is that they could easily become "jacks of all trades," and masters of none.

In every expedition to new territory, you'll want to include at least one explorer. Often the explorer is the one to put together and lead the expedition in the first place. Their enthusiasm and vision is infectious. But be sure to bring along strong personalities of other types to overrule the explorer who may want to lead the group astray into reckless and dangerous predicaments.

The Conqueror is a formidable traveler. His purpose is similar to the hunter, only instead of bagging the trophy and bringing it home, the way the hunter would approach it, he wants to completely dominate the entire field, and bring its will under his control. For obvious reasons, the Conqueror is a dangerous fellow. He wants it all, and will not be satisfied until he gets it. Conquerors can often be ruthless in pursuit of their goals, and use any means available to attain them. They are always looking for the advantage.

As learners, Conquerors are voracious. They gobble up new information, examine all the angles of every idea, and work diligently to incorporate new skills into their growing collection. Their urge to excel drives them to work harder or smarter than the next person. To the Conqueror everything is a competition, and he certainly doesn't want to lose. His drive to excel has a hard edge to it, becoming more of an urge to exceed, to beat the other guy.

Conquering guitar players tend to hog the limelight, and drown out the other players. The playing style tends to be clinical and a bit self-indulgent, though it will typically be perfectly performed. The Conqueror will not allow imperfections to mar his image. He is demanding of others and himself. He will invariably become a leader and seek to rule his corner of the guitar playing universe, and maybe someday the entire world.

The Warrior is the last and least common of the learning personalities. She finds it most rewarding to be on the cutting edge of new developments. The warrior is the adrenaline junkie of the group. The biggest thrill is the challenge of reaching beyond her current skill level and expanding her abilities in the process. Often highly disciplined, warriors cultivate awareness and hone their attention in order to be ready for any challenge or competition. Unlike the Conqueror, the Warrior is not interested in beating someone else *per se*. Competition to the Warrior is simply a way to test herself against someone representing the next level of skill. For her, competition is an opportunity to excel, not conquer.

Warriors are perhaps the purest learners of the personalities. They learn for the purpose of learning and getting better at what they do. They are more interested in the process of learning than the content of what they are learning. As guitar players, Warriors find beauty and satisfaction in the action of playing. The songs they play are less important than the thrill of playing a new style or technique. Warriors will seek out the most difficult passages and techniques to play and relentlessly devote themselves to achieving this new level of expertise. They tend to be relaxed, but intense, and sometimes aloof. Warriors live on a higher plane than the rest of us, and sometimes seem indifferent to the concerns of others. They are the most likely of all to become masters, yet Warriors are rarely impressed with themselves. To them mastery is the natural result of a great deal of time and effort spent seeking to improve themselves. Mastery comes naturally to the Warrior.

Of course, whatever personality you start with can change as you go along. The purpose of examining the various learning personalities is to get to know the variety of motives that people utilize to travel the road to mastery. Though there are no right or wrong motives, some will get you farther than others (see the chart at the end of the chapter). Adopt the style that fits your purpose, and gets the results you are looking for.

Keep in mind that when reading through the above descriptions, you may find yourself noting that you have characteristics that fit more than one of the learning personalities. This is perfectly normal. In some situations you may exhibit one learning personality and in other situations another. Don't leave out the possibility that you may change your learning personality as you proceed. Here's a simple example:

Perhaps, on a lark, you accompany some friends on an evening outing to a Sufi-dancing gathering. Like a tourist, you are there just for fun, but after participating a few times, you may find it so delightful and engaging that your attitude changes entirely, and you find yourself going back for more and becoming more deeply involved, adopting one of the other personalities in the process. It's your journey, have fun with it!

With the broad diversity of motives displayed by the personalities described above, you may be tempted to think that *everyone* is on the road to mastery. Are there any common characteristics visible in mastery travelers that distinguish them from others? You bet!

First of all, mastery travelers are ***going somewhere.*** They are people of action. While they may frequently be contemplative and take the time to nourish their visions, they are not idle dreamers. Mastery travelers have realized that there is something interesting and valuable to do in the world, and that by taking an active part in it, they can live richer and more fulfilling lives, while making useful contributions to the rest of us. What often starts out as a simple fascination with something new, soon becomes a quest to improve themselves, and perhaps the planet as well. As alluded to before, the road to mastery goes uphill, and the mastery traveler has willingly taken the challenge to climb above his or her current level of ability and see what new heights (s)he is capable of reaching.

Regardless of their motives for starting or continuing their journey, and the pros or cons of their learning personalities, true mastery travelers soon become ***dedicated enthusiasts.***

Enthusiasts are easy to spot. They are excited and passionate about what they do. A few minutes spent talking with enthusiasts about their interest area, or watching them perform, will quickly reveal the sparkle in their eyes and spring in their step.

Dedicated enthusiasts are committed to their interest area, and are willing to endure surprising hardships to continue to learn and grow and have fun with their discipline. Expanding their limits and learning about themselves never seems to grow old. Dedicated enthusiasts display both inspiration and determination, the key qualities of motivation that are examined in detail in Chapter 6.

Unfortunately, many people have not yet found something that provides that sort of stimulation for them. They wander aimlessly with little enthusiasm, or find themselves grinding their lives away, engaged in some activity that brings them little satisfaction or happiness. *The road to mastery beckons...*

Know Your Traveling Companions
EXAMINING THE LEARNING PERSONALITIES

HOW FAR WILL EACH PERSONALITY TAKE YOU?

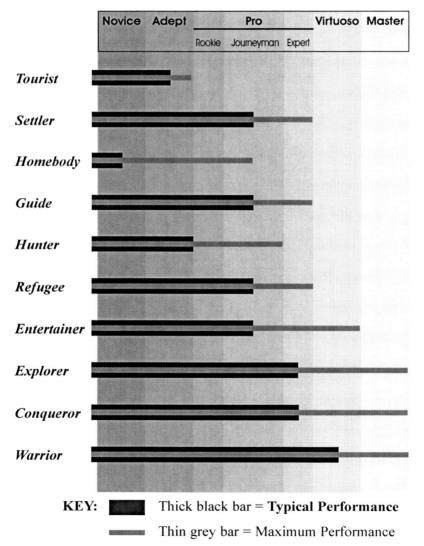

Novice	Adept	Pro			Virtuoso	Master
		Rookie	Journeyman	Expert		

Tourist

Settler

Homebody

Guide

Hunter

Refugee

Entertainer

Explorer

Conqueror

Warrior

KEY: ▬▬▬ Thick black bar = **Typical Performance**

▬▬▬ Thin grey bar = Maximum Performance

> *Never seem more learned than the people you are with. Wear your learning like a pocket watch and keep it hidden. Do not pull it out to count the hours, but give the time when you are asked.*
>
> — *Lord Chesterfield (1694 – 1773)*

Chapter 5:

Adopting a Learning Strategy
WHICH ARRANGEMENT IS BEST FOR YOU?

Starting something new can often be a frightening prospect. It helps to begin your new adventure in an environment that respects your unique needs and provides you with a comfortable and supportive foundation for further growth.

Though you may know little about the subject area you've chosen to explore, you probably know a fair amount about yourself. Are you a gregarious social person or a quiet loner? Do you thrive in competitive environments, or do you prefer an easy-going cooperative approach to learning? Do you have tight time or money constraints that may affect how much you can devote to your new field? Are you the sort of person who likes to live on the cutting edge of progressive ideas, or do you prefer proven, traditional approaches to learning something new?

What works best for you: having the complete attention of your instructor in a one-on-one setting; the varied interactions of a classroom of fellow learners; the dynamics of group exploration in a team environment; or having no instructor or anyone else around at all? The answers you provide for these questions will help you determine a learning strategy.

And the learning strategy you choose will have a dramatic effect on the results you generate, the ease with which you progress in your learning, and the enjoyment you derive from the process.

Your chosen strategy will need to fit the subject matter, your personal situation, and your learning personality. There are five basic approaches to choose from, along with a multitude of combinations of these five learning strategies.

1. INDEPENDENT STUDY

This approach begins with the accumulated knowledge and skills of the individual, and is usually self-guided. Since you are working independently, you can start wherever you wish, with no need to follow some set course structure. You work at your own pace, designing your individual learning process as you go.

Through trial and error and your own internal guidance, you determine the nature of each learning task, and decide independently how to proceed with each step. The assumption is that you are a good learner, and that you are successful in learning by yourself. You must also be self-motivated, and a terrific problem-solver to make this strategy work for you. Sometimes, the independent study process is guided by an instructor or mentor, who can help speed development and assessment of the learning achieved.

Advantages: If you are studying an area that is similar to one you are already familiar with (as in soccer and hockey, or clarinet and oboe, or advertising and marketing), then you may already know an effective approach to learning this new area, and need little guidance to proceed. By using this strategy, you will certainly not be retracing the steps of any predecessors, and you can thus discover new information, skills and concepts that others may not be familiar with. It is well suited to learning which involves the creative exploration of new environments, processes, or your own self-development.

This strategy is also effective if you are studying a brand-new area of learning, where there may not be anyone available to provide guidance to your process. As you work upward toward the mastery end of the learning scale, you will be on the outer fringes of what is known in that subject area, and you will need to strike out on your own to advance your knowledge and skills. Many of the boldest inventors, entrepreneurs, artists, athletes, philosophers and scientists have used this strategy to advance their fields.

Disadvantages: Since the process is designed by the learner (who may not really know what (s)he is doing), this strategy can be an arduous one. Expect to make many more mistakes than with other approaches, and to take longer to attain your performance goals. If you are not highly motivated, the learning process may stall when you are unsure how to proceed, or are repeatedly unsuccessful. Consequently, this strategy is not well suited to beginners. Despite that, many people start out independently, fiddling with the subject matter until they hit upon some true inspiration to study the discipline in earnest. It is usually at this point that the student realizes the inefficiency of the independent process and switches to one of the other strategies to accelerate his or her progress.

2. PACKAGED PROGRAMS

This strategy usually provides a comprehensive approach to learning the fundamentals of your discipline, designed by someone who has a high level of knowledge and skill. Packaged programs are available in the form of books, videos, CDs, DVDs, cassette tapes, computer software packages, internet learning courses, or in combinations of these media. Each provides a unique perspective or approach to learning your subject matter. The effectiveness of the package depends on the quality of the presentation materials and instructional techniques used, and their suitability to your goals and personality. Results experienced by students often vary widely, so it pays to choose such a program carefully.

Advantages: One advantage of packaged programs is that you are literally "buying the expertise" of the author of the program. Once the product has been available for a while, it will quickly acquire a reputation for its effectiveness that will assist you in determining its suitability for your needs. Reviews of the package by independent sources can help you choose an appropriate program easily.

Another advantage is that the student gets to work at his or her own pace, following the instructions provided, and making progress in pre-described steps. Thus the student is free to concentrate on the subject matter, and not on the learning process itself. Since there is no fixed schedule to keep, you can fit your learning into the times available to you. For these reasons, this strategy is often the easiest to adopt and is well-suited for the first two levels of mastery. The packaged program can also be among the least expensive alternatives, too.

Disadvantages: The disadvantages of packaged programs often correspond to the advantages mentioned earlier. The "expertise" that you buy in a packaged program is only as good as the author's presentation. Sometimes, famously talented individuals endorse (but do not write) the material in the packages, and thus the expertise enclosed may not correspond to the talents of the famous individual. Even more dismaying is the fact that famously talented individuals may not be equally talented teachers, and their expertise may be lost in the translation.

Working at your own pace and on your own time can be very attractive, but it invites a bit of sloth into the process. With little or no structure to the way you spend your time, it may become way too easy to put off doing anything at all! Strong internal discipline will be required to set and meet your own requirements for successful progress.

Consider the difference between a fitness program based on a home exercise machine and a similar program at a local health club. The mere presence of others in the gym can have an effect on your motivation. Depending on your personality, you could be spurred on through the comradery of other exercise enthusiasts or turned off by the implied competition with them.

Another disadvantage is the generally fixed nature of packaged programs. Since the learning is already packaged, it's usually not possible to alter the learning materials, or their order, or method of presentation. One-sized learning does not fit all, so you may find areas of a given package to be ill-suited to your personality or situation.

3. INSTRUCTOR-LED COURSES

This strategy is perhaps the most popular, and certainly is the most traditional and widely accepted learning strategy. Here the instructor is assumed to be the expert on the subject to be studied. He or she typically selects the books or other supplementary materials to use, devises the methods of presentation, and then actively leads the learning of the group of students. The number of learners taking part can vary from a handful of people in a small classroom to hundreds at a time in large lecture halls or seminar venues. Most "formal" instruction takes place using this format, and is often the only accepted method available for those seeking degrees, certificates, and other types of official validation of their learning.

Advantages: Perhaps the greatest advantage of this strategy is its familiarity to almost everyone, due to their extended exposure to it in grade school and beyond. Generally, most people entering a classroom environment know what to expect from the process. Its general acceptance, along with its requirement for many types of learning, cements its popularity as a learning strategy. But there are more advantages than just that.

Instructor-led courses can be highly flexible in meeting the learning needs of the students, by providing a rich and stimulating environment for learning that is often unavailable with other strategies. Interaction with multi-sensory presentation materials and methods can help insure that learning takes place on more than one level. The personal experiences and educational background of both the instructor and fellow students can lend a unique quality to each learning experience. Discussions and shared learning events can also contribute to a deeper level of learning. Since one individual leads the process, it can be altered relatively easily to adapt to changes in student needs or to accommodate unusual situations. Learning in a group setting also builds comradery with other students, and enhances the development of shared motivation.

Disadvantages: The major disadvantage of instructor-led courses is the complacency that often seeps into the process. In this strategy, the results are often dependent on the quality of instruction and the support materials used. Instructors who teach the same course over and over tend to get lazy and resort to unimaginative presentations and simple or rote explanations or demonstrations of the material. Inexperienced instructors can also get lost or get "in over their heads" during the teaching process.

Another factor that the student has little control over is the overall "classroom dynamic." Domineering, inconsiderate or disruptive students (or instructors!) can poison the learning atmosphere, reducing it to a painful experience for all concerned.

Also, in formal learning environments like colleges and universities, courses and degree programs can sometimes be constructed in such a way as to seem irrelevant or poorly suited to the needs of the student. For a learning situation where there are many hands-on skills to learn (like athletics, music, construction trades, etc.) this strategy is rarely the best one to employ. Usually, in such learning situations, one of the other strategies will be adapted to fit the setting. In short, the instructor-led course can be the best of all worlds, or the worst.

4. APPRENTICESHIP AND TUTORIAL

With the apprenticeship learning strategy, the student is seeking to absorb the knowledge, skills and wisdom of the master practitioner directly, by working with the master on a one-to-one basis. This is often a long-term investment of time and effort by both the student and master.

For thousands of years, this was the preferred learning strategy for almost any situation. In modern times, this approach has largely fallen from favor. The tutorial approach is a short-term version of apprenticeship, where instructor and student work together one-on-one with short-term learning objectives.

Apprenticeships make sense in an environment where the material and skills to be learned are well established and not subject to much change over the life of the student or master. In constantly changing situations, both student and master will be too busy adapting to new developments to devote much attention to each other. Once the learning becomes directed to the rapidly evolving knowledge and skills, the special relationship between master and student begins to break down and become superfluous.

Unfortunately, there are relatively few such learning situations left. Apprenticeships work well in some artistic disciplines such as painting or sculpture using traditional materials, or in religious or monastic traditions, or in the martial arts and some branches of athletics. Some of the older crafts and trades (such as jewelry-making, weaving, plumbing, etc.) still survive largely intact over the years, and provide appropriate settings for apprenticeship arrangements. Areas characterized by rapid technological development or shifting relationships change too fast for this to work well.

Advantages: "To learn from the master" is a special treat for the apprentice, since it affords the opportunity for a "pure" learning experience that is unpolluted by the interpretations of others who may not have the sophisticated level of understanding and skill of the master.

Therefore, apprenticeships provide what should be the fastest, most comprehensive and most rewarding of all learning environments. After all, by definition, the master has more to teach than anyone else, so it is best to learn from the one who knows the most. If you admire the master for other reasons beyond his or her advanced skills, then the chance to be "up close and personal" with the master can enable you to emulate other characteristics as well.

The short-term tutorial approach is widely used as an adjunct to other learning strategies, and takes advantage of the benefits of apprenticeships, without the long-term commitment involved.

Disadvantages: The limited applicability of this learning strategy is its greatest disadvantage. Modern fast-changing professions and short attention spans don't lend themselves to this relatively static, all-inclusive learning arrangement.

Many acknowledged masters face multiple demands upon their time, and are unwilling to pass on their knowledge in this relatively inefficient manner. In addition, many students are not interested in devoting themselves and their busy lives to shadowing a master at work. Another disadvantage may be the choice of master, who may not have the greatest teaching skills, or may have other character flaws that can make the learning process difficult.

Tutorial arrangements keep the directness and informality of the one-on-one exchange, but sacrifice the intimacy that builds between master and apprentice. Thus, the tutorial approach tends to have the feel of a temporary measure, designed to fill gaps in the student's learning, rather than forming a complete learning strategy.

5. TEAM LEARNING

Although team learning may seem like a modern invention developed by sociologists and trainers for cutting-edge businesses, this strategy can be traced back as far as stone-age hunting parties.

Buoyed by its link to the application of ecological principles, team learning once again is enjoying a comeback in a variety of learning environments. In team learning, a group of participants work together to assist each other in learning the subject matter. Often there is no designated leader, or the leadership role is rotated through the group.

One of the keys to team learning is the relatively equal status of the individuals in the group. Without the presence of an authority, the members of the group are free to learn the material directly, while sharing a variety of learning styles, observations, insights, and results of their progress with other members of the team.

Team learning experiences can be found in the contexts of: law students' study groups; climbing expeditions; project teams; popular music bands; "pick-up" or playground basketball; design, marketing or manufacturing groups; and software development teams, among many others. Team learning can be thought of as *group* independent study.

Advantages: Since team learning necessarily includes the interaction of the participants, the resulting learning experiences can be richer than that of other approaches. Members of the team are simultaneously learning the material to be addressed, the methods of apportioning parts of the project among the group members, coordination of the effort, the strengths and weaknesses of the members and how that affects the process, and their own participation in all of it. Properly designed, the team learning process can result in fun, creative, deeply enriching experiences.

Teams that are *coached* or *directed* by an outside individual who can set priorities for the group, and then send them off to participate as a team, can produce incredible learning results. Team sports, orchestras, plays and movies, construction crews, and restaurants are all examples of team learning that is guided by an outside director, who coordinates the activities of the group, but is not really an active participant. Many of the highest achievements in a variety of fields have been produced using this learning format.

Disadvantages: Like the instructor-led course, team learning can suffer from the same debilitating drawbacks related to the participants. Without the presence of an authority figure, domineering, inconsiderate and disruptive individuals have even greater opportunities to impose their own agenda on the process. Since the performance of the team is the collective result of the members' interaction, any disharmony among the members magnifies the problems.

Of course, some learning experiences don't lend themselves to group learning strategies. Playing the guitar is an individual learning experience until the guitarist gains enough skill and versatility to play in a band. Then the team learning strategy becomes a logical choice for further development. Some activities, like chess, are always going to be solo endeavors.

When the team does not contain a recognized authority in the subject area, the learning process can also be hindered by "the blind leading the blind." With many decision-makers and a variety of directions supplied by the team members, much time can be wasted in haggling over the process, and going down blind alleys of investigation. This is where the guidance of a *coach* or *director* can make a big difference.

By examining the advantages and disadvantages of the

various learning strategies (along with the chart at the end of the chapter), and the unique qualities of your field and your personality, you should be able to make an informed choice as to which approach to employ. Keep in mind that some combination of the above five strategies might prove to be ideal for your situation, providing a more personalized approach to learning.

Ask the advice of an advisor or mentor, a friend or relative who is successful in your chosen field, or a personal coach. Such people, who know you well and have some knowledge of the field you've chosen, can assist you in sorting out all the possibilities available to you. Armed with these recommendations, let your intuition be your guide.

Adopting a Learning Strategy
WHICH ARRANGEMENT IS BEST FOR YOU?

SUITABILITY OF EACH LEARNING STRATEGY

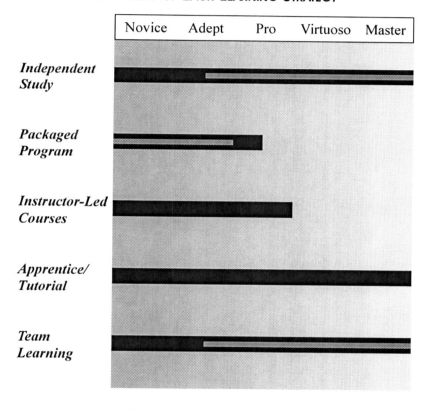

KEY: Thick black bar = **Guided Learning**

Thin grey bar = Unguided Learning

Guided Learning refers to the active presence of a director, coach, mentor, instructor, tutor or leader who shapes and directs the learning process for the student(s) involved.

> *A journey of a thousand miles begins with a single step.*
> — *Lao-tzu (604 BC – 531 BC)*

Chapter 6:

Getting Started

INSPIRATION AND DETERMINATION

If you've come this far in the book, you've probably chosen a discipline that *feels right* and inspires the passion within you. You've sized up your learning personality and made adjustments that will enable you to reach the performance level you desire. You've picked a method of learning that fits your unique situation, and you've begun to cultivate the character traits that will strengthen your spirit and ease your progress. You've even filed away those tips for creating success in multiple areas at the same time. You've made that shopping trip to the outfitter. You're ready.

What's left to handle before you begin your journey? Only one thing—*fuel.* To travel for any length of time or distance, you will need to plan for rest and refueling stops along the way. You may be all juiced up right now and anxious to get going, but sooner or later your energy will drain away, and you'll need to be prepared for that situation.

What needs to be fueled is your *motivation.* Your motivation to continue to learn is all you have to keep you going. Lose that motivation and your progress will fizzle out, too. For this reason, you cannot rely on chance to provide the motivation you need. Chance is far too fickle.

You will need to plan on generating your own motivation. Fortunately, like solar energy, motivation is a renewable resource that you can gather, store, convert to action and apply as needed for each situation you encounter.

What sort of energy is motivation? Motivation is *emotional energy.* Emotional energy has the power to *move you,* in both an emotional sense and a physical sense. This is why we can consider it to be a fuel source. *Positive* emotional energy will fill your tanks and keep you going. *Negative* emotional energy will just as quickly deplete your reserves and leave you spent by the side of the road.

Look around and begin to seek out and accumulate positive emotional energy. What you are looking for are feelings of *inspiration, excitement, passion, mystery and simple enjoyment* (to quote chapter two). These are but a few examples of positive emotional energy. There are many other kinds. Use any and all that appeal to you and fit your situation. *Love, companionship, affection, encouragement, fun, accomplishment, victory, generosity, loyalty, gratefulness, thankfulness, honor, bravery, humor, laughter, beauty, elegance, brilliance, subtlety, joy, exuberance, ecstasy, warmth, friendship, sharing, compliments* and more, are either examples of positive emotional energy, or simple ways to generate that energy.

Gathering positive emotional energy does not come naturally to everyone. Many people are wired in just the opposite way, acting like magnets for negative emotional energy and often dispensing it as they go. Fortunately, people can learn to re-polarize their magnets to attract positive emotional energy, store it, and re-direct it outward to shower others with its rosy glow. Please refer to the **Re-Polarizing Program** at the end of this chapter for a detailed approach to this problem.

For now, let's look at two of the most important and reliable types of motivational fuel sources, *Inspiration and Determination.* These twin fuel sources form the backbone of all motivation. Many of the other sources mentioned above can be thought of as ways to add to either your inspiration or your determination.

Inspiration: (from the Latin word meaning **to breathe life into**) **1.** *to produce, arouse, or fill with a feeling or thought.* **2.** *to influence, bring about, cause or impel.* **3.** a realization that what was once thought of as difficult or impossible is now possible or considerably easier than once thought. **4.** Literally: to **gasp** in wonderment or amazement at the possibilities.

Determination: (from the Latin word meaning **to hinder or prevent**) **1.** *the act of coming to a decision, or resolving something.* **2.** the settlement of a dispute or decision by an authoritative pronouncement. **3.** a fixed purpose or intention regarding a course of action. **4.** Resolute, unwavering, unaffected by life conditions or the opinions of others. **5.** Deterring, or turning aside other choices.

Inspiration and determination are important because of the unique ways they fuel your motivation. Inspiration *gets you going,* and determination *keeps you going.* In that way, inspiration overcomes *inertia,* and determination maintains *momentum.* Both will need to be replenished regularly.

The initial inspiration that motivated you to begin your new endeavor develops what is called *germination energy.* This eagerness to grow is similar to that of a seed that has been moistened and warmed. It bursts to life from its dormant state and sinks roots into the ground while sending its shoots skyward. Germination energy is the energy of youth. If you no longer consider yourself youthful, perhaps in beginning some new area of study you can harness that natural germination energy, reinvigorate yourself, and bring back your youthful outlook.

Once you've started the mastery process, any time your learning falters, your progress fizzles out, or your motivation drops down to zero, what you need is to refill your tanks with some *inspiration.* You need to be reminded that:

1. There IS something worth doing.
2. YOU can do it, and
3. It is NOT impossible or even all that difficult.

The only way to generate inspiration is to *change your perspective,* and see your situation in a new light. Renew your faith in yourself and the process you've undertaken, and then you can move forward again. Here's a simple way to change your outlook and restore your confidence:

Let's say that you are struggling with playing a particular melody on your guitar, and every attempt you make is worse than the last. As you flail away hopelessly, becoming more and more frustrated, you feel the urge to give up, and maybe smash the thing to pieces over a railing.

Whoa there! Take a moment or three to chill out. Stop playing your guitar and go find someone who can play the piece successfully (or watch a video), and just let go of your frustration for a little while. Watch and listen as (s)he plays the song. Put aside your self-criticism and really focus your attention. Spend some time just sitting back and listening to the sounds you hear. Get a feel for the fluidity of the movements of each hand as (s)he plays. Let the music play in your mind as you imagine your fingers running over the strings and strumming out the melody. Notice just what your guitarist friend is doing that you were not (or vice versa). Zoom in on those few little differences and then experiment with doing it differently.

Listening to your friend's smooth easy rendition of the tune, you will soon realize that: **1.** the song really was worth playing well. **2.** you can actually fix the flaws in your technique by relaxing into the feel of the music. **3.** when you break it down into its components, there were only a few little problems with playing that piece, and correcting those flaws is not so tough. Your fingers know what to do.

Voila! Renewed inspiration! Now you are "back in the game." All it took was to renew your faith in yourself and in the value you found in learning to play the guitar in the first place.

Generating motivation, like many other fundamental life processes, is a *yin/yang* movement. The companion energies of expansion *(yang)* and contraction *(yin)* work together to move you forward.

Imagine paddling a canoe. You reach forward with your paddle (*yang* expansion movement), dip the paddle into the water and pull towards you (*yin* contraction energy). As the paddle passes your waist, the pulling motion changes to a push as you follow through with the stroke *(yang)*. Releasing at the end of the stroke and withdrawing the paddle from the water, you return to the neutral position *(yin),* ready to begin the reach of the next stroke (yang again). Together, working in natural harmony, the seemingly opposing forces of *yin* and *yang* blend seamlessly to propel you through the water.

When creating motivation, inspiration provides the *pull.* Determination generates the *push.* Alternate them seamlessly and you will be propelled forward smoothly and easily.

Determination, as the definition suggests, implies that you are steadfastly focused upon your goal, and will not be deterred from it by any circumstances that might get in the way. You are determined to *push* your way through any problems that present themselves in order to reach your goal. Looking closely, you can see the different, yet complementary, energies that inspiration and determination utilize. Inspiration requires *imagination,* while determination demands *strength.* Together they build the *flexibility* and *endurance* needed to excel.

To build the strength of your determination to succeed, start with the original goal that inspired you in the first place (to play that dramatic solo on the guitar, to use our running example). By keeping the long-range goal firmly in mind from the start, your inspiration can build determination.

Next, break down that larger goal into smaller pieces that you can work on one at a time. Make sure that each small goal constitutes a recognizable and significant advancement in skill or knowledge. Identifying and successfully reproducing all the chords in the guitar solo might be one such smaller accomplishment. It is important to construct your smaller goals in such a way as to know when you have succeeded. If you're unsure what constitutes success, you invite confusion and frustration into the process.

By subdividing your goals into smaller pieces, you ensure that you keep a significant goal in sight at all times, while maintaining your vision of the inspirational larger goal that pulls all your efforts together. The power of your determination will see you push past all the mistakes and misdirected attempts you will make as you move closer to success. It is that laser-like focus on the long-range goal, fortified by smaller successes along the way, that will create the strength to endure. Renewing your inspiration builds stronger determination, which, as you overcome each hurdle, generates more inspiration, and so on.

Every once in a while, for a change of pace, create your own hurdles! Spice up your mastery process by inserting some sort of test or competition to act as a benchmark for your progress. In some fields the hurdles are already in place as a normal part of the process, whereas in others you may need to be proactive in developing your own benchmarks. In academics the learning process is littered with tests, projects and courses to pass that act as signposts to your progress. In sports, participating in some kind of competition to test yourself will quickly provide a reality check for the effectiveness of your game.

However, if you are walking two miles a day just to maintain your fitness, or learning the guitar to be able to play that solo, the idea of a test or competition may not seem pertinent. Yet, if you were gearing up for a 5-mile charity run/walk, or polishing your repertoire for open-mike night at the club, your motivation rises to meet the challenge, and you'll find yourself reaching *way* beyond the level you thought you could attain, and having a lot more fun in the process. Remember, motivation is your fuel, and generating more inspiration and determination any way you can will enable you to move farther and higher than you ever thought possible.

Two Secrets To Learning

As you begin your new studies, you may want to keep in mind two secrets to the learning process. They are presented as "secrets" because they may not be obvious, and they both seem counter to the prevailing common sense. They have to do with errors.

1. You MUST be willing to be wrong. In order to learn something new, it is necessary to let go of what you think you know. Only then can you discover if what you thought you knew was indeed correct. In other words, you must be willing to test your knowledge, your skill level, your theories and your unspoken beliefs to see if they are, in fact, true and optimal. When people stall in their learning, it is often because they have been unwilling to examine some of their basic assumptions about what is right, or what is the most effective way of doing something.

You see, we humans have a natural tendency to think that we are right—all the time! This left-brain/ego-based arrogance tends to creep in and take over the learning process, killing whatever progress you were making.

Think of it this way. If what you already know is correct, then there is no need for any new information or new ideas. If your technique is already flawless, then no improvement is possible. *Learning is literally impossible without first being wrong!* Even if you test your knowledge and skills and find that they are correct and successful, then you haven't learned anything new. You've just confirmed what you already assumed was correct. While this process is a valuable check on your progress, it will never be an eye-opener.

To counteract this tendency to be "right" all the time, cultivate a state of mind that is open, unassuming and contains no expectations. Zen Buddhists call this mental state *Beginner's Mind,* comparing it to an empty cup, waiting to be filled. Beginner's Mind has a child-like quality to it, since it does not pretend to know the answers, nor how to accomplish a new task. From this mental state of "not-knowing," comes the possibility of surprise, delight and wonder. When you are operating from Beginner's Mind, learning becomes interesting, fascinating and fun. In this mysterious way, firm, solid, tangible knowledge emerges from slippery, fluid, ephemeral "not knowing." *Not knowing is necessary to knowing!* How magical!

2. You MUST make mistakes. This is not optional. Making mistakes is a vital part of the learning process.

We were all taught (overtly or covertly) that making mistakes is a sign of weakness, clumsiness or stupidity. So it is no surprise that people want to minimize their mistakes. It's only natural to avoid the penalties and ridicule that often accompany the mishap, error or unsuccessful attempt. Our reward systems are generally not set up to encourage making mistakes. In academics, athletics, business and even personal relationships, if you make mistakes there are always consequences, and they are often severe. Mistakes can result in failing the test, losing the game, missing the sale, or upsetting your sweetheart.

Yet making mistakes is a natural result of straying from what is safe and well known. If you are going beyond what you are comfortable with—experimenting, exploring, investigating and discovering—then you are learning. And if you are going beyond what you know, then you are *sure* to make mistakes. But don't worry, this is not a disaster, it's just another step in the learning process.

What is the value in making mistakes? Very simply, when you make a mistake, you discover what does NOT work. If you are paying attention, you can then make adjustments to your knowledge or technique, try it again, and see what happens.

In a short time, most people become very clever at making mistakes. They discover that it is possible to *systematically make mistakes* in a way that will lead them to the correct technique or most effective action. This is an essential part of what is often referred to as *Practice.* What you are looking for in this process of systematically making mistakes is to *determine the boundary between what works and what doesn't work.*

Let's say that you are learning to shoot foul shots in basketball. You take your first shot. It falls way short of the hoop. Mentally, you tell yourself, *I've got to shoot it harder, with more effort.* Another shot, and this time the ball bangs off the backboard. *Whoops, too hard. A little softer next time.* You shoot again and this time it hits the rim and bounces off to the right. *Gently now, a bit to the left.* After each shot that misses, you compensate accordingly on the next shot until you sink one.

Then, once you've produced a successful shot, you try to duplicate it with the following shot. You sink into the feeling of the ball leaving your hands and softly, surely slipping through the air and into the basket. You feel the internal sensation of your body movements throughout the shot and just let your muscle-memory absorb the sensations. Repeat the process until the feeling of the successful shot becomes an integral part of you.

This is the essence of practice. Experiment repeatedly (making mistakes through trial and error), while looking for the most effective result. Bracket your efforts (as in the example above) so that your attempts surround the optimal action. Once you produce it successfully, then repeat that effective action over and over, gradually internalizing the skill.

This process may seem like a natural one to use in basketball, but it may be harder to see that this same simple technique of *systematically making mistakes* can be applied to learning anything. Practice is important because it provides the *space for learning.* In practice you can make mistakes in an atmosphere where there are few consequences and each is less costly to your tender self-esteem, since the results may not be visible to the outside world.

You are NOT a failure if you make a mistake! You've just discovered what doesn't work. Now it's time to take your new knowledge and put it to work by making adjustments, trying again, and noticing what happens.

The inspirational story of Thomas Edison's invention of the light bulb serves to illustrate the value of making mistakes systematically. Rumor had it that Edison experimented with 10,000 different materials to act as the filament of his new light bulb invention before he finally found a successful result.

Late in this process he was interviewed by a newspaper reporter. Seeing Edison's lab littered with the results of countless unsuccessful trials, the reporter remarks, "You've failed with your fantastic invention thousands of times already. You're wasting your time! Are you just going to fail again and again?"

Edison replied, "I haven't failed at all. I've just discovered another way NOT to invent the light bulb."

When you were a baby learning to walk, you made many painful mistakes. Each time you stood up tentatively, took a step, wobbled and then fell over. You repeated your trials many times before you got the hang of walking. It just took some practice before you mastered it. *There was never any doubt that you could do it.*

Now imagine what would've happened if you had doubted yourself, or if your parents had doubted that you'd be able to walk. Seeing you fall to the hard floor for the third time, your mom takes pity on you and rescues you once again. After picking you up and dusting you off, smoothing away the hurt with a kiss and a bandage, mom says, "Oh that's alright Dana, maybe walking is not for you. It's okay; you don't have to learn to walk. You're not very good at it anyway. Why bother with something so painful? Crawling suits you so much better. Come on, let's go crawling, instead!"

Thankfully, these thoughts never entered your minds, or you might still be scooting around on all fours. What if Edison had given up after just a few attempts—the way most of the rest of us do it? We'd still be fumbling around in the dark!

The critical part of Edison's learning process was that he *knew* that the light bulb idea would work; he just didn't know *how* to make it work. His inspiration was bright and true, his determination strong, and his experimentation relentless. *Successful results were inevitable.*

Another inspiring story is the tale of Englishman Sir Roger Banister. Banister was the first track star to run the mile in less than four minutes, back in 1954. For almost 70 years before that, little progress was made in lowering the record time. Athletes and scientists alike believed that it was *impossible* for a man to break the "four minute barrier." In the years preceding his record-breaking run, many of the top runners of the time regularly came close to the mark, recording times in the range of 4:02 to 4:08. So close, yet so far.

Banister figured out a novel way to improve his times. He noticed that he could easily run a quarter-mile in less than one minute (as could many other runners). His inspirational idea was simple. All he had to do was to string together four sub-one-minute quarter miles in a single run, and he'd break the four-minute barrier. So he concentrated on running fast quarter-mile times, and gradually put several together until the magic moment came.

What's even more interesting is that once Banister broke the four-minute barrier, in the next few months *over a dozen other runners also broke the four-minute mark.* Once they *knew* it was possible, they were able to reach beyond their self-imposed limitations and dramatically improve their times. Since then, more than 950 men have run the mile in under four minutes. Several have repeated the feat over 100 times!

Two lessons emerge from these twin secrets of learning:

1. Be humble, and keep asking questions. No one knows everything, so it's a good idea to keeping asking. Asking questions removes the cloaks of the unknown—one by one—revealing more and more of what is really there.

2. Persevere. Don't give up. It takes many wrong answers to determine the validity of the right one. Don't punish yourself for making mistakes. Just accept them as part of the process, learn from them and move on.

In fact, why not celebrate your mistakes? Making more mistakes actually means you are learning more. Become a champion at making mistakes, and you'll soon become a champion of success, too. It just takes a subtle shift in perception.

"Wow, that sure didn't work. But would you look at that result I created? Another great effort! Okay, time to rewind the mental tape. Let's see that again in slow-mo. See how close I was? Alright then, make a small alteration over here. Now give it another shot. At this rate I'll soon have the whole process surrounded. That way, when I do get it right, I'll really nail it. Onward!"

THE RE-POLARIZING PROGRAM

This series of exercises is designed for those who seem to be trapped in patterns of thought and emotions that are negative or self-defeating. Here are a few warning signs that your emotional energies may be magnetically polarized in a negative direction.

Do you find yourself frequently complaining about your situation, other people or your own inadequacies? Have you noticed that some people in your circle of workmates, friends, family and associates avoid you? Do you sometimes feel lost, miserable, ambivalent, angry or hopeless? Do unfortunate or problematic events seem to appear again and again in your life?

If you've answered "yes" to any of the above questions, then you may find these exercises to be helpful if you'd like to reverse your magnets and begin to attract positive or self-affirming energy. Please note that answering "yes" does not mean that there is something wrong with you. You may simply have run out of fuel, and have not been able to find a filling station.

1. Start a journal. Begin by writing a page or two in your journal every day. Don't be concerned with the content of your writings, just put down whatever comes to mind. Do not edit it in any way. Just let your thoughts and feelings flow onto the page. Relax into the process. There is nothing that you can do that is wrong. Give yourself the freedom to say anything you want in your journal, since no one else will read it. Continue writing in your journal through thick and thin. It will soon become your friend.

2. Notice what you have written. After a couple of weeks of consistently writing pages in your journal, sit down and reread what you've written. Notice the tone of your writings. That's all. Just notice, without further internal commentary. If you find that your internal commentary continues, just notice that, too. Then let those feelings go. Continue to reread your journal periodically every few weeks, noticing the tone. Rereading your journal shows you how you regard yourself and the people and events in your life. As you continue over the weeks and months, it will be easy to see the progress you are making. Over time, you will become less critical.

3. Begin to notice your thoughts as they are happening. Take a mental step backwards and calmly watch the thoughts you are thinking as they go by. Let go of the intensity of your thoughts. Like watching birds fly in the sky, simply observe your thoughts as you speak to other people, or silently talk to yourself. Practice this simple step as often as you can remember to do it. As you spend more time observing your thoughts, you will gradually become calmer and more relaxed.

So far, by doing the first three exercises on a regular basis, you will begin to notice how you are responding to yourself and the world. By distancing yourself somewhat from the thoughts and feelings you have, you can see that they are NOT you, they are just things that you do, and thus are changeable.

4. When you notice yourself thinking negative thoughts, simply stop. When you feel that you are ready for the next step, experiment with these next couple of exercises. As you are noticing your thoughts, if one goes by that you would prefer not to have, simply reach out in your mind and stop the flow of that thought. Like coming to a STOP sign on a roadway, simply halt that thought. It might help to imagine the STOP sign appearing before you.

5. Notice something else. Once you stop the negative thought flow, then immediately notice something in your surroundings. Put your attention on that item and begin to describe it to yourself. Describe the color, shape, features, size or whatever you discover in the physical attributes of that object. When your curiosity wanes, pick another object and describe it to yourself, as well. Continue as long as you like. As you gain more practice with this step you will enter a sort of "neutral" state of mind. Your cares and worries dissolve and you become even more calm and relaxed. You may find yourself fascinated by the objects you are observing.

With exercises 4 and 5, you stop the negative thought flow, and begin to take control. The "neutral" state of mind that you enter has no opinions, and thus no complaints, worries or problems. Practice with these exercises helps to create the ability to have "no comment" on the people and events in your life. This frees you from the effects of the ongoing negative internal commentary that can make your life miserable.

6. Begin to notice the beauty in the world. By now you are becoming skilled in watching your thoughts as they occur. In exercises 4 and 5 you began to notice the negative thoughts and stop them in their tracks. Now it's time to notice the positive, complimentary thoughts that you have.

Look around and start to notice the people, places and things that are beautiful to you, or that you appreciate in some other way than as beauty. For example, you may notice how delicate that frost pattern is on the windowpane, or how serene and unhurried the cat looks when she gets up and stretches after a nap, or the amazing balance of a squirrel running across an overhead telephone line. The world is bursting with examples of such beauty.

When you notice these positive thoughts of appreciation passing through your mind, stop for a moment, just as you did in exercise 4. Only this time, repeat that thought again slowly, luxuriating in the pleasant feelings that it evokes within you. Move your head slightly and let the sparkle of light dance across the frosted panel of glass in front of you. Imagine the simple satisfaction of the cat as you mimic her stretch in your mind. Feel the perfect balance and confidence of the squirrel as he dashes across the wire.

Wherever and whenever you notice yourself thinking positive thoughts, take a bit of extra time to "stop and smell the roses," and enjoy the feelings that accompany these experiences. Soon you will find that you are experiencing the pleasant effects of your positive thoughts *as they happen,* instead of repeating them afterwards. Practice this exercise often.

You will soon find yourself surrounded by beautiful objects and scenery, even though you've not spent an extra dime. The people around you become more pleasant, and more fun to be with. The events of your life become richer and fuller. Everyday occurrences begin to take on a special significance. Before long, everywhere you look you will find something to appreciate. *The only real difference between a person with a genuinely positive outlook on life, and others with gloomy dispositions, is the amount of time they spend* **appreciating**.

7. Practice compassion. Begin to appreciate the commonality of our human condition through your compassion for others. To access your compassion and further build its power, use this simple, yet powerful exercise from the book *Resurfacing®,* by Harry Palmer, ©1994, used by permission, and reprinted here:

Compassion Exercise

Honesty with yourself leads to compassion for others.
Love is an expression of the willingness to create space
in which something is allowed to change.

Objective
To increase the amount of compassion in the world.

Expected Results
A personal sense of peace.

Instructions
This exercise can be done anywhere that people congregate (airports, malls, parks, beaches, etc.). It should be done on strangers, unobtrusively, from some distance. Try to do all five steps on the same person.

Step 1: With attention on the person, repeat to yourself: "Just like me, this person is seeking some happiness in his/her life."

Step 2: With attention on the person, repeat to yourself: "Just like me, this person is trying to avoid suffering in his/her life."

Step 3: With attention on the person, repeat to yourself: "Just like me, this person has known sadness, loneliness, and despair."

Step 4: With attention on the person, repeat to yourself: "Just like me, this person is seeking to fulfill his/her needs."

Step 5: With attention on the person, repeat to yourself: "Just like me, this person is learning about life."

You may wish to approach the above exercise in a progressive manner. To start, choose a person who might benefit from your compassion. Everyone is eligible. Begin first with friends or loved ones, then move up to strangers, then to people you don't seem to understand, and then finally to people with whom you have disagreements or upsets. If the person is not present, simply picture the person in your mind's eye; pause to feel his/her presence, then proceed with the five steps.

If you find yourself squabbling with a friend, spouse, family member or associate, you may find that when both parties involved perform this exercise, a lot of the tension and bitterness will simply melt away. However, it's not necessary for both people to use the exercise to notice its benefits. Use the Compassion Exercise anytime you feel tension building between you and another person. Your increased compassion can often be felt by the other person, even without their participation. That alone may be enough to resolve the situation.

8. Be grateful. Support others. As you practice appreciation and compassion, you may find your heart filling with emotion. Sometimes it feels as though your heart may burst. As this feeling wells up in you, let it overflow. Give it away. From this feeling of gratefulness, return your fullness back to the world in the form of a simple acknowledgement, a nod, a smile, a compliment, a warm touch, an expression of love or friendship, or any gesture of gratitude, kindness or support that seems appropriate for the moment. We each have been given the gift of life. Being grateful for the opportunities available to us can become a naturally fulfilling and spontaneous response to each moment.

These final three exercises assist in developing your ability to see and appreciate the richness and fullness of life, and how others share our bittersweet predicament in living as human beings. Practice this series of exercises, and before you know it, you'll find your life becoming more positive and rewarding, with an expanding sense of gratefulness for all the rich moments that you used to take for granted.

Practice and thought might gradually forge many an art.
— *Virgil (70 BC – 19 BC)*

Level 1: The Novice

Treat Your Subject Area as a **Practice**

Level 1: The Novice
TREAT YOUR SUBJECT AREA AS A **PRACTICE**

Objective: To learn the basics of your subject area by heart.

Process: Divide the material to be learned into component parts. Study the unique language, terminology, background information and basic principles until they become second nature to you. Practice component skills over and over until you can perform them successfully "without looking." Focus on *content*.

Expected Results: Solid basic knowledge of your subject area. The ability to perform fundamental skills automatically.

Action Steps: As a Novice, what you lack most is experience. To advance, you simply need to acquire more experience in your field. So immerse yourself in all aspects of your interest area. *Gather lots of information, ideas and principles.* Study them thoroughly. *Study, study, study.* Practice basic skills, building a solid base of core capabilities. *Practice, practice, practice.*

Keys to Success: Find and *follow a proven approach* to learning the basics. Cultivate *mindfulness* and *patience*. Seek guidance from successful pros. Use only high quality equipment and services.

Words of Praise/Encouragement: Go get 'em! You can do it! Good work! Alright! OK, you're making progress! (Acknowledge/praise *all* efforts.)

How you can help others: You are not in a position to assist others who are farther along, but you can share your emerging knowledge and skills with others at the Novice level, and encourage them and yourself at the same time. Become co-learners. Your greatest asset at this point is your enthusiasm. Spread it around!

Chapter 7

Level 1: The Novice
TREAT YOUR SUBJECT AREA AS A **PRACTICE**

The mastery traveler lingers for just a moment longer, her gaze fixed on the shining mountain peak in the distance. With the siren song of this climbing challenge still ringing in her ears, she finally turns away, still seeing the puff of clouds surrounding the proud summit that's now etched into her memory. Silently she whispers a vow to stand at the top of that range and soak up the vast beauty of the surrounding valleys and plains. She swallows once as she eases forward onto the wide road before her, ready to begin the long trek into the hills. "Well, here goes," she thinks. Soon the mountains disappear from view as she plunges into the thick woods around the next bend...

Mastering a whole new area of interest can be a huge project, especially when you are brand new to the field. There's so much to learn that it's hard to know where to start. You just can't swallow it all in one gulp. Perhaps by nibbling away, with one small bite at a time, you can begin to make some progress in learning your subject area, while you get a taste of what it's all about.

The first step is to break down the vast depth of knowledge and all those intricate tasks into simpler, more elemental forms. This Aristotelian approach assumes that a very complex field, which is difficult to understand, can be dissected into smaller pieces that will be relatively easy to learn. While that assumption begins to break down at the later, more sophisticated stages, it serves well at this early stage of learning. By studying the small pieces one by one in the appropriate order, you will gradually form a preliminary understanding of the whole field.

At this first stage of mastery, there's a lot to do. What you are after at the Novice level is to learn the **basics** of your area **by heart.** This overall objective can be realized in three ways:

1. Familiarize yourself with the specialized language and terminology of the subject area, so that you can communicate effectively in your field. **2.** Learn the guiding principles and background information that will ground you in your subject's foundational knowledge. **3.** Practice the key component skills that form the basis of every performance, so that you can produce those skills successfully and automatically.

With all three components of your objective, the key is to learn everything *by heart.* Learning something by heart means to infuse the knowledge or skill so deeply within you that you no longer have to think about it. Instead, you can *feel* the correctness of the process you've learned *as you use it.*

Here you've moved beyond the mental deliberations and "taken it to heart," where the knowledge or skill becomes *second nature.* In its original form, the knowledge or skill is encountered as an external item or event—its *first nature.* As *second nature,* you *feel* the knowledge or skill from the inside out, as part of yourself and the way you think and act. Here are a few examples:

You know you've learned how to walk *by heart* since you rarely think about the process of walking. *How* to walk never crosses your mind. You just get up and do it.

In basketball, you know that you've really learned to shoot when you can *feel* whether the shot will go in before it ever leaves your hands. You go up for the shot, and as your arm extends and the ball rolls off your fingertips, you hear yourself say, "Swish!" Then the ball arcs through the air and drops into the net without touching the rim, just as you predicted. Now you've really gotten a *feel* for shooting.

When playing music you may wince when you hit the wrong note, or when the timing of your chord progression is too fast or too slow. You know it *by heart* when you can sense the error as you are making it.

You've learned the sales technique *by heart* when you find yourself saying automatically, "How would you like to pay for that, sir? Cash, check or credit card?" Such simple closing techniques come smoothly and naturally when you know the principles *by heart.*

In general, you know when you've learned something *by heart* when, if it's a fact or some information, *you can recall it instantly.* If it's an idea or principle, *you use it without questioning it.* If it's a skill or technique, *you can feel the correctness of the process as you perform it.*

Far more than mere memorization, this depth of learning provides the stability of a foundation of deeply integrated understanding that you build on as you progress. Let's see how that foundation is built.

Every field has its own specialized language, code or terminology that describes its unique qualities. Music has its own written symbolic notation in notes, staff and time signature. The computer field speaks in bits, bytes and a bewildering array of acronyms and programming codes. Sports have their own specialized terminology, from downs to smashes to moguls to falls to grinds to swishes to RBIs. Biology, marketing, customer service, law, politics, auto mechanics and every other field also has its own unique way of communicating its subtleties.

Building fluency in your new language helps you develop a sense of rapport with your subject matter. Knowing the language will also help you become accepted as an "insider" within the existing society of initiates. At the same time, using that unique terminology will acquaint you with the subtle nuances of your subject area. Interwoven into the language are the broad concepts and principles that serve to hold the field together and provide the "rules of the game."

For example, experienced house painters know about the "coverage area" of different types of paint on a variety of surfaces, the preparation techniques, and the various primers, sealers, base- and top-coats of paint. These specialized terms imply that there are a variety of factors to take into account when painting a specific wall surface that will help determine the cost, projected longevity and final appearance of the finished paint job. These important concepts are actually built into the language.

Learning the specialized terminology of your subject area provides some of the keys to understanding your whole field, so don't skimp on this step. Many people find that the easiest and most enjoyable way to accomplish this vital step is to dive right in and immerse yourself in your new field.

Reading trade magazines and books, special interest publications, and field-related web sites can quickly bring you up to speed in the current issues, vocabulary, and overall direction of your field of interest. Studying the guiding principles and background information pertaining to your subject area can be even more enjoyable when shared with other interested mastery travelers. Joining a club or professional association related to your field can help you make valuable contacts, find partners for further exploration into common areas of interest, and help you feel like you "belong" in your new field.

In addition to learning the terminology and fundamental principles of your field, at the Novice level you'll also break down the physical and mental performance of the expert into elemental skills that you can learn one at a time.

It's clear that some elements must be assimilated before others can be understood and applied. In tennis, for example, learning the proper way to grip the racquet will make it much easier to generate an effective stroke when hitting the ball. Carried further, learning the mechanics of the stroke will lead to smooth execution of volleys. This entire sequence (and much more) will need to be integrated thoroughly before you can even think about winning a match.

There is a natural progression to learning the elemental skills that is unique to each field. The learning strategy you use will guide you in this process, by providing exercises that build on one another and develop the foundational knowledge and skills you will need for later progress.

This is where some form of guidance becomes very valuable (see Chapter 5: Adopting a Learning Strategy). The experience of an instructor, coach, textbook author, mentor or other professional in your field will help establish a sequence and progression to your learning that will let your budding competence come together smoothly and cohesively. Using a progressive approach to learning will enable you to forge a more integrated understanding of your field, while facilitating higher performance levels in your basic skills.

As a Novice in your field, your initial assignment is to ***gather information*** and ***gain experience.*** In terms of the information and concepts that form the basis of your field, that means you simply have to study this material. *Study, study, study.* Read everything you can get your hands on. Attend conferences, expos or classes; join discussion groups, subject related chat rooms, or anything to help get you involved in your field. Jump in with both feet.

One of the best parts of being a Novice is that you can learn from almost anyone! Since most people who are active in your field have more experience than you do, you can pick up facts, tips, ideas and techniques everywhere you go.

Perhaps surprisingly, many experienced practitioners would be excited and happy to assist you in getting a handle on your new field. Most people will feel flattered by a request for help. This gives them a chance to display their knowledge without seeming to brag about it. Not only do they get this satisfaction from helping you, but they also get to clarify their own understanding of the material at the same time. It's a double bonus for all concerned.

To *perform* well in your interest area, begin by concentrating on learning and integrating each elemental skill into your accumulating set of basic performance techniques. Focus on performing each little skill successfully and consistently. Repeat the action again and again, making adjustments to your technique until you're sure that you've "got it right." The guidance of an experienced pro can help speed this process, since that person can point out the subtleties involved that you may not notice.

Once you've "got it right," that's just the beginning! Now repeat this "correct" action over and over until your mind and body can perform the whole process automatically. You'll know that you've achieved this "automatic" level of performance when you no longer have to "think about it," or "watch yourself doing it," while you're in the midst of the action.

For example, to play a particular chord on the guitar, you'll need to press your fingers onto the appropriate strings between the proper frets. At first, you'll do this with deliberate attention and care. Place the fingers just so. Strum the strings with the other hand. Does it sound right? How hard do you have to press?

Adjust your playing technique until the chord sounds clean and clear. Then do the same for another chord. Moving back and forth between the chords will train your fingers to make the transition between the sounds that might be the key part of playing a favorite song. Repeat this sequence of movements until you can do it blindfolded.

The watchword for this entire process is ***Practice.*** Perform the task repeatedly, making adjustments as needed, until you achieve success. Then perform the successful action over and over until you've integrated it completely. *Practice, practice, practice.* Some techniques will require considerable practice to gain fluency, while others can be assimilated quickly.

In any case, additional practice will serve you well. As you continue to practice beyond the "automatic" level, you will begin to develop greater fluency and confidence in your performance, while increasing your appreciation for the subtler aspects of the techniques involved.

Maybe you've heard the story of a famous concert violinist who had played at the highest levels of classical music with the finest orchestras from around the world for many years. His performances were truly exquisite, even to the untrained ear. After a very full career of masterful performances and memorable recordings, he retired from the concert circuit. Years later, he was interviewed by a reporter when he was in his late eighties. The reporter asked the violinist how he spent his time now that he was happily retired.

The master musician replied that he still practiced the violin two or three hours a day. His response took the reporter by surprise. So he asked, "After all these years, why would you still want to practice, even into your retirement?"

The master replied, "Well, I think I'm beginning to make some progress..."

Clearly, practice was no chore to this master violinist. He simply loved to play. And after continued practice over all those decades of accomplished musicianship, he was still discovering additional levels of perfection in playing the violin. Practice may not make perfect, but it will continue to uncover deeper layers of subtleties and generate additional satisfaction for the dedicated enthusiast.

Make friends with these small skills. Since you will be practicing them a lot over the years, it's important that you enjoy the simple process of training yourself in these small ways. If the training is not enjoyable once you've "got the hang of it," then you will find yourself bowing out of your endeavor without even noticing it. You'll simply stop doing it, and that will be that.

The results you create at this level will be limited in their satisfaction, since only a small piece of the full task is performed and learned at one time. Learning the notes and chords to play the chorus of a song can be dull and tedious until it begins to come together smoothly into a melody.

In the early stages of learning tennis, shagging the ball time and time again can be quite draining. It is not until you've progressed to the point of being able to volley the ball back and forth with your partner that it really becomes enjoyable. So as you begin to learn a new field, be patient with yourself and remember that the best parts are yet to come.

To maximize your satisfaction and speed your progress, use only high-quality equipment, training products and services. This enables you to have the best possible results with the least wasted efforts. Be wary of "cheap" products and training services. What may seem like a bargain now might generate inferior results later.

Since you will be investing a considerable amount of time and energy in learning your new field, matching that with a corresponding level of excellence in your training and equipment just makes sense.

Using great equipment actually facilitates your enjoyment of the learning process. You can demonstrate this to yourself quite easily. Ride a department-store bicycle around the block, then go to a bike store and ride a high-quality, brand-name bike. There's no comparison! Likewise, if an experienced instructor or quality training program can save you a week's worth of misplaced efforts, how much is that worth to you? When you're investing in yourself, you deserve the best assistance you can find.

When assisting others, you'll also want to provide all you can. One of the best ways to learn anything is to attempt to teach others. At this early stage of the game, though, you don't really have much knowledge or many skills to share. Clearly, you are not in a position to offer assistance to those who are farther along, so the only people left to assist are your fellow Novices.

This can work out great, though, since there are probably some skills and ideas that you've picked up that your fellow Novices have not, and vice-versa. Become co-learners and you can help guide, explore and encourage each other through this early stage of mastery. Enjoy making mistakes together!

Yet, if the mistakes continue and little progress is being made, it may be time to defer to more knowledgeable and experienced practitioners or instructors. With just a quick tip from someone who is more advanced, you can avoid mishaps and wasted efforts for all concerned. Your most valuable asset at this point is your enthusiasm, not your expertise, so be generous with the former and frugal with the latter.

To help insure your success at the Novice level, it will be helpful to focus on developing two of the ten character traits mentioned in Chapter 1, namely: *Mindfulness* and *Patience.*

In the excitement of beginning a new endeavor, it can be difficult to concentrate on any one thing. Too many fresh ideas and experiences clamor for your attention. Cultivating *mindfulness* and the ability to control your attention will thus be crucial to your success. Since at the Novice level you are working with one small chunk of information or one component skill at a time, it will be necessary to be able to focus on that task without interference from other thoughts or concerns.

The term *mindfulness* brings together two aspects of this ability to hone in on the task at hand. The first is the notion of bringing your *full mind (and body)* to bear on the material you are working on. Handling other concerns before putting your attention on your study or practice can clear some mental space for what's to come. Utilizing all five senses also helps to enrich your learning experience, and aids your ability to make new mental connections. The process of clearing mental (and physical) space and concentrating all your faculties assists in making the most of each learning experience.

The other important aspect of *mindfulness* is a sense of being simultaneously involved in the current task, and also reserving some part of yourself to act as the "witness" to what is taking place. "Watching" yourself perform as you practice a skill can help you progress by providing feedback from "within" and "without."

Feeling yourself performing the skill from within enables your muscle memory and mental/emotional memory to make the proper connections needed to internalize the skill. At the same time, by "witnessing" your performance from the outside, as if you were a spectator to the event, you can gauge the effectiveness of your performance as it appears to the outside world. Balancing both types of feedback gives you a clearer and more accurate estimation of your progress.

Patience is the other character trait that will be tested at the Novice level. When first beginning to explore a new interest area, there is a natural tendency to mis-judge the depth and complexity of the area to be studied. Since you do not really have a full grasp of what your field is all about just yet, these kinds of mistakes are common. When seen from the outside, the basic information and skills that you are studying at this level seem so simple that you could easily master them in a short time. But once you dig in and become involved in these tasks, you will discover subtleties and complexities that you didn't know existed. Impatience with the whole process can then set in and undermine your satisfaction.

Since it's all new, everything at the Novice level seems complicated. That's why the progress of the Mastery Traveler at the Novice level is symbolized by traveling through a dense forest. At this early stage the Novice can only see the individual trees, not the whole forest. It's easy to get lost in woods, and the Novice will frequently feel confused and overwhelmed by it all. Progress can be agonizingly slow as you begin to realize how much there is to learn. Comments like these are often heard:

"I didn't realize that to become a concert pianist, I'd need to practice four hours a day for years!"

"To draw like my favorite artist, there are mountains of techniques to learn. I don't know if I'll ever be that good."

"Management? I can't even manage myself and my own responsibilities, much less all that goes on in this department."

"I thought cooking would be simple, but now I realize that to be a good chef, I'll need to learn a lot more than I thought."

These disappointing realizations can lead to ***discouragement.*** This difficult topic is addressed in the Repair Kit of Chapter 12.

Experience has shown that one reliable rule of thumb is this: *Whenever performing an unfamiliar or seldom-used skill or task, count on it taking THREE times the amount of time you think it should take.* Perhaps this is the universe's way of reminding us that the world is a much more interesting place than it seems at first glance. You've probably heard this quote: "God, grant me patience, and I want it now!" Surprise! Cultivating patience takes time...

The following section examines the types of learning tasks and experiences encountered by people at the Novice Level in a variety of subject areas. These subject areas were chosen to cover a broad range of topics and illustrate the progression of learning with specific examples that are appropriate for each area. Use these examples as a guide to the type of learning experiences you may encounter in your chosen field. These same subject areas are provided as examples in all of the mastery level chapters.

THE NOVICE PIANIST

At the very beginning, the Novice Pianist learns how to position her hands over the keyboard and how to strike the keys in different ways to produce variations in timbre. She'll also learn to identify and play the individual notes and chords, while keeping a sense of timing with each keystroke. Along the way, she'll be learning the language of the piano, including the names of notes (A, B, C, etc.), chords (C major, D minor, etc.), white and black keys, and the expressions for how the keys are struck (staccato, legato, etc.)

Most people learn to read sheet music during this early stage, as well. This is necessary for the budding concert pianist, and quite useful for the more casual performer interested in modern popular music. Being able to read the musical score will enable you to learn songs when there is no one available to guide you in the process. Then you can simply play the music as it has been written, since the notation is literally a symbolic shorthand for the music.

As in any field, the goal is to learn the basics by heart, and in terms of playing the piano, that translates into developing an easy familiarity with the pianist's terminology, and the ability to play the correct notes and chords in proper sequence without looking at the keyboard. Association of the notes with the keys must become automatic, so your conscious thinking can move on to more advanced aspects of playing the piano. With all the possible combinations available, this will likely take a considerable amount of time to accomplish.

With most musical instruments, including the piano, students learn to combine the notes and chords into simple songs at first, and then progress into more complex music involving a wider variety of notes, chords and more challenging playing and timing sequences. This actually involves many of the principles used at the Adept level. In general the Novice learns the component skills (like notes and chords), and the Adept merges those small skills into integrated techniques that result in complete results (like songs or stanzas). Here the progression results in simple songs at the Novice level and more complex music at the Adept level.

THE NOVICE BASKETBALL PLAYER

The Novice basketball player begins by learning the rules of the game, the fundamental principles of play, and the basic skills of dribbling, shooting, passing, rebounding and man-to-man defense. Since this is a very physical sport, most beginning players will also need plenty of conditioning work to train their bodies to run, jump and move laterally or backwards in ways that correspond to typical basketball situations. Developing speed, agility and endurance will also be a key part of that conditioning.

Practice in the elemental skills of dribbling, shooting, passing, rebounding and defense will assist the budding player in acquiring the hand-eye coordination, agility and ball control needed during later phases of play. Being able to dribble the ball without looking, while running the court at full speed should be one of the goals at the Novice level. Likewise, passing and shooting while on the move will be vital to successful game play. Practice in jumping, positioning, timing and anticipation will build the skills needed to become a successful rebounder. Learning the principles, stance, footwork and reactions needed for man-to-man defense equips the new player with the basics required to play at the defensive end of the court.

Even though basketball is a team sport, at this early stage of development, individual skills are stressed. Only when the individual skills are learned to an adequate level can they be applied to playing as a team. As in most other fields, basketball players never outgrow the need to practice these fundamental individual skills. Even the most accomplished pros still spend a considerable amount of their daily practice time on the basics of dribbling, shooting, passing, rebounding and defense.

THE NOVICE ARTIST

Beginning artists first work on capturing the shape of the

objects they are drawing. Typically, this starts with what is known as *gesture drawing,* reproducing the outlines of objects, living things or people. The outlines serve to distinguish the object from its background, while giving some definition to the shape or form of the item. Later, the budding artist will incorporate the more sophisticated skills of shading, coloring, texturizing, and highlighting (among others) to distinguish one area from another.

In the process, she will learn about the principles and terminology associated with value, form, balance, hue, saturation, brightness, contrast and lots more. Most art students also get some exposure to art history and the various styles of art that were developed by different cultures over the years. Each style typically uses its own techniques, tools and materials.

At the Novice level the artist concentrates on content—drawing and/or painting simple items so that they are immediately recognizable and life-like. Successfully reproducing any object in a realistic manner constitutes the primary goal at this level. The ability to see deeply into the complex visual subtleties of the items you draw or paint, and then faithfully capture and reproduce what you see provides you with the mental and physical skills you'll need later on to produce truly dynamic visual art.

Even if you are not interested in realism as an artistic style, be sure to concentrate on developing your skills in visual realism at this stage of your learning, since every technique you learn now will help form the basis of any other style you wish to develop. As in other fields, considerable practice is required to internalize the skills involved and absorb the knowledge needed to enable those skills to be developed even further. There is no substitute for practice.

THE NOVICE CHEF

Cooking food seems like such a simple activity until you begin to delve into the complexity of knowledge and skills involved. The culinary field is one of the few that involve creating a multi-sensory experience. In preparing a dish, the chef must take into account the taste, aroma, appearance and texture of the food he creates. Thus, the chef has a very broad array of factors to balance in the preparation of each dish.

As a Novice Chef, you will need to familiarize yourself with all the various characteristics of different plants and animals that are eaten as foods in a given culture. Fruits, vegetables, grains, seeds, nuts, fish, birds, mammals and a wide variety of herbs and spices present a fantastic array of food possibilities.

Likewise, there are many different methods of cooking, including boiling, baking, frying, sautéing, roasting and many other variations. These different cooking methods impart their own unique flavor, texture and appearance to the food. Learning about these methods, as well as various preparation methods like chopping, slicing, mixing, kneading and tenderizing, provide a rich background of information, principles and techniques that will form a foundation for your culinary endeavors.

Along with absorbing all this background knowledge and fundamental skills, the primary task at this Novice level is to prepare various dishes exactly according to the recipes provided. At the Novice level you want to make sure that you can create the food according to the recipe, so that you know what it is "supposed" to taste like.

Similar to the idea of playing music exactly as it's written in the score, performing recipes exactly as written grounds you in the basics of the culinary field. It could also be said that until the Novice Chef fully recreates the gastronomic visions of the chef who created the original recipe, he has no right to alter it to his own tastes. After all, if you can't prepare a dish according to its recipe, what makes you think you can improve it?

THE NOVICE MANAGER

Most managers start their management careers by taking on a supervisory role as a project manager, workgroup supervisor, or department manager. Ideally, you will have worked on similar projects, within similar workgroups, or in the same department as the people she is now supervising. In any case, you'll want to gather information and experience related to the tasks that your group performs.

If you are that Novice Manager, you'll be asking and finding answers to the basic questions of: Who? What? Where? and When? as they relate to your group. Who is in your group? Who do you report to? What is the group's function? What tasks need to be performed? Do you need to coordinate your work with other groups? What reports or documents need to be prepared? When are they due? Do you have deadlines to meet, or production schedules, sales goals, or work cycles to work within? What are the standards of quality or regulatory requirements that your group must meet? What is your group's budget, and do you have responsibility for it? Where do you and your group work? Where do you get your raw materials and business information? Where does your completed work go?

This seemingly endless series of questions hints at the depth of responsibility you have now assumed. At the Novice level, your task is to get a handle on the content of what and who you are managing. Successfully managing the tasks of your group is your primary responsibility, so concentrate on those functions at this early stage.

If you have the opportunity, practice those primary functions within your group before those results "count" in the workings of your company. *Practice* is the watchword at this stage, as it is for anyone else performing at the Novice level. Few Novice managers take the time to practice their group's functions, so the result is that their inevitable mistakes occur during the normal course of business, and the fallout from those mistakes can damage their careers, the company's bottom line, or the safety of fellow workers.

Study and practice your tasks until you (and all the members of your group) know them by heart. In the business world, this kind of conscientiousness pays great dividends in the progress of your career and the success of your company.

*I am always doing that which I
cannot do, in order that I may
learn how to do it.*
— *Pablo Picasso (1881 – 1973)*

Level 2: The Adept
Treat Your Subject Area as a **Craft**

Level 2: The Adept
Treat Your Subject Area as a CRAFT

Objective: To develop a deeper, more complete understanding of your subject area, while combining your skills in ways that generate whole, complete, successful results.

Process: Step back to see how what you've learned fits into "the big picture." Assemble concepts, ideas, and information into an integrated understanding of your field. Join component skills into whole techniques, then practice those techniques as complete routines. Carefully craft more and more successful results. Focus on *process*.

Expected Results: To understand your field as a complete entity, and successfully craft a portfolio of products or techniques.

Action Steps: To advance your understanding, *ask lots of questions*. Your basic question is, "how does this work?" To integrate your component skills into whole techniques, *observe closely*, and explore the subtleties of the process. *Practice those complete techniques*, looking for the essential nuances of each method that make it successful. *Build a portfolio of your successes*.

Keys to Success: Engage in discussions that explore the workings of your field. Seek understanding. Cultivate *discipline* and *confidence*. Develop relationships with others in your field. Find some pros to emulate. Model your techniques on their successful methods.

Words of Praise/Encouragement: You did it! Very good work! That's great! (Reward increasingly successful results.)

How you can help others: Strengthen your command of the basics by assisting Novices. *Demonstrate, encourage and guide*. Since you are still putting it all together, avoid the role of instructor. Simply assist where needed.

Chapter 8

Level 2: The Adept
TREAT YOUR SUBJECT AREA AS A **CRAFT**

Growing weary, the mastery traveler slows her pace. As she looks back, she notices that the road has been gradually rising for some time now. No wonder she's tired. Ahead stands a sign announcing a scenic overlook. At last, a place to rest and gather strength. She stops and sits on the bench, letting her gaze sweep over the sea of trees below. Far away beyond the forest rim, she sees the highway emerge from the woods onto the plain. "Hey, that's where I began," she says to herself. "I've come a lot farther than I thought."

Turning around, she can see that the road she's on curves up the mountain, winding back and forth across its slope. That peak can't be far, now...

You can recognize your advance into the Adept level by noticing a shift in your perspective. As a Novice, you began with a narrow focus, concentrating on the basics of your subject area, learning one thing at a time. You studied a series of terms, concepts and principles, and accumulated a lot of information. You practiced a number of small skills and internalized them. At that early stage, you studied the *micro* elements of your discipline, viewing your field through a close-up lens.

At the Adept level, your perception shifts to seeing the "big picture," the *macro* elements of your craft, as though viewed through a wide-angle lens. This shift comes naturally as you gather more and more skills and knowledge. At some point you will sit back and take stock of what you have learned so far. You'll ask yourself, "How does what I've learned fit together? What can I do with all I've gathered? How do I carry it through to a successful conclusion?"

The primary concern of the Adept is to **assemble** the

knowledge and skills that have been gathered at the Novice level into viable results. You are putting together the simple elements that you studied as a Novice. The result forms the completed whole product, the assembly of the parts, the "big picture." The emphasis is on the *process* of assembly. Which methods work well, and which do not?

A simple example that illustrates the Novice and Adept levels of learning is the process of putting together a jigsaw puzzle. The puzzle comes in a box with the picture to be assembled shown on the front cover. Beginning at the Novice level, you dump the pieces onto the table, turn them "right-side up," and begin to sort the pieces into piles related to the colors and other features of the picture. Along the way, you may practice fitting some of the pieces together to get a feel for the subtleties of shape and color that allow two or more pieces to connect correctly. As a Novice, you are focused on the individual pieces and their unique characteristics.

Once these preparatory steps are completed, your perception shifts to the "big picture." At the Adept level you step back and regard the picture on the box again. You begin to assemble the outside edge of the picture from the pieces with the straight sides. You're literally building a framework for understanding and assembling the puzzle. From there it's on to the subtler and more complex relationships between the interior pieces. These pieces now need to join on all four sides, with the shapes and colors of adjacent pieces matching perfectly. More sophisticated spatial, color and pattern recognition skills are employed. Your goal at this Adept level is to correctly fit all the pieces together into the finished picture.

Throughout this process, your attention shifts back and forth between the narrow view, focusing on the specific features of each individual piece, and the wider view of how that piece might fit with others to form the entire image. Thus the Adept level involves a review of material learned as a Novice, but now with an emphasis on the broader goal of combining the knowledge and skills learned earlier into complete, integrated techniques.

To build an understanding of your field from all the

information, concepts and skills you learned at the Novice level, it will help to develop some *clarity* in your knowledge. If things are clear, then the pieces of your understanding start to snap into place and everything begins to *make sense.*

When cleaning a windowpane, clarity is achieved by wiping away the dirt and smudges on the glass. In a similar manner, clarity of knowledge is achieved by wiping away errors, misconceptions and distortions in your understanding.

Questions are the rags to use in wiping away the dirt that interferes with your understanding. Asking questions helps to clarify any points that you missed, and reveals new subtleties in the ideas and applications you are examining. At this stage, your basic question is: *How? How does this work? How should I approach this problem? How does this concept relate to that other information? How do I apply what I've learned to this situation?* Keep asking questions, and your understanding will become crystal clear. With a clearer understanding of what you are doing, you'll be able to progress faster and easier, while making fewer mistakes.

The goal at level two in any field is a comprehensive understanding of the nature of the discipline, and the production of quality products or performances. What you're looking for are *results!* In a sense, results *become* the "big picture."

Generating results is the purpose for attempting some action in the first place. The reason to execute the play in football is to score the goal. The purpose of strumming the guitar is to play the song. The bottom line in completing a profit and loss statement in accounting is to see how much money was made. Generating results is the name of the game at this stage, and that is what separates the Adept from the Novice. The Adept is able to put it all together into useful results.

At this level, you are learning to determine the methods and techniques that culminate in successful outcomes. You are "separating the wheat from the chaff." The key to this essential step is to pay close attention to the details involved in performing each technique, and to tinker with the elements to determine which combinations produce the desired results.

Study how accomplished professionals do it, and note the subtleties of their performance. Model your techniques on those of someone whose skill you admire. See if you can copy the pro's methods. By using that ideal performance as a benchmark, you can deepen your understanding of the process, and steadily improve your results.

At first it may not be obvious how the pro's techniques work so effectively. It all seems a bit magical. How does the accomplished presenter get the audience to loosen up and feel comfortable so easily? How did the pro tennis player learn to place his shots at the edges of the court? How does the black belt martial artist get her moves to blend together so smoothly? In general, what are the key aspects to emphasize in performing each technique?

Here the guidance of a professional instructor or coach can be invaluable. From a broad base of previous experience he or she can quickly point out the important points to concentrate on that may have escaped your attention. While learning the basics in level one can often be accomplished with little fuss by using a prepackaged training program of some sort, the subtleties of understanding and performing a complete routine or producing a whole product can be difficult to obtain from such a static approach.

A trainer or instructor can see the subtle, yet crucial flaws in your performance that you may never notice. At this stage, you are concentrating on the *process* of putting it all together, and you don't have much attention left over to "watch yourself" perform. The trainer/instructor can play this role well. He or she can watch you carefully and evaluate your performance impassively. Since that person also has more experience with the same struggles you are going through, he or she can provide the insight needed to avoid a long period of fruitless trial and error.

Regardless of the learning strategy you've chosen, you will need to develop a high level of ***discipline*** to navigate this stage successfully. Since the best way to learn is to make a lot of mistakes (and of course, learn from them), a measure of discipline will help you weather this unrewarding period.

By setting aside a particular time slot for your study and practice, you can begin to develop the regularity needed to ensure that your learning process endures. By practicing at the same time of day and in the same place, you are providing your mind with subtle cues that help put you in the proper frame of mind to perform. The routine that you develop in "going to the gym for a workout," for example, helps establish the sort of discipline that bypasses the need for excessive willpower.

Doing your study or practice in the company of others will also assist you in maintaining your discipline. Going to the library or a coffee house to study written material, for example, helps reinforce the fact that you are not alone in your labors. Even though the folks there are not necessarily concerned with the same type of study that you are, the energy of a group of people pursuing their own (similar) goals is contagious.

Of course, if you can gather a small group of people who are involved in your field to study or practice with you, that will prove even more effective at generating discipline and quick results.

Since your goal at the Adept level is to learn to create successful results, it pays to treat your subject area as a *craft*. To *craft* a birdhouse from a collection of lumber, as an example, implies that you will measure, cut and prepare the wooden parts precisely, then skillfully assemble the pieces into the complete structure, and carefully apply the finishing touches to bring both aesthetic beauty and practical utility to the final product.

The qualities of precision, care and skillful attention to detail are what distinguish a finely crafted product or performance from a lesser effort. Treating your subject area as a *craft* will help guide you in producing increasingly successful results.

Attention to this kind of quality craftsmanship at level two yields the satisfaction of a job well done. Producing a quality product or performance can be very rewarding, helping to build your confidence and fuel your desire for further accomplishment.

Increased *confidence* might seem like the natural result of producing some successes, but that is not always the case. Confidence arises from the *recognition* of your own successful efforts and *rewarding* those efforts appropriately. Many people fail to notice the significance of their own accomplishments, remaining mired in doubt about their abilities. It seems much easier to pay attention to the flaws in your performance than to notice when things go right.

Most people find that their internal critic tends to work overtime, finding fault with everything they do. The trick to developing confidence is to interrupt this habitual process, and begin to notice the aspects of your performance that *are working.*

Some people might say that this is not realistic, that looking for something good in a flawed performance is just sugarcoating the poor results. But don't forget, this is a *learning process.* Making mistakes is normal and valuable. Could you have done better? Of course. Were there things that went well? Of course, again.

It's all a matter of where you place your attention. Try making a mental or verbal acknowledgment of the progress you are making: "OK, these parts of the performance are working well. I've got those down pat. Now a bit more practice to integrate these other aspects. I'm making progress, now, just a little at a time."

When you are noting to yourself what worked and what didn't, be specific in both areas. **Example:** *You are learning tennis, and volleying with an opponent. She hits the ball to your backhand. You run to get it, but your return goes into the net. Instead of telling yourself, "Oh s---, I screwed up my backhand again..." try, "OK, I hustled over to the ball, got my feet positioned right, with the backhand swing coming smoothly, but I was a little slow with the swing, and I need to adjust the stroke angle a bit to get more lift."*

The second assessment is much more accurate than the first, by noting both the successful and unsuccessful aspects of the play. It has the advantage of pinpointing just what went wrong, as well as recognizing what went right. Now, do this type of self-assessment *every time* you make another attempt. Before long it will become a habit that will boost your confidence and provide direction for further improvement at the same time.

As you advance through level two, you are gradually becoming more ***adept*** at your craft. This is good, since you become *adept* at something when you can produce successful results more than once. Being able to repeat your successes demonstrates that your accomplishments are not flukes, and that you really do know what you are doing.

Reaching the pinnacle of the Adept level signifies the end of the "training phase" of your learning. You have enough knowledge and skills to be able to perform effectively in your field. You've got the ***know-how***. In many disciplines, demonstrating your complete successful results in some form constitutes a "rite of passage" or "graduation" into the next level.

In many martial arts, you graduate by attaining a *black belt*. In formal education and training at the trade or college level, there is a graduation ceremony to honor this achievement. In music, you are now ready to play or sing with other musicians in a band, group, choir or orchestra. In athletics, it's time to compete with others in some type of official contest.

In less formal learning environments this achievement is sometimes overlooked. If you are involved in this type of setting, make sure that you reward and honor yourself (and each other, when in a group) for your very significant accomplishments. Celebration is in order! You've demonstrated that you are indeed *Adept...*

THE ADEPT PIANIST

In playing the piano at the Adept level, the budding musician begins to put together the notes and chords and musical notation into songs that can be recognized and enjoyed. As mentioned before, the Novice Pianist is concerned with learning the keystrokes and scales, and playing simple songs to practice those basic skills.

Once the keystrokes have been learned, the subtleties of

various stanzas can be explored. Much of the nuances of music are to be found in the transitions and interplay between the notes and chords. In music, as in many other areas, timing is everything.

So the level two pianist must broaden her awareness to include the entire piece being played. A great deal of time will be spent practicing these transitions, becoming ever more sensitive to the smoothness and accuracy of pacing and timbre, and the gentle but firm fingering of the keys. The emphasis shifts from the keystrokes themselves, to the *process* of playing those keys in a harmonious manner.

At the Adept level, the music being played gradually becomes more complex and interesting. You learn to use both hands and work the footpedal at the same time. The range of sounds you make broadens and deepens to deliver a fuller, more complete sense of the music. Your results become far more satisfying as you blend the three (or more) voices played by your hands and feet into harmony.

Just as you did at the Novice level, your attention will shift back and forth from the focused learning of a new chord sequence, to the broader view of the piece in its entirety. Only now you will spend less time with the individual sequences and more with the integration of the entire piece.

You reach the peak of accomplishment at level two when you can successfully play moderately complex music at a satisfying level of competence. At this point you can play the music without mistakes, and play it in a manner that is true to the emotional "feel" of the original score. Congratulations!

THE ADEPT BASKETBALL PLAYER

At the Adept level, playing basketball becomes a lot more interesting. All that time spent learning to shoot, pass, dribble and play defense can now be put into action in a more meaningful way. It's time to scrimmage! The fun and excitement increases dramatically as you put all your skills together to play the game.

Since scrimmaging simulates game play, you'll be practicing all your individual skills in ways that demand a broader perspective on the sport. At the Novice level you practiced in isolation, or in one-on-one situations. Your attention was confined to perfecting your individual performance of each skill, one at a time. Yet, sinking shots when there's no one around is relatively easy compared to trying to get off a shot with two defenders swarming around you, sticking their hands in your face and batting at the ball.

Similarly, when you first learned to execute a bounce pass, the goal was to deliver the ball to your teammate quickly, smoothly and accurately, so he could catch it easily. But at the Adept level you look beyond the successful execution of the pass to learn when and where to use that type of pass.

Your skill in dribbling the ball takes on a new sense of urgency when you must not only dribble, but keep the ball away from defenders, size up the position of all the players on the court, and use that dribble as a prelude to a drive, pass or shot. Putting all those skills together in successful and harmonious ways presents the major challenge at this stage.

Clearly, most of your attention must now shift to noticing the positions of your teammates as well as the actions of the other team. There will be little attention left over to spend on the individual skills that you recently learned. Dribbling, passing and shooting must come instinctively now, so you can be ready to execute those skills when the opportunity presents itself.

To accomplish this, your vision will have to open up to be able to see situations developing on the court. The Adept's ability to see the "big picture" takes a literal turn here. Rather than the narrow focus you've used thus far in concentrating on those solo skills, you'll need to develop your peripheral vision to take in all the action.

Maintaining that broad perspective throughout the course of the scrimmage will play a key role in your success. Any time your attention collapses back to a narrow focus on an individual event, you'll become vulnerable to steals, blocked shots or other types of preventable errors. Your own "tunnel vision" can become a bigger threat than the opposing team!

If you haven't perfected your individual skills to the point where you can perform them "without looking," you simply won't be able to expand your attention to "see what's coming." Continued practice of those individual skills will be the only answer to that particular dilemma.

In order to "see everything," shift your gaze from the players and ball to the gaps between them. Since all the action takes place in the spaces surrounding the players, noticing the spaces instead of the players will alert you to any new developments before others see them. That way you'll also be noticing the actions of *all* the players instead of just one.

Just as in the piano example above, at the Adept level your attention shifts to the transitions between events, rather than the events themselves. In music you work with the transitions between notes and chords to develop accurate timing and harmony in performing a song. In basketball you work with the transitions between dribbling, passing and shooting, and the harmony of players cutting to the basket, and setting picks and screens to develop a successful play.

Even the definition of success changes with the territory. At the Novice level, your concern was to successfully perform those solo skills. Now your personal performance must integrate with the larger goals of the team. The *individual* act of shooting expands to become the *team* act of scoring. You begin to see that the shot that swishes through the net is only the final act of the scoring play.

At the Adept level most of the work goes into developing plays that allow one player to shake his defender long enough to set up an easy shot. Creating a high-percentage shot becomes the focus at the offensive end of the court. At the other end, players work together on defensive techniques that keep everyone on the other team covered, so they take only poor low-percentage shots, or none at all.

Throughout this period of learning to work together as a team, players will still be continuing to practice their individual skills, while adding new techniques like setting screens and picks, cutting and driving to the basket, and passing in traffic. At Level 2 you develop the individual and team *tactics* that enable your success. The tactics involved in "getting open," rebounding, scoring and team defense will all coalesce as you scrimmage to improve your game. The results come in the satisfaction of smoothly executed plays that result in points on the board, and the camaraderie that accompanies great teamwork and shared accomplishment.

THE ADEPT ARTIST

Once you can accurately draw or paint still life objects, capturing the likeness of their shapes, proportions and colors, you're ready to move to the next level. Now it's time to place those object into a *scene*. As an Adept artist, your vision widens to include the relationships between the items in the scene. You actually start to pay more attention to the spaces between the items than the items themselves. Much of the drama of a fine drawing or painting comes from the skill that the artist uses in generating a three-dimensional scene on a two-dimensional surface. When done effectively, the scene will appear to "pop out" of the canvas and take on a palpable quality of realism that makes the viewer want to "reach out and touch" the items in the painting.

The three-dimensional qualities of the scene are reproduced mostly through the play of light on the objects portrayed and the various techniques that can be used to demonstrate the differences between those items or people in the foreground and the other elements comprising the background. To portray these complex relationships, you will learn techniques of layering, proportion, perspective, foreshortening, shading, highlights, shadows and chiaroscuro. Color shifts and variations of detail and focus can also be used to indicate these subtle changes from front to back within the scene.

At the Adept level you also delve into the much more complex arena of life drawing. Learning to portray the human form effectively will help you craft your skills in the intricate areas of shape, proportion, shading, texture, and subtle variations of color. The process of capturing people's expressions, stances and features can be amazingly subtle, so the ability to insert these details into your art will often serve to demonstrate the depth and breadth of your skills.

The Adept artist has a tremendous amount to learn at this level, and it usually requires a lengthy period of practice and experimentation. Fortunately the visual nature of drawing and painting provide instant feedback for your efforts, enabling you to see the progress you're making as you hone your skills.

It's not easy, but the rewards you earn are terrific. Artists who successfully traverse the Adept level leap ahead of their lesser counterparts and become instantly recognizable as "real" artists. Even those who are not very knowledgeable about art can easily spot the additional accuracy and sense of realism that the Adept can create in her work. All that extra craftsmanship you invested in each piece pays off as you begin to fashion superior works of art.

THE ADEPT CHEF

As a Novice chef your primary concern was to learn the many techniques needed to enable you to prepare a wide variety of dishes exactly according to their recipes. The emphasis was on developing practiced precision in the basic skills of measuring ingredients, mixing and blending, knife-work, and various cooking methods. Once you can perform these skills smoothly and consistently, preparing any *new* recipe becomes much easier.

By the time you've practiced these techniques enough to develop a recipe collection of your favorite tasty dishes, the next step that naturally emerges is to put some of those dishes together to create a complete meal for your guests. While this might not sound like such a big deal at first, you'll soon find that the process of preparing a successful meal involves much more than simply cooking the individual dishes properly.

The Adept chef steps into a whole new world as he shifts from concentrating on producing a single dish that tastes good to creating a complete *dining experience* for his guests. To begin with, consider what type of meal you're preparing and the overall character of the foods you select.

Will the meal be the highlight of the evening, where the guests are expected to linger over their food and savor each bite, or will it be a prelude to a more active evening of dancing and revelry? What about the texture and temperature of the food? Will this be a warm, hearty, stick-to-your-ribs, comfort-food meal, or a cool, crisp, light-grazing type of affair? Will the mix of flavors and aromas in the dishes you prepare be intense and spicy, or subtle and delicate? Do you plan to stay within a particular regional or cultural style of cuisine, or will you lead your diners through a smorgasbord of culinary styles?

Choosing *complementary* dishes for each meal goes way beyond mere flavor considerations. You'll want to balance the nutritional content, select the textures, juxtapose the colors, dress the ingredients with sauces, artfully present it all on the plate and then accent each dish with a simple garnish. To create an outstanding meal, the food needs to look as appetizing as it tastes, while providing a nourishing repast for your guests. A fine meal appeals to all of the senses and tickles your pleasure centers on every level.

The Adept chef also learns about the importance of atmosphere and service to the dining experience. Providing a comfortable environment that includes an attractive decor, subtle lighting, music and friendly conversation contributes a great deal to the overall experience. Eliminating noises and interruptions while offering prompt and efficient service also adds a special touch that your guests will appreciate.

Harmonizing all these ingredients into a complete dining experience will take considerable practice and involve many subtle adjustments. To put it all together successfully, timing is everything. Just as in music, preparing and serving several dishes at once calls for precise interweaving of efforts and critical attention to the smooth flow of the process.

In both the kitchen and dining room, you may be working with others in preparing the meal. At the Adept level you must learn to coordinate your efforts with the rest of the cooks and servers. As in basketball, teamwork comes into play as you adapt to your position and begin to work together effectively.

The Adept chef plays a much bigger game than he did as a Novice. Taking responsibility for creating a complete dining experience demands a much deeper understanding of the culinary field, and a more comprehensive approach to integrating all the myriad factors involved.

When it all comes together successfully, the results can be particularly satisfying for everyone. You set an inviting table in comfortable setting. The aromas that waft from your kitchen arouse the taste buds of your guests. Preparation of the food goes smoothly and the service is timely. Your guests find the meal to be a delicious feast for all their senses. Everyone is delighted, and goes home full and happy. Cheers all around, as your efforts have contributed to creating the kind of fulfilling culinary experience that lies at the heart of every culture.

THE ADEPT MANAGER

As a Novice manager you concentrated on the content of your job—the tasks to be performed, the quality standards to be met, the sales or production quotas, and the reports that must be generated. Basically, you had to figure out exactly what your group was supposed to do, and then make sure that the work was completed.

Now that you have a handle on all the components of your group's responsibilities, the next step is to work on the *process* of how that work gets done. At the Adept level, it's time to step back and look beyond the tasks to be performed and begin to examine the people and procedures involved. The Adept manager shifts from addressing *what* needs to be done to dealing with *who* is doing the work, and *how* well that work is being performed.

How should you organize the work flow? How do you make sure that the work gets done on time? How can you motivate the group to cooperate with you and each other to get the work done? How do you handle the frictions that develop between people? What does it take to satisfy your boss and make sure your group gets the rewards they deserve?

This is where all those business books, management theories and project software you studied have a chance to be put into practice. If you haven't had the opportunity to explore the theoretical side of management, then that might be a good step to take. Read some management-related books and arrange to have a senior manager coach you as you progress.

New managers typically start out in one of two ways. The more formal method of entering the management profession is to enroll in a business related program at a college that leads to a degree in management. If you choose this method, then you will be exposed to some of books, theories, charts and software mentioned above. Your business degree studies will thus form the basis for your progress at the Adept level. Some programs even offer an internship or externship course toward the end of your program where you get the opportunity to learn and work in a real-world business setting. This helps to ease you into your new career and build confidence in your abilities.

In many other instances new managers get their start in a much less formal way. You may have worked in a particular staff, sales or production position for a period of months or years. Over time you've become quite accomplished in your work. Then, when a supervisory position opens up, you apply or are appointed to fill this post. Bingo! You're now the next supervisor or manager of your group.

If this is your situation, then you face a different learning curve than the business school graduate. Since you have jumped into the management fray by taking this new position, you now need to compress all the learning that occurs at the Novice, Adept and Rookie levels into your new situation. To make matters more difficult, you may not get any sort of formal training for your new position, either.

Since you have demonstrated that you can do your job well at the staff level, it may seem natural to assume that you would be the best choice to manage others doing the same job. Unfortunately, this is not always the case. Performing a job and supervising others doing that same job are totally different tasks, and involve different knowledge and skill sets that don't even overlap all that much. It may even call for a person with an entirely different temperament.

So the business school graduate and the veteran worker both begin their new managerial positions as Rookies at their positions. Each has a different background containing strengths in some areas and weaknesses in others. Both will likely need to begin at the Novice or Adept level in some aspects of their jobs.

The business school graduate has completed her training and emerges from college with an Adept's level of competence in the art of management, yet her knowledge and experience in the field where she's managing may be lacking. She may know little or nothing about the nature of the work done at her new company. Her learning curve thus involves putting together a knowledge base in this new field at the Novice level and building upon that through the Adept level.

Just like in the other fields, Adept managers also shift their focus from handling the minutia of their group's work parameters to the broader concerns of how their group's performance relates to other groups within the company. This expanded view also includes examining the relationships the company maintains with suppliers, service vendors, consulting firms, and of course, your clients or customers.

Where does your group fit in? How does your group's performance affect these other relationships? If some aspects of these relationships could be improved, are you the one to initiate those changes? What changes can you effect, and what are the limits of your influence?

As an Adept manager, you look around and discover yourself in the thick of all these relationships, shuffling around to find your place within all of them. As you can imagine, this often takes a while, and sometimes results in some painful moments as you bump into the limits of your influence and the limits of your budding skills as a manager. It's a tumultuous time.

With practice, patience and a little guidance from more experienced senior managers, you can work on integrating all these relationship parameters into the performance of your job. As you gradually get a handle on *how things work* in your company, you'll be crafting better performance for both yourself and the group you lead.

Unlike some other fields where the transition from the Adept level to the Pro level is marked by producing whole successful products (like complete, tasty meals), or performing at a competent level (as in playing a moderately challenging piece flawlessly on the piano, or executing a successful series of plays in basketball that score points), the Adept manager may find it difficult to determine just how well she is doing in an overall sense.

The field of management (like many other service professions) doles out it's rewards in smaller doses. When your group meets its work deadlines or quotas, that's an indication of your competence as a manager. This is also true when the monthly reports you generate look good to upper management. When you solve a problem in production, or come up with some good ideas in a meeting, or work through a personnel issue successfully, you are certainly making progress. Yet, seldom do all these things happen at once. Most often the kinds of events that mark your graduation from Adept to Pro will be sprinkled in with other not-so-successful moments where things don't go all that well.

So remember to make note of your successes as they arrive. Congratulating yourself for a job well done is a necessary step for developing your confidence. Keep a notebook or spreadsheet that chronicles your most effective decisions and actions, along with the outstanding accomplishments of your group. You'll want to remind upper management of your successes from time to time, and being able to add written detail to your memories will be especially helpful when your review is due!

An expert is a person who has made all the mistakes that can be made in a very narrow field.
— Neils Bohr (1885— 1962)

Level 3: The Pro
Treat Your Subject Area as a **Science**

Level 3: The Pro
TREAT YOUR SUBJECT AREA AS A SCIENCE

Objective: To integrate your knowledge and skills into a comfortable, reliable and effective approach to your field that produces winning efforts. To generate consistent, high quality results with a minimum of time, effort and resources.

Process: Integrate the theory and practice of your field by applying various theories to your performances, and in turn, altering your theories based on your results. Continue to practice complete techniques to internalize entire performances. Focus on *optimizing results.*

Expected Results: A comprehensive understanding of all aspects of your field and a personal philosophy of action that leads to success. The ability to consistently deliver excellent performances in demanding circumstances.

Action Steps: To integrate your knowledge and skills, *explore the basic question of: Why?* "Why do it this way? Why not try a different method?" Challenge yourself. In a scientific manner, *examine* and *dissect* all aspects of your knowledge and performance back to elemental levels, and *reconstruct* new, more effective techniques. *Practice those revised techniques* to forge consistently flawless performances.

Keys to Success: Expand the scope of your knowledge by exploring related areas. Develop your resource base. Devise *strategies* and *tactics* to generate "winning" performances. Cultivate *desire* and *perseverance.* Find a mentor/coach to guide your progress. Follow his/her advice.

Words of Praise/Encouragement: Superb! Excellent! Terrific! Delicious! (Reward excellence when achieved.)

How you can help others: Test the coherence of your philosophy and the breadth and depth of your skills by teaching Novices and Adepts. Learn from them.

Chapter 9

Level 3: The Pro
TREAT YOUR SUBJECT AREA AS A **SCIENCE**

With an extra surge of effort the mastery traveler finally reaches the summit of the mountain. Elation! Triumph! "I did it!" she shouts to the world. To her surprise the booming echoes of her victory cry ring out over the landscape. She laughs out loud as the peaks reverberate with her joyous exclamation.

Looking back down the mountain the way she came, the enormity of the view before her begins to sink in. Breathing gently and easily now, her voice softens to little more than a whisper. "Sure, that was a tough climb, but will you look at that view? Amazing. I can see every tree and road for miles. No wonder it took so long. The road I took winds back and forth all over the place."

*After resting awhile she walks around the summit and explores the view in all directions. Off in the distance beyond this crest loom the giant snow-covered slopes of a mighty mountain range, its upper reaches shrouded in fluffy clouds. "Now those are the **real** mountains. This is just one of the foothills of those big boys. Wouldn't it be amazing to climb to the top of those mammoth peaks? Imagine the view from **there.***

"But you know, I'd really have to get into better shape to tackle that much climbing. It looks cold there, too. I'll have to gather a bunch of equipment to take on this new trek. And then there's the long roller-coaster ride over the vast hilly plateau between here and there. Traversing that seems like it would take forever. Well, every road leads downhill from here, so I might as well head someplace interesting..."

The descent from the peak of accomplishment in level two comes initially as a bit of a shock. You've worked hard to learn everything necessary to generate those first few successes. And those results came at the price of a great deal of time, effort and concentration. Your euphoria starts to wear off as you begin to compare your best efforts with the routine accomplishments of proven performers in your field. Placed in that different perspective, your early successes don't seem so impressive.

As you continue to practice, you begin to realize that being able to put all the pieces together into a successful result is only scratching the surface of what your field is all about. The concentration you've been using to merge those component skills into a whole performance required every ounce of your attention. But as you practice those complete performances until they too become routine, your attention is gradually freed from the absorbing task of proper assembly. Then the resulting attention becomes available for other things.

Once you can perform the whole routine "without looking," your continued concentration and practice reveals an entire world of subtleties that were hidden from you just a short time ago. It's as though your vision expands, and you can now see farther and deeper into the nature of your discipline.

From your elevated view at the peak of the foothills, the enormous depth and breadth of the high plateau and the majesty of the giant mountains beyond offer an awe-inspiring glimpse into the full range of possibilities that stretch before you. With your first taste of this realization comes an exquisitely humbling moment of genuine wonder. Who knew that such magnificent beauty and such deliciously elaborate intricacies were hidden just below the surface of the obvious?

As the sense of wonder begins to fade, a new and stronger respect grows within for the accomplishments of the many masters who came before you. It was their discovery and exploration of this vast landscape that paved the way for you to follow in their footsteps.

Now, humbled by a glimpse of the enormous scope of the journey you've begun, you see that a decision must be made. What will you do now? Which way will you go? From this peak of success it's all downhill in every direction. Upon closer inspection you find that there are only three paths to choose from.

The first choice is to go back down the same road that brought you here. This direction leads you out of the wilderness and back home to the safety and comfort of the familiar. The second choice is to explore the other foothills in the area. You may not reach any higher elevations on this route, but the extended trek will surely prove interesting. The third choice is to dig deep and head for those tall peaks far in the distance. This is a much longer and more arduous journey, but it offers the possibility of higher achievement and the certainty of new adventures.

The mountain metaphor and the dilemma of the three paths can be expressed in a different, and perhaps more pragmatic way. Now that you've gotten a sneak peek of the enormity of what can be learned in your field, and you've achieved some modest success in the process, the three alternatives before you look like this:

1. Quit while you're ahead.
2. Continue as an Amateur.
3. Turn Pro.

Of course you could always quit, since you already have some initial accomplishments behind you. That might be enough to satisfy you if your enthusiasm is wearing thin. Maybe the struggle to get this far has been more trouble than it's worth for you. The new skydiver who has his first successful jump can now say, "I've done it, and that's enough for me!" If you choose, this is a great point to bow out of your field, as you will have put in enough time and effort to have "given it a fair shot." *If you quit now, you can still hold your head high.*

But what if you truly enjoy playing with your newly expanded capabilities, yet for whatever reasons, this new field is not so important that you wish to make it your life's work?

Perhaps you took up the flute so you could play softly as you hike in the woods. Or, you may have started doing woodworking as an escape from your stressful job, with the reward of creating your own coffee table as a bonus. Maybe you took a gardening class at the local free university so you could learn to grow your own flowers and vegetables, but you have no desire to become a farmer. Or perhaps your doctor suggested that you get more exercise, so you started running, and began to enjoy it so much that you don't want to stop, yet you have no great ambitions to star in the next Olympics.

If these examples describe your level of interest and commitment, then it may be best to continue in the same vein that you have been comfortable with as an Adept. Simply continue as an amateur.

The terms *Amateur* and *Pro* are used here to distinguish between differences in *intent*, not between levels of talent, dedication, accomplishment or compensation. In this sense, *an amateur is one who performs primarily for his or her own satisfaction,* reveling in the quiet pleasures of engaging in his or her field for its own intrinsic benefits. In the examples above, the flutist, woodworker, gardener and runner chose to continue with their fields simply for their own enjoyment. Just participating in their interest areas is reward enough for them. Typically, these areas of interest evolve into pastimes, hobbies, or sidelines. The activities serve to round out a fuller life that may be dedicated to other, more pressing concerns.

There is something pure and noble about the pursuits of amateurs. Since they are only doing what they do to please themselves, amateurs can go about their endeavors without the concerns of fulfilling the expectations of others, competing for victory, or making their efforts pay the bills.

With dedication and perseverance, amateurs can sometimes outperform their professional counterparts. But since amateurs are not really interested in competition, it's often difficult to make that determination. To the amateur, it doesn't really matter. That's not the point, you see.

If you do decide to continue as an amateur, just proceed with the methods described in the previous chapter to continue to craft successful and satisfying results. Though the rest of this chapter is oriented towards those who turn Pro, you may find some of the techniques and processes described later on to be of value to you in maximizing enjoyment of your pursuits.

There's one thing to keep in mind, though. Many amateurs find that sooner or later their enthusiasm for their interests starts to wane. Even when things are going well and there seems to be no difficulty generating good results, your passion will start to taper off. Before you know it, you've stopped your flute playing, woodworking, gardening, running or whatever you began doing.

The problem is a lack of *incentive*. Once you can perform successfully, the natural next step is to improve even further, and become more consistent in the process. For a while you can sustain this progress on your own, since you probably have an innate sense of the pace of your own development and improvement.

However, as you get better and better, further improvement generally comes in smaller and smaller steps. After a while the steps become so subtle that you may not notice any improvement at all. Then, without further incentive, your fascination with this field may peter out altogether. You find yourself asking, "What's the point?" Now you are down to one of the other two choices.

The third alternative is to turn **Pro.** This is a big step. You can say goodbye to the casual approach you may have been employing thus far in your learning. By turning Pro you are entering a world where the stakes are dramatically higher than before.

Initiation into the Pro ranks begins when you decide to test yourself. Depending on the activity you are involved in, this can take several forms. In each case you are *putting yourself on the line,* testing your knowledge and skills against some additional standard besides your own.

Perhaps the most obvious way to turn Pro is to land a **job** in your field. Now you *must* perform. No longer can you just putter around at your own pace, fiddling with the results simply to satisfy your own urges. By signing on with an employer, you are going to have to learn how to do things the employer's way. In return for your pay, you'll have to get up to speed quickly and then continue to perform at a high level to satisfy the demands of your position.

There are other ways to "turn Pro," though. The prospect of entering into a *competition* could be the test that launches you forward to a higher standard of performance. If you are involved in athletics, martial arts, or other areas where contests or competitions are held, this can propel you into the Pro ranks, even if there is no prize money to compete for. It doesn't matter whether you are competing against an opponent, racing the clock, or performing in a contest to impress the judges.

Becoming a Pro involves a shift in the way you regard yourself, and a new more focused and serious approach to your discipline. By performing to standards that are set by others, you automatically broaden and deepen your commitment to the task at hand. You begin to challenge yourself to perform at your *personal best*. While Amateurs may also strive to improve themselves, the Pro has "upped the stakes" so that nothing less than his or her personal best will suffice. It is that change in circumstances that marks your advancement to the Pro level.

Another way that this shift to the Pro mode of thinking can happen is through joining with others to perform with, or lead a team. The musician who joins a band or orchestra, the actor who lands a part in a play or movie, the worker who becomes the supervisor or team leader, or the climber who volunteers to lead the expedition, all step up to a new level of responsibility that goes beyond themselves to encompass the welfare of the other members of the team. The added responsibility brings with it an expanded sense of dedication to your discipline. Now others are counting on you. You *must* perform to the best of your ability, or you will let down everyone else, as well as yourself.

A shift in consciousness occurs when you challenge yourself to perform to standards set in that broader context. You begin to realize that in this new setting, everything you do affects the success and welfare of others. (Actually, this was always the case, though now it's easier to see.) By expanding your thinking to include the effects you have on others, you become a *bigger,* less selfish person. This process of adapting your knowledge and skills to better serve others could be considered the very definition of *professionalism.* Of course, once you make that shift into the larger world of performing for others, there are additional steps that mark your advancement as a professional.

The stand-up comic raises the bar a few notches each time he plays to larger audiences at more impressive venues. The stakes get higher in moving from telling jokes at a party to performing at the local "talent night," to becoming a regular at the comedy club, to headlining at a Madison Square Garden extravaganza. Yet these steps (as significant as they are) mark levels of *achievement* for the Pro, rather than any shift in approach to the performance involved.

As you've probably already realized, the Pro level covers the most territory of all the mastery levels. It becomes the eventual home for the vast majority of people who continue to participate in their discipline.

Within the broad range of knowledge, experience and capability represented by Level 3 are three distinct sub-levels. These three sub-levels of **Rookie, Journeyman,** and **Expert** correspond to successive stages of development within the Pro level. Each signifies a subtle shift in orientation and emphasis within their development. Though these stages have their unique qualities (as we shall see shortly), the learning methods used and the overall approach is common to all three stages of the Pro level.

The term Pro is used to describe Level 3 because of the many concepts that apply to this mastery level that begin with the prefix *"pro-."* Some of the attributes that people strive for at the Pro level are to become: *pro*ductive; *pro*fessional; *pro*ficient; *pro*fitable; *pro*found; *pro*gressive; *pro*lific; *pro*minent; *pro*sperous; *pro*vocative; and to demonstrate their *pro*wess. Being a Pro covers a lot of ground, doesn't it?

In Latin, the prefix "pro-" means: *ahead* or *forward;* to go forth, as in the verbs pro-ject, or pro-mote. Clearly, *getting ahead* is a key feature of the Pro mind-set. This forward-thinking orientation will serve you well as you continue to apply yourself. Like a compass, the thought of *moving ahead* can direct you forward to the next set of challenges that mark your progress.

The overall objective at this third level is to expand your capabilities and refine your performances to a higher standard. Once you can create *some* successful results, it's natural to take the next step, and improve the quality and consistency of your efforts.

And, as your quality and consistency develop, you'll become increasingly *pro*ficient, *pro*ductive, and *pro*lific, which are key qualities of the *pro*fessional. The core goals of *refining* the quality of your results, *optimizing* your efforts, and *expanding* your capabilities will guide your learning process at the Pro level.

Reaching those goals can be frustrating, though. The difficulty is that further improvement at this stage comes in smaller steps and arrives at a slower pace. After all, as an Adept you made great strides in putting together those first few laudable performances. That's going to be a tough act to follow. Additional progress will require **refinement** of your already successful results.

And **refinement** is often a long and difficult process. It requires tremendous attention to detail. That's why a *scientific* approach is recommended. To improve on a process that already works well, you'll have to examine every detail of your performances with the intent of finding all the imperfections. Once found, the blemishes can then be polished away.

This process is a literal description of the *scientific method.* Armed with a theory of how your performances *should* turn out, you closely examine the whole process to see how well your performance compares with the ideal. All that time spent assembling the component parts of your whole routine at the Adept level is now reversed. For the next step, you'll need to dissect it all, and re-examine how each piece contributes to the whole.

Discrepancies are discovered. Changes are introduced—slowly—one at a time, so as to determine the effects of each change. Subtle alterations in technique are tested again and again, with careful attention to the results they produce. The most successful results of each trial are then combined all over again and re-tested to gauge if any progress has been made. It is this painstaking procedure that lends validity to the scientific method. It is rigorous! However, when you are done, you can be confident that you've "left no stone unturned" in arriving at your successful solution. You'll have "done your homework."

The process often proceeds erratically. Improvements in quality typically come in fits and starts. Practicing the same routine again and again may not result in any improvement at all. Then suddenly you may notice some detail that is not quite right. Making the necessary alterations can then result in a noticeable gain. Any progress you make can thus be inconsistent and unpredictable.

This intermittent and slow improvement will test your commitment to your field. To see you through this plateau of relatively slow progress, it will help to cultivate the twin qualities of *Desire* and *Perseverance* mentioned in Chapter 1.

When the going gets tough, and it's not easy to see what to do to make any further progress, only your *desire* will see you through. *You've really gotta want it.* You've got to know exactly what you want from all your study and practice. What is the ultimate result that you are looking for?

If you look deeply at this question, you'll find that at the root of your desire for accomplishment in your field there is a very special feeling. This desire is not so much a high level of attainment, or some reward that accompanies that attainment. Rather, the ultimate result you desire is the *feeling* you get when you are performing at your very best.

Hidden beneath your desire to: *win the contest; beat your opponent; impress the audience; receive the standing ovation; gain the respect of your peers; make tons of money; see your name in lights; or on the cover of Time magazine;* or whatever seems like your ultimate goal, is the feeling that washes over you at your finest moments. This elusive feeling can take many forms. It varies with each person and the nature of the goals you long to achieve.

The examples of achievement mentioned above are the outward manifestations of the inner feelings that enabled those rewards to be attained. It is the exquisite, deeply emotional feeling of *performing perfectly, triumphing over obstacles, and exalting in a sense of greatness beyond what you suspected you possessed,* that lies at the heart of your desire to participate in your field in the first place.

To determine the nature of your innermost desires, try this deceptively simple method. Ask yourself *why* you want to achieve your goal. When you get your answer, then ask yourself why you want that. Keep repeating the question, *"Why do I want that?"* for each response you generate. As you delve deeper and deeper into your own motivations you will find that your answers will all revolve around some version of the experience of *ecstasy.* The greater the effort, the deeper the sacrifice, and the higher the hurdles, the more rewarding that feeling becomes.

Desire is the urge to experience ecstasy in one of its many forms. Remembering the particular feeling of ecstasy that moved you to begin your mastery journey will help fuel that desire. When you recall that emotion, spend some time visualizing and deeply feeling the ecstasy that accompanies the very moment when your goal is fully realized. This exercise will actually draw the result you seek closer to you.

[For a full examination of the process of generating the feeling of ecstasy and increasing happiness in your life, please refer to the forthcoming book *The Ecstasy Principle,* by the author.]

In between those alluring moments of desire, you'll want to make sure that you have plenty of *perseverance.* When your determined efforts don't produce the results you are looking for, just keep at it. Look a bit deeper, see even more subtleties, and be open to any possibilities that present themselves.

Keep practicing. Don't give up. Persevere.

You've probably heard that success is 10% inspiration and 90% perspiration. Your sweat and toil will indeed buy you the results you desire—eventually. There's just no telling how long it will take. Sometimes you stumble upon some valuable improvements without too much trouble. The rest of the time it may not be that easy, and you'll just have to keep plugging away. Using a scientific approach guides your perseverance by providing a systematic method of chipping away at the improvements you seek.

Perseverance is just the price of admission to the Pro level. Pros are not fair-weather practitioners of their trades. To be a Pro, you have to perform day in and day out. Nobody said it would be a walk in the park. Successful mastery travelers are able to set their sights ahead, on the prospect of gaining greater expertise and higher levels of satisfaction. They understand that traveling the mastery road is more like a marathon than a sprint.

Remember that in the fairy tale, the tortoise eventually triumphs over the hare. And the way that the turtle wins is by *never giving up.* The turtle keeps his desire alive while he perseveres, slowly putting one foot in front of the other, until he finally crosses the finish line. *The hare was a dilettante, but the tortoise was a **Pro.***

THE PRO STAGES: ROOKIE, JOURNEYMAN AND EXPERT

When you take that first step into the Pro level, you begin as a **Rookie,** then progress further to become a **Journeyman,** and then at the upper reaches of the Pro level, you can develop into an **Expert.** The process often takes many years, but the rewards are plentiful, and the improvements you make along the way are truly remarkable. Let's explore how this progress takes place.

As you emerge from the Adept level, you have just learned to successfully complete an entire performance. You have a pretty solid grasp of the principles and techniques used in your field. In short, *you know what you are doing,* at least theoretically. The trouble is that most of your knowledge is based on the training you have just completed, and you've only recently put that all together into successful results. Your new capabilities are still fresh.

Like making lasagna, you've chopped and prepared the meats and vegetables, then layered the pasta, sauce, cheese and fillings in the pan. You have all the ingredients of lasagna. You've put it all together as an Adept. Now it's time to add some seasonings, and bake for a period of time to let all the ingredients reach their peak flavor and texture, while the various tastes and aromas mingle together to become one in the delectable main dish. To continue on the road to mastery you'll need to merge your raw talents and capabilities into a fully baked finished product. Development at the Pro level backs up your training and theory with more real-world experience.

Now you begin all over again as a **Rookie,** with a solid background of knowledge and skills, but relatively little familiarity with the tasks and performance requirements of a working Pro. As a Rookie, your goal is to broaden and deepen your newly acquired capabilities to firmly establish your *competence.* You are looking to emphasize your strengths, shore up your weaknesses, and utilize the very best of the techniques and skills you've learned to give yourself every advantage you can find.

It is tempting to think that you *know it all* at this point in your development. After all, you can point to the successful results you've generated to prove your point. Yet so far you know "just enough to be dangerous." You know how things are "supposed" to work, but lack the experience needed to apply that knowledge in new and different circumstances.

As a result, Rookies are often the butt of jokes and pranks played by their more experienced colleagues. If this happens to you, try to be patient and not take offense. This "hazing" process is just another initiation rite. Often without fully understanding what they are doing, your colleagues are administering their own test to see if you are worthy of joining them as an *insider* in the field you share. If you can handle the razzing that they dish out, then you can be included in their ranks. You become "one of the boys."

Thus the most pressing task for the Rookie is to *prove yourself.* If you are to have a future in your field, you'll need to prove yourself to your colleagues, your bosses, and yourself. You will want to know that you really *can* perform at this new higher level that is now expected of you.

To create this sense of confidence in your capabilities, you'll need to increase the quality of your work to reach or exceed the prevailing standards. To accomplish this, use the refinement process described earlier. Now you have the performance standards of the group to use as the baseline for your improvement. As you adjust to your new situation, your *confidence* and *competence* will arrive hand in hand.

If you are smart, you'll enlist the assistance of one or more of your colleagues in guiding you through this Rookie period. After all, they already "know the ropes." Who would be better qualified to offer advice and guidance in your unique circumstances? You may as well use every advantage available.

Besides, there are some sneaky psychological advantages to enlisting the support of your peers as you learn the sometimes unspoken rules and standards of the group. Part of the behavior of your colleagues revolves around the psychology of the existing insider group. Everyone here already knows each other, and what each person is capable of producing. *You* are the new and unknown quantity. *You* are a threat to their security, so you'll want to defuse the situation, and reassure them that you are not the enemy.

Your peers will want to probe and prod you to "see what you're made of." The hazing and other initiation rituals are part of this familiarization process. By asking for advice and guidance from your colleagues, you will be helping to sate their curiosity about who you are and what you can do. At the same time, your inquiries reaffirm their status as the established, dominant players. They will actually be flattered to answer your questions, because then they get to offer their knowledge and demonstrate their skills without appearing to "show off." Soon the hazing will stop as you become integrated with the group.

Thus, by simply asking questions of your peers, you are fulfilling their unspoken needs at the same time that you're filling gaps in your own knowledge. Before long they will be so comfortable with you that they will begin to ask for *your* opinions and advice. Without anyone even noticing what happened, you could gradually turn the tables and become the new authority, the new "go to" person.

Once you've proven yourself to your colleagues and anyone else who has an interest in your development, you can now regard yourself as a **Journeyman** in your field. Your performance meets the existing standards, and you've attained a measure of consistency in the process. In short, you can perform what is required, on demand.

So now the pressure is off. Once you can perform as well as your peers, there is no longer any need to prove anything to anyone. The Journeyman is finally able to relax and begin to enjoy his craft a bit more than before.

In fact, you can recognize Journeymen by their easy confidence and the comfortable way that they go about their tasks. Journeymen have learned their entire craft "by heart," and have developed their performances into a well-oiled routine. After so much struggle to learn, you can at last take it easy.

When you can perform consistently and reliably to a high standard, as Journeymen can, what is there left to learn? At this point, it appears that you've got it all handled. You can perform at a very competent and satisfying level, so there is no great need to go any farther down this Mastery road.

The Journeyman stage of development is symbolized by the flattest portion of the Pro plateau. The Rookie portion of the road runs through some rocky terrain, and includes some significant hills, and the Expert section requires still more climbing, but the Journeyman stage offers a welcome respite from all that elevation change.

The learning that occurs at the Journeyman stage consists primarily of *adaptation, expansion* and *optimizing.* Over time, the circumstances governing where, when and how you perform will change. Every time you get a new boss, address a new client, confront a new competitor, or play at a new venue, you'll have to make adjustments to your routine. This involves the familiar *refinement* process (where you painstakingly introduce subtle changes and evaluate the new results), only this time you may have to adapt to the shifting circumstances *on the spot.* If your adjustments are not successful, then you'll have to review and revise later, after your screw-ups have been endured.

As you are adapting, you'll also be expanding your repertoire of skills and accumulating more knowledge. Learning to play new songs, adding new moves to your game, or taking on new responsibilities in your job are all part of the gradual expansion of your abilities at the Journeyman stage. This process of learning new techniques and routines will broaden your base of skills and add to your command of the field.

Another adaptation that comes naturally at this stage is the streamlining of your efforts. In the midst of refining your techniques, you will notice ways to accomplish your tasks that take less effort, time or resources. Since we are all lazy by nature, these more efficient methods will be eagerly adopted. Clearly, *optimizing* your techniques so that you can accomplish more with less will be to everyone's advantage. To the newcomer, your ability to perform at such an elevated standard, with such ease and comfort, will seem wondrous.

Performing at the Journeyman level is indeed a comfortable and satisfying experience. For most people, that comfort and satisfaction is so endearing that they remain at this level for the rest of their lives. It is the Journeymen who settle down along the banks of the rivers on the high plateau and populate the small cities and towns. They have found their place in the world.

It is interesting to note the origin of the term *Journeyman*. During the Middle Ages, apprentice cabinetmakers would spend years under the tutelage of their masters, painstakingly learning their craft. As the young woodworker neared the end of his apprenticeship, he would be required to produce a special *journeyman's piece*. This unique product was a miniature version of his woodworking specialty, such as a table, cabinet, bureau, or chair. The apprentice would invest every bit of his skill in producing the very finest piece possible. If the master pronounced it worthy, then the young craftsman would be able to end his apprenticeship and *journey* to another town, where he would set up his own cabinetry shop. There the journeyman's piece would sit prominently in the shopkeeper's window, as his signature effort.

If you are excited about your field and eager to strike out on your own and set up your own business as an entrepreneur, shop owner, consultant, coach or independent contractor, then take some advice from the original Journeymen and learn the ropes first as a Rookie before making that big leap to independence. You'll want to be able to consistently produce a quality product or service before staking your career on the results.

Starting a new business demands a tremendous amount of time and effort. It is only at the Journeyman level or above that you have gained the ability to perform effectively without really thinking about it too much. At all the earlier stages your complete attention and concentration was needed to learn the nuances of your trade. Now, at the Journeyman stage, you finally have enough free attention to begin thinking about striking out on your own.

So if you wait and let your employer pick up the tab for your Rookie training, you can avoid making those inevitable Rookie mistakes when it counts toward the bottom line in your own business. In fact, once you have proven your competence on the job, then you can begin studying the other aspects of the business you are in, and prepare your business plan while you are still earning a paycheck. By doing this "homework" while still on your employer's clock, you can hit the ground running when you have gathered all you need to start your own show.

Of course, many people find plenty of satisfaction and rewards—and a lot fewer headaches—in a career where they work for others. In a world where most everyone who is employed resides at the Journeyman level, you'll find a wide range of talent, skills and attitudes on this plateau.

Much of the difference in competence between individuals at this level can be determined by noticing if and when they *stopped learning.* Since Journeymen can perform well without much effort, there is a point where some people stop learning altogether, and begin to just "go through the motions."

As you become so skilled that you can do your job in your sleep, then the tendency is to simply nod off! This phenomenon is responsible for all the people you see who appear to be sleepwalking through their jobs. These Journeymen act like zombies sometimes, because their minds are literally off in a dream world, thinking about something else entirely.

Ironically, most of the people who are dissatisfied with their work *used to* find it interesting. They were truly fascinated with their job while they were busy learning everything and getting up to speed. Then, once they reached the Journeyman stage and could do their jobs blindfolded, they simply stopped learning. Amazingly, their work suddenly became boring!

Remember this when you become bored with your work, or your relationship with your significant other, or your life in general. *Things are boring only when you've stopped learning about them.* This amazing world we live in is infinitely rich in detail and subtleties. There is *always* something more to learn about any topic, person or phenomenon you care to explore.

Realizing this, there is no reason to be bored *ever again.* Just bring your full attention to bear on this present moment, observe and deeply *feel* whatever presents itself, and a whole new depth of intriguing nuances gradually reveal themselves to you. *Seek, and ye shall find,* was the biblical admonition. Our deeply mysterious world cannot help but give up its secrets to an inquiring mind.

The best scientists, musicians, artists, craftsmen, writers, directors, poets, inventors, entrepreneurs and athletes have realized this truth, and then they spent their lives showing the rest of us what their inquisitiveness has revealed. Simply put, *learning something new, and then demonstrating what you've learned to others, gives life meaning and satisfaction.* Without this simple process in place, life quickly dissolves into a pointless exercise in futility.

When this sense of boredom and futility takes hold for you (and rest assured, sooner or later it will), then it's time to move a little farther down the Mastery road.

To revive interest in your field, you can take the next step and become an **Expert.** Journeymen typically perform in a solid, reliable and competent manner, yet are rarely outstanding. Though the Journeyman's technique may be beyond reproach, and serve as a terrific complement to the work of others, it lacks the sheen of excellence that the Expert can bring to his or her performance.

As a result of years of diligent effort, and an almost fanatical attention to the subtleties of the discipline involved, the Expert manages to take his or her performance a couple of notches higher, to the point where it borders on perfection.

Yet, advancing to the realm of the Expert involves much more than that little bump in the quality of your performance. Using the same scientific approach that is inherent in the *refinement* process, the Journeyman becomes an Expert by applying those processes to a broader and deeper range of topics that surround the field that he or she is studying.

All along the way from Novice to Journeyman, you have been gradually learning how to perform within your field. Yet this represents just *one way* to approach it. Your techniques will reflect the methods of those who taught you. Your instructors, the authors of the books you read, your boss and colleagues, all have molded your performance to reflect their methods and theories about how it should be done. You have assembled your particular methodology from all you have gathered on your journey thus far.

Experts cast a wider net. They investigate beyond learning *how* something is done, and begin asking the question, *"Why?"* By studying their fields from a variety of perspectives, they find themselves exploring and learning a number of different strategies in the process. Using this multi-faceted approach, their understanding and skill set becomes deeper and richer. With these expanded experiences, Experts can develop the *expertise* to select the correct strategy to use for each situation.

So the Journeyman marriage counselor expands her perspective to include study and practice in adjacent fields, like developmental psychology, sociology, communication theory, perhaps neurolinguistic programming (NLP) and even economics. From her broader knowledge and experience, she can now assist couples in examining their problems from these additional angles.

Here are some examples of situations where the faultless

performance of the Journeyman may still fall short of the mark:

In football, the offensive team may execute the play perfectly, only to find that the defense has shifted into another formation, resulting in an interception or a fumble. You may be able to play one song beautifully, yet another song using the same chords in a different sequence, style and tempo may prove troublesome. As a stand-up comic, you may have developed a great routine that delivered a ton of laughs last night, but tonight, at a different venue with a different crowd, all those same jokes are falling flat. The terrific sales presentation you gave last week to Able Software's executives resulted in a fat contract. But now, at Corporate Consulting, your LCD projector's bulb burns out and your fancy PowerPoint© slides are shrunk to the tiny screen on your laptop. Corporate Consulting's executives are unimpressed, and your presentation dies a painful death.

Only the broad and varied experience of the Expert can get you out of these kinds of situations intact. In these situations you'll have to shift gears and pick another, more appropriate strategy from your bag of tricks. By studying a wide variety of theories, strategies and approaches, the Expert becomes an excellent problem-solver. The bonus that arrives with this expertise is a palpable sense that you know your field *inside-out*. A true Expert can dazzle and amaze others in the field by applying some little known technique that manages to snatch victory from the jaws of defeat. By pulling a rabbit out of the hat, Experts sometimes appear to be able to do the impossible.

With these kinds of wide-ranging abilities, it's no wonder that Experts are the ones who are singled out to become spokespeople, and represent their field to outsiders. Experts are often interviewed by TV, radio, net and print reporters who want to understand some new development in the Experts' field. Journeymen may not have the broad experience needed to explain all the technicalities to a layman.

So the Expert stands at the pinnacle of development at the Pro level, armed with an encyclopedic knowledge of the field, wide-ranging problem-solving skills, and the capability of performing with precise, near-perfect technique.

Experts epitomize another aspect of performance at the Pro level that is worth mentioning. Pros take what they have learned at the earlier levels and *apply it* to some higher purpose beyond the mere performance itself. This shift into utilizing your knowledge and skills to accomplish a particular goal is another factor that distinguishes the Pro from the Amateur.

It is this concentration on *purpose* that shapes the refinement process, and reveals inefficiencies in the techniques used. Focusing on a strong purpose also enables the development of strategies and tactics that combine to achieve a specific result.

At the Pro level, the economist shifts from attempting to understand the world of economic policy to using that knowledge to accumulate a pile of money. The athlete turns from learning various plays to utilizing those plays to win the game. The woodworker beings to apply those new joinery techniques he just learned to improve the appearance and functionality of the cabinetry he builds.

As a developing Pro, the martial artist gradually begins to feel and direct the movement of *chi* (or as it is known in Japanese martial arts, *ki*) in her body. With this new, deeper awareness, the moves learned as part of the form she has been practicing suddenly come to life. Now she can *feel* how the application of those techniques in a combat situation can help her subdue an attacker.

Despite the adult-oriented professional image of the Pro level, Level 3 is not reserved for those in any particular age group. Although it may be easiest to see the example of the college graduate moving into the professional world as the stereotype of entry into the Pro ranks, people at almost any age can become Pros, depending on the field they choose.

In some endeavors, people start very early and their careers tend to peak at a young age. Swimming, gymnastics, figure skating, diving, popular music, and many other fields all have players who peak in their teens or early twenties. These fields all require exceptional flexibility, balance, power, and/or a youthful mindset.

Those involved in most other sports, construction trades, performing arts like singing, dancing and acting, and professions that use emerging technologies, like software development, web design, or computer animation, all tend to peak in their late twenties and thirties. This age range corresponds to the period of life when we are at the pinnacle of our physical strength, mental acuity, and emotional power.

Professionals in traditional careers like art, law, politics, marketing, architecture, engineering, photography, medicine, science, teaching, and trades such as plumbing, auto mechanics and the culinary arts continue their development right along into their forties, fifties and beyond. Many great classical musicians, managers, writers, researchers, designers and inventors don't peak in their fields until they are almost ready to retire. These are all fields where the benefits of broad experience outweigh the advantages in physical capability that may be displayed by younger practitioners.

By the time you've reached the Pro level and settled in as a Journeyman or Expert, you've accumulated a wealth of experience that could serve as a valuable resource for those who are at the earlier stages of development. You are now at the perfect stage to offer your knowledge and skills to others as an instructor or coach. By doing this, you will not only help pave the way for others to reach their goals, but also deepen your own knowledge and skills in the process. There's nothing like trying to teach your craft to someone else to reveal those things that you don't fully understand.

Don't worry about locating students. If you are open to sharing what you know, you will find that people will be attracted to you who need just what you have to offer, at a level that will challenge you both. Just let people know that you are willing to assist, and opportunities will start popping out of the woodwork.

THE PRO PIANIST

As the Adept Pianist continues to add to her repertoire of songs, she begins to match her growing skill with a sense of ease and confidence in her abilities. With increased confidence, she may consider turning Pro and playing her music for paying audiences.

Whether it's a simple gig in a bar or coffee house, or a more elaborate opening with a larger band or orchestra, the first experience of playing before a "real" audience is a nerve-wracking event. That flock of butterflies fluttering in your stomach is a sign that you're about to take a giant leap in your musical development. Regardless of how that first big event turns out, you've shown your courage in taking that huge step. Now you're a Pro.

There's no turning back! If you stumbled and floundered with your performance, then you know it can only get better. If it turned out great, then that should provide the boost in confidence that can turn loose your talents. All that's needed in either case is (guess what?) continued practice—to polish your skills, tame those wild nerves, and expand your musical repertoire.

Practicing with other members of your band or orchestra provides plenty of opportunity to work on your timing, harmony and precision. During your Rookie period you will also learn how to handle your "stage fright" and the moods of various audiences, as well. Seek out advice and tips from those who have already "been there and done that." After all, they survived somehow. The stories they have to tell are often tragically amusing, and offer pearls of wisdom that can guide you through your Rookie period to the Journeyman stage. With continued practice, achieving routine excellence is well within your grasp.

You can then advance to become an Expert Pianist. All it takes is to become inspired by a certain style or genre of music, or to concentrate on a specialty like teaching or composing your own music. Then your continued efforts can lead you deeper into the rich fabric of musical history and the vast array of playing styles and rhythms available on the world stage. By making one of those styles your own and developing rich skills in that area, you can rise to the level of Expert in your specialty. *Then* the world will come knocking on your door.

THE PRO BASKETBALL PLAYER

First, keep in mind that the term Pro Basketball Player above does not necessarily imply that this level is reserved for NBA players. Certainly, all NBA players are pros, both in the sense used here, and in the fact that they are well paid for their work.

The key feature that distinguishes the Adept from the Pro in athletics is the emphasis on *winning*. As an Adept, you learn all aspects of the game, and concentrate on putting those skills to work in executing successful plays. Now at the Pro level, what counts is using those plays to win the game. So the term Pro would likely apply to most college and some high school players, along with the more serious players in the playground wars and amateur leagues.

The adjustment to this higher level of thinking and performing demands considerably more dedication to the game than you have needed thus far. Of course you will still continue to practice all your individual skills and team plays, just like before. But now the emphasis on winning brings into focus the development of *strategies* that will enable you to press your advantages over the other team.

These advantages are exploited through individual matchups, player substitutions, and offensive and defensive strategies. Players move from learning to play together to assisting each other in creating scoring opportunities on offense and disrupting their opponent's play on defensive. Strategies are developed that take advantage of the tactics you learned at level two.

In order to maximize your chances of winning, you must be willing to sacrifice your own glory for the good of the team. At level two you learned many scoring plays and polished your shooting skills to become an offensive force on the court. Yet at the Pro level each player's skills are meshed together to develop a winning team effort. The successful basketball team operating at the Pro level knows what it takes to win, and delivers.

At both the individual and team level, you will need to develop a series of moves and plays that can be counted on to take advantage of your strengths and minimize your weaknesses. Once you develop your "favorite" techniques, you'll want to expand your repertoire to include variations on those special moves and plays.

The variations will be needed to counteract the adjustments that opponents will inevitably make once they get burned by your success.

Taking apart each move and play down to its most fundamental level will enable you to discover the real heart of each technique. Honing in on these gems will add power and precision to each move. Using the scientifically oriented *refinement* process to examine and test the effectiveness of each component skill will go a long way toward gaining that little half-step that can keep you ahead of the competition.

Beyond refining your own play, studying your opponents' past performances can provide further fuel for your efforts. Coaching strategy and tactics become vitally important to the success of your team at this stage, since it's the coach's assessment and guidance that will steer the efforts of the team.

Just like in other professions, optimizing your efforts will pay big dividends at the Pro level. For athletes the question becomes, "How can I maximize my effectiveness, while minimizing my energy expenditure?" The most successful Pro players learn that they can still be an asset to their team, even if they are tired or hobbled by a minor injury.

For me, one such tip came from watching the play of Boston Celtic great John Havlicek. After seeing him consistently burn my favored New York Knicks, I noticed that one of the keys to his success was to never stop moving. Most players jog back to their end of the court after a scoring play, and take up their positions. Not Havlicek. He kept going at a smooth and steady pace, jogging around the court, running his defensive opponent into other players, making the guy stop and start, fight through picks and try his best to keep up.

When I mimicked his technique, I was amazed at how effective it was. Even though I was moving all the time, it was at a relatively constant pace, whereas my opponent would wear out quickly, since he had to use much more energy to keep up. The result allowed me to get open much easier and to stay fresher longer. I had learned one secret to optimizing my efforts. The real Pros in basketball utilize many other subtle techniques of gaining position, protecting the ball, and "closing the door" on defense. These hard-won advantages often spell the difference between starters and benchwarmers in a world where sheer talent abounds.

THE PRO ARTIST

Moving from the Adept to the Pro level as an artist begins with a shift in the way you regard yourself. As an Adept, you worked hard to develop your ability to draw everyday scenes with accurate perspective, realistic detail, and a good sense of depth generated by subtle variations of shading and color.

Now, to move to the Pro level, you'll need to make the mental leap from "being able to do art" to considering yourself to be "a real artist." If you expect to be paid for your work in the arts, the mentality of "dabbling in art" is no longer sufficient. Even though others may have expressed their admiration for your artistic efforts, the transition to the Pro level is not quite complete until you begin to believe it yourself. *"Yes, I **am** an artist!"*

Perhaps because of the phobias that many people attach to creativity and the generation of art, it can sometimes take a long time to make this shift. Most people seem to think that they could become successful in business, athletics, the building trades, or any other field they choose if they put in the appropriate amount of time and effort. Not so for art, music, design or other so-called "creative" fields. The prevailing view here is that you have to have a *special* talent or ability to be successful in the arts, since creativity can't really be taught.

Of course, this is absolutely false. Creativity is a natural talent that *everyone* possesses. The trick is learning to get in touch with your own inherent creative abilities, and to apply that creativity to the task at hand. Both of those aspects of creativity can be taught.

Learning to be more creative is similar to learning to meditate. It's more about getting out of your own way than adopting any special methods. In both cases, you learn a few basic techniques, and then spend the rest of your life gradually *letting go*.

The process of enhancing your creativity is a broad and deep subject that deserves a fuller treatment in a future book. Beginning with a brief survey of the works of Edward de Bono, Julia Cameron, Michael Michalko, Win Wenger and other writers in the creativity field should provide you with a good background in this growing subject area.

If you are having trouble at this stage in believing in your own artistic abilities, review the section on generating confidence in the previous chapter. With added confidence, you can more easily come to believe in yourself and the talents you bring to the world.

Once you've made the mental shift into considering yourself a "real artist," the Rookie phase unfolds as you simply apply what you've learned as an Adept to meet the needs of your employer or clients.

This might sound simple enough, yet this process will require a higher level of organization of your time and efforts, and greater attention to all the little details surrounding each project. You will now need to schedule your projects, meet deadlines, relate to clients and be more flexible with your artistic vision in order to accommodate their varying needs. In addition, you'll have to keep track of expenses, negotiate business deals, and bill your clients. You may also need to promote yourself, push your company's products and services, and pitch each individual project along the way. In short, you'll need to learn the "business side" of art.

Many artists find these new "non-artistic" duties to be too stodgy or confining for their freewheeling creative minds to handle. Consequently, they avoid performing those essential steps as much as they can. Yet these duties are necessary for the successful running of any business, even a freelance artistic one.

Your only real choice is to buckle down and learn to perform these new business responsibilities as well as you create your art, or to shuffle those other duties off onto someone who does them well, and can assist you in transforming your art into your business. Ignoring your business responsibilities is not really an option if you intend to be successful. The evidence is clear from the sheer number of artists who have failed to adequately address these issues. Their failures have given rise to the term "starving artist."

Don't let this happen to you. There is no reason why you can't make a fruitful living from your art. After all, it doesn't take too many sales of $500-$3000 paintings (as an example) to pay the bills and provide a healthy income. Just learn the basics of the art *business*, and you'll be on your way.

Of course, in order to sell your artistic creations to your employer or your clients, you'll also want to improve the quality of the work you produce. Naturally, greater quality commands higher prices and appeals to more potential clients, as well. Refining your techniques and learning new "tricks of the trade" will pay off in increased revenues, as well as greater personal satisfaction.

As in any other field, at the Pro level of development you'll be refining your knowledge and skills to a higher degree than before. At the Journeyman stage you'll be concentrating on improving the subtle skills that enhance the realism and the distinctive style used in your creations, while expanding your repertoire and streamlining your efforts to improve productivity. In the world of visual arts, the key to this refinement process is the cultivation of both your curiosity and your attention.

Once you have perfected most of the techniques of accurate drawing and painting as a Journeyman Artist, the tendency is to apply those techniques in every instance. This is the blessing/curse of the Journeyman. It's a blessing that you now have the skills to create excellent pieces, and a curse that this very success tends to limit further development.

At this stage you've settled into a style that works for your purposes, and now you can crank out new pieces quickly and easily. The problem is, that in the process, you have unconsciously *generalized* the appearance of common subjects. As a result, each new piece of artwork you produce will tend to look similar to your previous pieces. All your buildings look alike, the faces you draw don't really change all that much, and the details of the scenery behind your subjects all appear generic.

In order to improve further and develop into an Expert Artist, you'll have to see deeper into the subject you are depicting. Use your curiosity to discover the unique qualities of each object in the scene you are drawing, and the special overall visual *atmosphere* that pervades the entire panorama. To stimulate your curiosity and enhance your attention levels at the same time, use the following simple exercise.

THE REALITY ENHANCEMENT SHIFT (Hi-RES)

1. **Choose some item in your immediate environment.** *Give it your full attention.*
2. **Describe the object to yourself.** Describe each successive detail that presents itself to your awareness. Notice the shapes, colors, materials, reflections, shadows, textures, patterns, relationships between component features or anything else that you discover through your observations.
3. **Continue to describe the object to yourself.** Notice even more details. At some point you will feel that you have thoroughly described the item, and that there is nothing more to notice. Dig deeper and concentrate on discovering more. Describe a few more details of the item, then...
4. **Pick another item and describe that item to yourself.** Repeat the above three steps on another item, spending a few minutes on each item you pick out.
5. **Continue describing items to yourself until you can notice NEW features of any item you choose to observe.** Fifteen to twenty minutes is a practical time frame for completing this exercise.

After performing this exercise for 15–20 minutes, you should feel calm, focused and highly aware. You may also feel some surprise at your discovery of the intricate details of the items you have observed. By stimulating your curiosity and focusing your powers of attention, this exercise enhances your sense of reality, furnishing a powerful sense of involvement in the depth of everyday objects in your environment.

If you perform this exercise by studying the people or items in scene that you are attempting to draw or paint, more of the subtle details of your subjects will reveal themselves, challenging you to improve your artistic treatment of the scene so it can sparkle with the deeper sense of realism than you can now notice. The overall effect of this exercise is similar to viewing the entire scene at a higher resolution, as if it were much closer to you and more vividly detailed than it originally appeared. The Hi-RES abbreviation for this Reality Enhancement Shift helps to remind you of the increased observational powers you can summon by using this exercise.

Variations of the Hi-RES exercise can be utilized to refine the discernment skills involved in using any of your senses. This can be a boon to your development in any area where increasing your sensitivity leads to improved skills. Imagine what gains you could make in the culinary arts with improved sensitivity of taste and smell, or in pottery or sculpture with improved sense of touch, or in music, as you develop greater tonal accuracy, or in interior design using enhanced powers of discernment in color and texture. This little exercise can improve your performance in just about any area where you choose to apply it.

THE PRO CHEF

In a manner similar to that of other disciplines, the transition from the Adept Chef to the Pro Chef occurs as you shift from cooking for family and friends (or your culinary instructors) to preparing food for paying customers. Paying customers provide the true test of your abilities, since their dining satisfaction translates directly into your establishment's bottom line.

Your first job as a chef initiates the Rookie phase of your professional development. At this point, your primary concerns are to follow the recipe for each item on the menu precisely, without making any mistakes, while coordinating with other kitchen and wait-staff personnel to produce each meal promptly and accurately. Timing is crucial in this process, as you balance the preparation of each course so that all the items ordered for each party reach the peak of perfection at the same time. It won't do to have three orders wilting under the warmer while the last one is still cooking. Your paying customers will surely notice that sort of *faux pas,* and in this business you rarely get a second chance to please your customers. If they're not happy, they simply won't come back!

As you work on improving the quality and consistency of your efforts, perhaps the most difficult adjustment you will need to make is to adapt to the pressure of handling many different orders at once, while fielding conflicting demands from what seems like everyone else in the restaurant. Everybody wants something, and they all want it NOW! Aaargh!

So, when the rush hits, take a few deep breaths to calm yourself and then use the simple exercise below to *relax and broaden you perspective.* To handle all the tasks needed to complete the rush of orders, you'll need to be calm, collected and working smoothly and efficiently. You can't get stuck on one task, because the rest will back up and then you'll be behind the proverbial eight ball. Remember that doing each task *right* is more important than doing it *fast.* Your customers will be willing to wait a few extra minutes if necessary, as long as the food comes out hot, tasty and looking scrumptious. They will be less forgiving if you rush their order and lower the quality in the process.

In order to perform multiple tasks at the same time, you'll need to fan your attention out over your workspace so you can prep one dish while others are cooking, and not lose track of it all. The key is to *broaden you perspective.* If your attention is too tightly focused on the task at hand, you'll miss what's going on with all the other orders you've begun to prepare. To shift your perspective into a wider field, try the simple **PEA** exercise below:

THE PERSPECTIVE EXPANSION ADJUSTMENT (PEA)

1. **Choose some item in your immediate environment.** *Let your attention linger for a moment on this item. Relax.*
2. **Fan your attention out to the edges of your perception.** *Tune in to the full breadth of your senses.* With your attention centered on the item in front of you, notice the entire scene that resides between the edges of your peripheral vision. At the same time, tune in to the sounds you hear around you, noticing the faintest of them.

Likewise, notice the aromas wafting through the air around you, and the taste sensations forming in your mouth. Feel the rustle of your clothes against your skin and any faint breeze as it flows through your hair.

3. Return to your previous activities while maintaining this expanded perspective. *Notice what's happening all around you as you continue with your activities.*

With a bit of practice using this exercise, you will find that you can easily shift into the *expanded perspective* state of consciousness in the space of just a couple of deep breaths. As you return to your work in this relaxed, expanded state, it will be much easier to *flow* with the activities and handle the rush of new tasks you face without becoming irritable, frustrated or confused.

The PEA exercise is not restricted to Chefs, though. Anyone can benefit from a broader perspective from time to time, especially when you are feeling upset, bewildered or overwhelmed by your situation. A short pause while you relax and perform this exercise will serve you well in restoring your calm, confident demeanor. With a broader perspective, you can more easily see where your current efforts fit in with all the others.

Once you are able to calm your jitters and go with the flow of the kitchen, you'll be on your way to Journeyman status. Journeymen chefs typically fill most of the culinary staff positions from line cooks to sous-chef. As you work on the quality and consistency of your food preparation and the integration of your efforts with other members of the kitchen staff, your responsibilities will tend to expand, as well.

Moving up to the Executive Chef position, with responsibility for managing the entire kitchen, will require the knowledge and skills of an Expert Chef. As in other fields, the Expert Chef not only knows the art of cooking and food preparation inside out, and can rely on a fabulous repertoire of recipes and techniques, but has also studied all the other aspects of the business. To run the kitchen effectively, the Expert Chef will need to advance to at least the Journeyman stage in his kitchen management skills, as well.

As in basketball, developing a winning strategy for the restaurant becomes a major part of your success as an Expert Chef. A key part of that strategy is to put together a menu of compatible and complimentary foods with an attractive theme that offers a variety of tastes and experiences for your diners. You'll then need to place considerable attention on the perfection of those recipes and their consistent preparation—day after day. The ability to produce the same outstanding dining experience for your customers each time they order is the key to building a successful restaurant. Many chefs can prepare excellent meals, but the ones who are capable of building successful restaurants are the ones who take the time and effort to concentrate on consistency. Few experiences are more disappointing to your patrons than to order a meal that they enjoyed the first time they visited your establishment, only to find that this time it tastes or looks different than they remembered.

By developing high standards for food quality, preparation techniques and service procedures, you can maintain outstanding quality while providing for smooth and speedy flow through the kitchen. As you develop your skills, your overall goal as a Pro Chef soon becomes identical to the goal of the restaurant, which is to provide a consistent, high quality dining experience for each patron, while utilizing a minimum of time, effort and expense.

THE PRO MANAGER

As mentioned in the previous chapter, the new manager typically arrives at her new position in one of two basic ways. The more formal method involves obtaining a business related degree from a college or university, and then finding a managerial position as a business school graduate. The other method grows the manager from an existing staff position in the company. A new management position opens up at your company and in the scramble you land the new job as the next step up in your career progression.

What makes the management profession unique is that in either case described above, your first management job condenses the Novice, Adept and Rookie levels all into a single experience. If you are a business school graduate, you enter your first management position at the Rookie level in field of management, yet you may know little about the business that your new company engages in. So you will have to learn about the nature of this novel business as a Novice and then an Adept before you can come up to speed in your new position. You have to have a handle on what you are managing before you can become an effective leader.

On the other hand, if you advance from a staff position to a management position, you are probably already a Journeyman in your previous job, and now you have to learn the art and science of management from scratch. So you will have to go through the Novice and Adept stages in this learning process.

Because of these complications, the Rookie stage of the management profession typically takes much longer than it does for other fields. Remember that when it's your turn to make this important step in your management career. Be patient with yourself. It'll all come together in due time.

To assist you in successfully traversing this difficult stage of your development, find an experienced manager in your company to mentor your progress as a Rookie manager. Most smart companies realize the problems you face in your new position, and are willing to help with this process. By having a senior manager in another department assist you, you can relax a bit more, knowing you are not alone in dealing with your new responsibilities.

Before you know it you'll be handling your tasks smoothly and easily. It's this internalization of your new management skills and responsibilities that marks your advance into the Journeyman level. Now you not only know what you're doing, but you're busy proving it through your performance!

Once you've shown that you can do the job well, you've passed the first big hurdle in your Pro development. As a Journeyman manager your continued success will hinge directly on the bottom line. Now that you can "deliver the goods," let's see if you can improve on that initial benchmark. As in other professions, the Journeyman stage unfolds as you refine your already successful performances. With continued experience and attention to all the details involved, you can pick apart each aspect of your performance and improve on your abilities to manage the people in your group and the tasks your department performs.

One of the keys to your ability to improve as a manager is to measure your progress. A vast array of measurement techniques have already been developed to assist you in charting every aspect of your group's performance. Just consult the shelves of business literature at your local library or bookstore for the specifics that apply to your situation.

This emphasis on measuring all facets of your group's performance reflects the need to optimize the productivity of your department. In most companies, senior management will analyze your success primarily by reviewing those reports you generate that chart your group's progress.

By treating your profession as a science, you seek to gain more knowledge by measuring everything in sight, so you can use this new knowledge to your advantage in streamlining your operations. Being a Pro Manager in the business world is all about generating quality results in the most effective way possible. The bottom line becomes both the judge and jury in this process. Can you do it better for less?

Once you've spent a few years studying your profession and all the measurements you've taken, a few patterns will emerge. These patterns demonstrate what is valuable to the success of your business, and what is not. For instance, if you plot the rate of turnover in your department against it's productivity, you will probably be able to determine what the optimal rate of turnover might be. Then you can take steps to keep turnover at that optimal rate.

Likewise, if you analyze the productivity of the individuals in your group and examine where these people came from, you can decide whether it is best to hire new graduates, experienced veterans from other competing companies, or to promote from within the company.

As you measure and examine all these parameters and draw conclusions from your observations, you gain expertise in the management game. It takes plenty of experience to develop methods of motivating people and techniques for handling disputes that arise. Sometimes you'll be pleasantly surprised at your own abilities, and other times you'll be disappointed with the results.

Your progression into the ranks of Expert Managers comes as you discover which management theories and techniques work effectively and which are no more than hot air. After years of recording all those measurements, you'll be able to tell which parameters are the most valuable to track, and which just get in the way of the very productivity you are trying to measure.

By continuing to question the validity of the methods she uses and experimenting with new techniques, the Expert Manager develops an instinctive knowledge of what will work in any situation she is likely to encounter. Troubleshooting problems as they come up across the company, and mentoring new managers in the organization thus becomes the natural domain of the Expert Manager.

Do the one thing you think you cannot do. Fail at it. Try again. Do better the second time. The only people who never tumble are those who never mount the high wire. This is your moment. Own it.

— *Oprah Winfrey (1954 –)*

Level 4: The Virtuoso
Treat Your Subject Area as an **Art**

Level 4: The Virtuoso
Treat Your Subject Area as an Art

Objective: To develop your ability to *lose yourself* in your work, maintaining this state throughout entire performances. *Move people* with your vibrant *passion*.

Process: Immerse yourself thoroughly in your practice. Become so involved that nothing else matters, and you'll *lose yourself* within the activity. Work on maintaining that concentration. Let go of fears and inhibitions. Cultivate your unique expression and wisdom, guided by that intuitive voice or feeling. Focus on *going with the flow.*

Expected Results: Development of a uniquely artistic style that defines a new niche in your field. This can inspire a following of both fans and colleagues. *Leadership.*

Action Steps: Recognize and cultivate the feeling of *losing yourself* in your activities. Practice it. Though you may already have all the knowledge and skills you need, study and practice the unique interpretations of other Virtuosos and Masters to enhance your emerging style.

Keys to Success: Remove all distractions. Discover what factors enhance your concentration and use them to develop an environment that is conducive to your undisturbed practice. Focus completely on the activity. *Detach* yourself from the outcome of your efforts and practice being *courageous*. Go for it! Be fearless and passionate. Allow yourself to switch from work to *play.*

Words of Praise/Encouragement: Wow! Brilliant, Exquisite, Mesmerizing! (Respond to authentic passion and style.)

How you can assist others: Thoroughly develop your unique contributions. Inspire and guide others through your integrity and authenticity. Be a mentor or coach.

Chapter 10

Level 4: The Virtuoso
TREAT YOUR SUBJECT AREA AS AN **ART**

After trudging along for what seemed like ages, the mastery traveler finally comes to a halt. She doesn't really have much choice. Before her hangs a battered and rusty road sign nailed to a young aspen sapling. It says simply, "Dead End." That was not at all what she had been anticipating. From the last mountaintop she scaled, it looked like the road went on forever, winding through the valleys on the high plateau, and up and down the hills in between. But now, after crossing the entire length of that broad plateau, she stood at the base of a ring of giant mountain peaks, literally at the end of her road.

"Now what?" she thinks to herself. "I didn't come all this way to turn back now. But how will I ever find my way among all the trees and rocks, without even a path? I could easily get lost up here, and no one would ever know."

She puts down her pack and fishes inside to find a snack. Looking for a place to sit down and rest, she spies an old log that looked inviting. Arranging her things around her, she relaxes in the shade, munching on an energy bar. As she sits there and begins to consider her options, she notices the wrapper of her energy bar. Strangely, it bore a "Star Wars" theme, with spaceships, aliens, and the familiar characters from the movies. She muttered to herself, "It seems like everything has some commercial tie-in these days. I can't get away from it, even way up here."

The back of the label mentions some sort of game or contest, with clues printed on the inside of the wrapper. Turning it over, she stops chewing abruptly. Her clue reads, "Trust the Force, Luke."

In a flash, she realizes what she must do next. "It's time to proceed on my own, road or no road. I'm an excellent traveler. I can carve my own path. You know, 'boldly go where no man has gone before.' Whoops, that's Star Trek, not Star Wars. Whatever..."

Stuffing the wrapper in her pocket, she slings her pack onto her back, and strides forward into the woods and up the sloping terrain, not really knowing where she's headed next, yet feeling oddly unconcerned.

Up to now, it has been easy to see the progression of learning that occurs between the Novice and Expert levels. At each point you built upon the knowledge and skills you had incorporated at earlier levels—studying, practicing, experimenting, building, integrating and polishing all along the way.

Advancing to the Virtuoso level takes you off that familiar path. The Virtuoso makes a qualitative leap, rather than a quantitative step. At this point, it's not about learning *more*. Rather, it's about learning in a different way altogether.

Once a high level of skill has been obtained, the Pro can produce excellent performances on a regular basis, *and* achieve the desired result in the process. But performing flawlessly, and winning the game, or a contract, or applause from the audience, is quite a different result than winning the respect and admiration of your competitors, the confidence and trust of the client, or the hearts and minds of the audience. This is what the Virtuoso can do, while *still* winning the contest, the account or the standing ovation.

In classical music circles, when a reviewer describes the orchestra's performance as "technically flawless," he is damning the players with faint praise. Top orchestras all have musicians who are experts with their instruments. Being capable of playing at an expert level is the *minimum requirement* for any orchestral chair. What the reviewer (and the rest of the audience) is looking for is to be *moved* by the performance. Technical excellence cannot accomplish that. Technical excellence may be admirable, but at least in this case, *passion* is what rules the day.

As a Pro, your first responsibility was to get your *competence* down pat, performing as precisely and accurately as possible, according to the rules, theories and techniques you've been studying all along. This scientific approach slowly chips away at the development of *comprehensive knowledge* and *perfect technique.* The Expert has even developed a variety of approaches and near-perfect techniques to choose from. Yet this persistent pursuit of perfection has a dry, flat, mechanical flavor to it.

Virtuosos manage to transcend the merely perfect, and add a personal, emotional element to their performances that transforms the performance, the performer, and the audience, all at the same time. Virtuosos tap into our feelings, and play those heartstrings as surely as the guitarist plays the steel strings of his instrument. The Virtuoso performs with a sense of drama, or humor, or colorful animation that invites the emotional participation of the audience.

He or she performs to the beat of a different drummer, so to speak. The result is magnificence, power, beauty, and inspiration. The result is *art.* And art works its magic by slipping invisibly into our souls and stirring up the juices into a passionate cocktail. That's what's missing from the Pro's otherwise flawless performance.

It's the difference between Spock and Kirk, or Data and Picard from the old Star Trek series. The technical excellence of Spock and Data made them invaluable to their crews, yet their lack of emotion made them blind to the motives and operations of those who didn't act in a rational manner. Kirk and Picard balanced their broad knowledge and excellent skills with a deep passion, subtle perception of emotional complexities, and a creative sense of action that their more precise and scientific colleagues lacked. It was this flexibility, along with their ability to inspire the passion and dedication of others, that enabled them to lead their crews so effectively.

In any subject area you care to examine, most of the **stars** of each field are the Virtuosos. It's not enough to be technically perfect to become a star. It is the independent style, the artistic flair, the emotional appeal, the passionate dedication to a cause, the captivating message, or the uniquely creative methods they use that allow Virtuosos to inspire a following of fans. Stars are capable of "wow-ing" both their audience *and* their colleagues.

How do they do it? What does it take to move from the Pro to the Virtuoso level? What is happening "behind the scenes" that makes this qualitative leap into stardom possible?

It all starts simply enough, but the change in approach seems to sneak up on you. Once you practice your techniques so often that you can perform successfully without thinking about it, a curious thing sometimes happens. You begin to *lose yourself* in the activity. You become so involved in what you are doing that the sense of you (as an individual) performing your tasks (as a process) begins to fade. The three separate entities of you, the task to be performed, and the process of performing it, all merge into one event.

Perhaps the surest way to recognize this shift in consciousness resides in your perception of time. When you *lose yourself* in the activity you're doing, your sense of time goes with it. Hours can go by in what seems like minutes. Minutes pass as quickly as seconds. You begin to act spontaneously, responding to events without hesitation or deliberation. The need to plan, analyze and control what is happening dissolves, leaving only a profound unity of thought and motion, performer and performance.

This immediacy brings with it an intoxicating sense of heightened awareness. Your senses become sharper. Your appreciation of the subtleties of your performance increases. Suddenly, everything begins to shine just a bit brighter, twinkling with an arresting beauty that seems to lie just below the surface, in some mysterious way. You can feel your body acting from within, seemingly on its own, with power, poise and precision. You marvel at the magnificence of it all.

Even if you make a mistake in your performance, it all seems to flow without interruption, as though the error was scripted into the overall plan. It feels as though you are an essential part of an elaborate dance that includes everything within your awareness. You enter a world that looks a lot like the regular world, but shimmers with a sense of magic and wonder. Amazingly, it seems even more *real* than the "normal" reality you know so well.

At first, this delicious sense of *losing yourself* in your work may last for just a fleeting moment, flashing past your awareness like an apparition. You may wonder what just happened. Who spiked your coffee? Was this a dream, or some oddity of the mind?

But that kind of handy, dismissive explanation proves insufficient for you. There's more to it than that. You *felt* it. That was no fluke, no trick of awareness, no jive. The intoxicating allure of that fleeting moment drives you to seek more such moments, if only to prove to yourself that you were not dreaming that first time.

Recreating that moment of *losing yourself* proves elusive at first. The more you try to feel it, the farther it retreats into the distance. Then, once you've forgotten about it completely, and you are busy practicing your craft, there it is again! Startled by your sudden recognition, the magic bubble bursts once more.

After a while, though, you begin to catch on. Never mind about *creating* that special moment. Just do your thing, get completely immersed in what you're doing, and the enhanced awareness will arrive all by itself, without you having to "do" anything special.

So you continue to practice your discipline. That special feeling comes and goes. Sometimes you manage to complete an entire performance while in the "spell" of this heightened awareness. You begin to notice how expressive your performances have become. When you are in this state of consciousness, the spontaneity of your actions brings out some of the inner charm of your personality.

More of who you really are starts to seep into each performance. By now you are deviating somewhat from your script, improvising as your mood and intentions shift from day to day. Your performances start to take on a personality of their own, adding a different and unique feel to them that varies from the technically perfect ideal. Gradually, you develop your own *style*.

The style you generate will remain authentic and true to your unique interpretation as long as you "trust the force," and remain in the spell of *losing yourself.* As soon as you begin to recognize the special qualities of your interpretation and try to capitalize on that uniqueness of style by deliberately adding to it, the spell will be broken. Your performances will feel fake, contrived and hollow, as though you were an actor doing a poor imitation of yourself.

There's no faking this genuine feeling of *losing yourself.* If you were to try, it would be painfully obvious to you *and* your audience. Some stars have "made it big" when they stumbled into outstanding performances that surprised everyone, including themselves. Then, when they struggled to recreate the magic, they lost sight of what made their performances great, and tried to force it, or employ some gimmick. Stars like this quickly fade from view. They become known as "shooting stars," "one-hit wonders" or perhaps as a "flash in the pan."

Real Virtuosos have staying power in their fields, because they don't have to rely on gimmicks. *Losing yourself* in the inexhaustible *flow* reaches into deeper levels of awareness, intelligence, harmony and beauty than any gimmick can offer. Wise Virtuosos don't have to worry about what the critics say, either. Since they are *done with* striving for perfection, they realize that what they do or say will resonate with some and not with others, and are not concerned with who "gets it" and who doesn't.

Don't worry if you are not familiar with the process of *losing yourself.* You may know this feeling in different terms. Being *in the groove,* or *in the flow,* or *in the zone,* or *in the moment,* or *in harmony,* or *on form,* or *on top of your game,* all refer to this same sense of being fully immersed in what you are doing, and the special qualities of performance that emerge from it. Mihaly Csikszentmihaly offers a comprehensive examination of this feeling of *losing yourself* in his book, *Flow.* In a similar manner, Herbert Benson and William Proctor refer to being *in the zone* as entry to a state of consciousness that precipitates peak experiences in their book, *The Breakout Principle.*

Here's an example that you'll probably be able to relate to. Have you ever had the experience of narrowly avoiding an auto accident? Most people have been in this harrowing situation at one time or another. Remember a scene like this one?

You're driving along smoothly with the rest of the traffic, perhaps absorbed in thought. Suddenly, you notice another vehicle about to cross your path. In an instant, your surprise gives way to a sudden shift in consciousness.

Everything slows down as if it were a slow-motion scene in a movie. You vividly see the shocked expression on the face of the driver in the other car. You hit the brakes and turn the wheel to avoid the crash that's about to happen. For an agonizingly long moment that seems like minutes (but actually flashes by in a fraction of a second) you see, hear and feel every sensation with heightened intensity. Every fiber of your being becomes involved in the drama of this moment, where nothing else exists except the two cars careening towards each other. Your heart and breathing stop. All the details of the scene become etched in your memory with crystal clarity.

Somehow the two vehicles slide by each other without touching. You can feel the swirl of wind as you pass by. Then, just as suddenly as it began, you pop back into normal time, and the dramatic moment is over. You stop by the side of the road and gather your wits. Whew, that was a close call!

For that dramatic moment, you shifted into the *flow* state, and *lost yourself.* Subtract all the heart-stopping fear and surprise, and you have the essence of *flow.* Virtuosos learn how to shift into this heightened level of consciousness while in the midst of their performance. Gradually, through continued practice, they learn to turn it on and keep it on for as long as needed.

Another way to recognize your own shift into the Virtuoso level is to note how it *feels* when you perform. At every stage from Novice to Adept to Pro, whenever you sought to improve, it always had the unmistakable feeling of **work.** Each new advance came at the price of considerable *effort, struggle, hardship and sacrifice.* It was tough! Yet you hung in there, worked hard, and held out for the payoff at the end. You were ready to grab the brass ring.

You may even have gathered considerable rewards already, in the form of a healthy paycheck, or a row of trophies, or kudos from audiences, coworkers, or your contemporaries. Any rewards you've received have been well earned, and they brought with them the considerable satisfaction of a job well done.

Yet Virtuoso performances feel decidedly different. For one thing, they're *easy.* Not easy in the same sense as the Journeyman, who can perform so easily he can do it in his sleep. It's not *easy-hohum-boring-trivial,* but *easy-smooth-harmonious-vibrant-rich.* Gone is the struggle to integrate the next new trick technique. Instead, it's the genuine thrill of **surrender,** as powerful inner forces move through you, giving life to the artful expression of your innermost desires. The brass ring was already within your grasp. You had only to *let go...*

When that delicious sensation of *losing yourself* takes hold in your performances, it brings with it a sense of **surprise, delight** and **wonder.** You may find yourself saying inwardly, "Wow, that was amazing. It's hard to believe what just happened. Was that really me just now? I could feel myself going through all the motions, but it felt like a much better version of me had slipped inside and taken control, guiding me to perform beyond my natural ability."

Friend and Virtuoso seminar leader Luis Cordoba once put it this way, "When I'm up there on stage conducting the seminar, it feels like the material just plays itself, and I'm the loudspeaker. It plays *through* me."

Imagine that you are a sculptor. At the **Novice** level you struggle with the unfamiliar tools and hard marble of your masterpiece-to-be. Just working the hammer and chisels to dislodge a chunk of material is a chore. Long hours of practice are needed to become familiar with the grain of the stone and the action of each hammer stroke and chisel angle.

As an **Adept,** your hammer strokes come with more confidence as you meticulously chop away at the marble, gradually bringing your final figure into recognizable shape. Attention to careful craftsmanship insures that you don't remove too much material at this early stage.

With the sure and deft strokes of a **Pro,** you carve the subtle details into your statue, revealing the power and purpose behind your creation. By now, each stroke you deliver is much more precise, removing exactly the right amount of material each time. The bold stance, expression and muscle tone of your figure emerges as you shape and polish the smooth marble surface.

Now that most of the hard work is over, and your statue nears completion, the **Virtuoso** within you steps back and regards the figure anew. With an impish grin, you dive back into performing the finishing touches, humming to yourself as you caress your tools into performing their magic. Hours pass unnoticed as you delicately add and subtract subtleties from certain areas, until the unique personality of the figure stands before you. No longer a perfect human likeness, the minor imperfections somehow make the statue seem even more *real*. At last, the cold stone warms under your gaze, and speaks to all who view it.

At the Novice level you *struggle* with the new material and skills, twisting your mind and body around in unfamiliar ways, in an attempt to make each new piece work smoothly and comfortably. As an Adept, you *tinker* with various ways to string together the ideas and skills you've learned into something more complete and whole, so it stands on its own. At the Pro level, you bring greater precision and efficiency to your work, as though you have switched tools from a butter knife to a scalpel. Your persistent efforts *chip away* at perfection.

The Virtuoso sidesteps this relentless drive for perfection, and rediscovers the simple pleasures that hide beneath the drudgery of all that work. As you let go of the subtle uptight hesitation that accompanies the inner fear of making a mistake, a new fluidity emerges, carrying each thought, movement and moment smoothly into the next.

Unshackled at last, you can gleefully throw caution to the wind. Your fearless performances blossom into enthusiastic celebrations of your newly unleashed brilliance. With your anxieties behind you, what had seemed for so long to be *work, work, work,* now becomes *play, play, play.*

So far, the descriptions of *losing yourself* in your work have emphasized the physical acts of performance. In more intellectual pursuits such as writing, researching, counseling, teaching, managing and other areas where thinking counts more than physical action, there is a corresponding sense of *losing yourself.* This sense often goes by the name of *intuition.*

One definition of *intuition* is: *the process of knowing, without knowing how you know.* At one moment you are busy doing your tasks in the normal familiar manner. Then the next moment arrives with a sudden awareness, a new idea, or an unusually smooth flow of thought that brings with it more knowledge, greater insight, and a deeper level of understanding than you knew you possessed.

As seminar leader Cordoba suggested, this recognition of sudden abilities beyond your normal standards feels as though this intuitive knowledge is acting *through* you. Your wisdom, creativity and attunement to the situation advance in a dramatic leap. Totally tuned in to it all, you know just what to do or say, at the perfect moment, in a smooth and unhurried manner that resolves any lingering dilemma and sets you and those around you on course to their greatest potential. Looking back on the whole episode can leave you breathless. And yet, there is more...

To advance at the Virtuoso level it helps to treat your subject area as an *Art.* This shift in approach from Science to Art captures the essence of the Virtuoso. Once a high level of skill has been obtained at the Pro level, the practitioner has captured and can communicate almost all of the *information* available in his or her performance. This complete and accurate communication goes straight to the heart of the matter and delivers the results in a no-nonsense manner. The result is quite satisfying to the *intellect,* but the *soul* remains unnourished.

So the shift naturally begins to occur toward the communication of *feeling* as well. It is the job of science to ferret out all the information possible. What's left is *feeling.* And the translation of information into emotion is the province of art. *While science informs, art moves people.*

The goal of the Virtuoso is to go beyond informing, or

entertaining, or getting results, to the far more complete and satisfying act of *inspiring or moving people.* Your development as a Virtuoso proceeds as you become more familiar with performing under the spell of *losing yourself.*

The pinnacle of the Virtuoso level arrives when you can deliberately place yourself into this magic state of consciousness and maintain it. Then you are no longer at the whim of chance when you perform. Like the Journeyman, you can now perform at this elevated state day in and day out. Only now your performances captivate and delight while they get the job done.

To smooth your transition into the realm of the Virtuoso you will need to cultivate two special qualities of character. Since the key to becoming a Virtuoso lies in your ability to *lose yourself* in what you do, the development of **courage** and **detachment** will serve you well. These two qualities of character work together to open the door to the *fearlessness* that all Virtuosos display. Perhaps that is part of what makes Virtuosos so captivating to others.

You see, most of us live under the influence of fear all the time. This fear is not necessarily anything too debilitating. Most of the time we can go to work or school each day and perform without much trouble. We can interact with others and have a reasonable personal and social life. The really big fears have either been handled somewhere along the line, or carefully tucked away in our psyches so they won't get in the way of our everyday activities.

The fears that we are dealing with here are usually much more subtle. When learning something new you may encounter such fears as: *the fear of failure; the fear of success; the fear of embarrassment; the fear of not-being-good-enough; the fear of exposing your flaws;* or simply *the fear of making a mistake.*

These kinds of fears rear their ugly little heads at every point of development, from the Novice on through to the Master. You may actually encounter the same fear again and again in subtler forms as you proceed. Peel off one layer of fear, and underneath lies another juicier version at a deeper level. Like peeling onions, uncovering each new layer can be enough to make you cry.

The qualitative shift that the Pro undergoes as he or she enters the Virtuoso level brings the difficulties involved with these fears into focus. At least in the areas surrounding your discipline, you will have to drop those fears altogether in order to make the shift.

That's where courage and detachment come in. As mentioned in Chapter 1, courage is *the quality of mind or spirit that enables a person to face difficulty, danger, or pain, without fear; bravery.* Courage is the ability to get out there and perform **despite** your fear and uncertainty.

As long as you are worried about how your performance will turn out, the Virtuoso level will be unavailable to you. That fear, worry or concern acts to inhibit you, so that the full depth of your capabilities are never realized.

Luckily, courage has a "fake-it-till-you-make-it" aspect built into it. Note that the definition of courage includes both fearlessness and a sort of bull-headedness that says, "Get in there and do it anyway. Never mind about your fears and uncertainties. Everybody has those. Who cares?" It turns out that the folks at Nike© got it right with their tag line. *Just do it!*

If you *just do it,* you will surely get some kind of results. Perhaps they're not the ones you had hoped for, but you get results, nevertheless. Once you have some results, then you can make adjustments. But if you don't perform, then you won't have any results to examine, so no new changes can be made. You're stuck!

What helps to develop courage and the willingness to *just do it* is **detachment.** The fears that inhibit us in performing are all tied to the outcome of the performance. "Oh, what if I fail? What if everyone sees how terrible I am at this? What if someone makes some rude comment about my performance? What if I make a fool of myself? What if no one cares? What if I succeed? Then I'll have to keep performing superbly again and again, and I don't know if I can do that." *Oh, ye of little faith...*

Give up your attachment to the outcome and these types of fears dissolve into nothingness. Who cares if you look silly, or screw up, or somehow don't perform as well as you know you can?

Is that the worst that could happen?

Haven't you looked silly, screwed up and underperformed before? *Oh yeah.* Well, you survived those experiences just fine. What's so different about this time? Give up your vanity and get out there and do it and see what happens. You may surprise yourself.

Try changing your relationship to fear altogether. Instead of resisting the feelings that come with anxiety, turn that fear into your friend. Use it as a sign. Whenever you feel the fear of performing, then that's the signal to step up to the plate and *just do it!*

Once you can **detach** from the outcome of your efforts, then courage comes easily, and you'll find yourself getting lost in your activities before you know it. As you surrender your fears and attachments, you become one with the activity at hand, and the wonders that expanded awareness can bring. That awareness, in turn, will make it easier to be courageous in detaching yourself from the results you create. You'll be on your way to developing another deeper layer of your capabilities that will prove to be the most satisfying yet. By riding this happy spiral, you can reap rich dividends.

Sometimes an extraordinarily talented individual comes along in a particular field who takes full advantage of this upward spiral. This person's exceptional aptitude can often be recognized early at the Novice or Adept levels. He or she may possess superior physical or mental gifts, enhanced perceptual abilities, or a special affinity for the field involved. Such people are often referred to as "prodigies," or "whiz-kids," or "quick studies."

If such gifted individuals have been able to tap into the *flow* state early in their development, they may be able to jump straight from the Rookie stage to the Virtuoso level, bypassing the intervening stages. These highly touted "stars in the making" are often celebrated in the fields of entertainment and athletics, where their exploits are most often in the public eye.

Because the advance to the Virtuoso level involves a qualitative shift instead of a quantitative one, the jump to the Virtuoso level can happen from any stage of development, ranging from Rookie to Expert. This leap does not exempt you from the learning that occurs at those levels, though. You'll just have to go back and traverse those stages at some later time in order to become truly effective.

The supremely talented individuals who make the jump early in their careers are sometimes "blinded by the lights" of stardom, and the advisors and handlers who are often attracted to the glow of fame and fortune. They fail to realize that their continued success depends upon learning the full range of knowledge and skills that other pros have absorbed as Rookies, Journeymen and Experts. When they attempt to continue on their raw talent alone, it may not be enough to take them much further by itself. The steps they skipped earlier turn out to be valuable ones after all.

In any learning experience, the cycle of expansion and contraction alternates back and forth to move you forward at the speed that is right for you. First there is a short period of advancement, followed by a longer period of consolidation of what was just learned. The faster you advance, the more time must be spent backfilling and consolidating to cement the learning in place. The expression, "two steps forward, one step back" is sometimes used to describe this process of advancement and consolidation.

The development of your sense of *losing yourself* can be a key factor in how swiftly you advance. Those who move into this expanded awareness early in their mastery journey often blaze to the top of their fields in short order. Others who take more time with this development can be seen to "come out of nowhere" and suddenly become a force in their subject area. People in the latter group are the ones who become "overnight successes, with ten years in the making." In either case, the development of your ability to *lose yourself* in your work will enable you to gain a foothold at the highest levels of your profession, and carve out a unique contribution that you can call your own.

THE VIRTUOSO PIANIST

After practicing at the piano for years, playing beautiful music comes naturally to the aspiring Virtuoso Pianist. She has learned proper technique quite well, and her fingers know just how and where to go next as she skillfully progresses through the score. Yet, the more she plays her favorite pieces, the more she is swept away with the power and beauty of it all. Surrendering to the *soul* of the music, her fingers begin to dance along the keys, teasing still more harmony and expression from the ivories until the room resonates with the rich melodies playing deep within her, now released for all the world to hear.

What had been a standard piece of music that many have played over the years suddenly becomes an instrument of joyous release for the Virtuoso Pianist. The music that emerges now carries the indelible stamp of her personality, her history, her emotional cry, all folded into the pages of the score. Whoever composed the music retreats to the back of the auditorium as the Virtuoso Pianist crafts the piece anew, making it *her music,* delivering a new interpretation truly worthy of the term *art.*

As long as the music she produces stays true to the thrum of her own heartstrings, she is assured an appreciative audience whose souls resonate to the same beat. More than that, she will have found a way to unleash the chains of mortal living, and for a few moments at least, let her heart burst with exuberance. There is no better feeling available to a musician.

THE VIRTUOSO BASKETBALL PLAYER

When a basketball player performs while immersing himself fully into the *flow* of the game, an amazing transformation takes place. The Virtuoso Basketball Player (or any Virtuoso athlete, for that matter) seems to play the game from the inside out. The most obvious aspect of this shift can be described in one word: *Smooth.*

Suddenly you find yourself in the right position at the right time doing the right thing. This shift of consciousness brings with it a sense of natural fluidity, where there is complete alignment between you and the process you are engaged in. When you are *in the flow,* winning becomes the path of least resistance.

Without even concerning yourself about the outcome of the game, the scoreboard keeps racking up the points. Perfect passes, intuitive plays, unstoppable moves, and shots that cannot miss, all merge together into a symphony of extraordinary basketball. You subtly alter each move as needed—in the moment—so that the play comes off effortlessly, leaving your opponents gasping in bewilderment.

A basketball player or team performing at level four is a joy to behold. It seems as if they can do no wrong. There is a grace and artistry to the play that captures the imagination of the fans and other players as well. Highly skilled teammates begin to slip into the same sense of *flow* that began with a single player. The synergistic effect of an entire team playing at the virtuoso level grows into a sort of *tour de force* that carries the game into the realm of the "highlight reel." The roaring enthusiasm of the crowd shakes the arena, fueling the momentum of a team on a roll...

THE VIRTUOSO ARTIST

Since art is the process of translating information into emotion, it is only at the Virtuoso level that the true vision of the artist can begin to be realized. When the Virtuoso Artist surrenders to the inner forces that speak to her and stir her passions, the real *art* that lies dormant within her work gradually comes to the surface.

In drawing or painting, the Virtuoso artist starts to color her work with her own perception of reality. Exaggeration, emphasis, and subtle nuances of color, shape and shading combine to create an individual interpretation of her own. Drawings begin to take on a deliberate flight of fancy connected with the artist's perception of reality and what is important to her. An artistic style is forged.

Combine your highly developed skills and techniques with an effervescence of emotional energy directed by your own inner voice, and the results can be staggering. As your true *artistic talents* begin to emerge, the world can suddenly begin to sit up and take notice of your work.

One of the sure ways to recognize the efforts of a Virtuoso is to notice the effect that it has on people. Virtuoso performances seem to light a fire beneath those who view it. It carves its mark in your soul. Only the most insensitive can walk away unscathed by efforts of this magnitude. Even if the style may not be your cup of tea, chances are that you will be able to recognize the emerging genius behind the work.

THE VIRTUOSO CHEF

While there are many thousands of highly competent professional chefs out there making delicious meals for their patrons, the plates created by the Virtuoso Chef will be instantly recognizable as something very special. Virtuoso meals tantalize your senses with a feast of aromas and flavors that tickle your taste buds with a touch that is at once delicate and powerful.

Sampling Virtuoso dishes reveals an intimate depth of flavors and textures that are sure to fill you with delight. There seems to be an almost magical quality about the food. Shimmering and tingling on your tongue, the sensations dance their way into your memory.

In virtually every culture you will find considerable folklore that refers to the *love* that is stirred or baked into certain dishes that may be the specialty of the local Virtuoso Chef. When you taste the food you can feel the depth of love and passion that went into the dish's preparation. The aromas and textures arouse juices within your body and soul that seem to flow from a depth that began long ago in the blood ties of your personal cultural heritage.

Indeed, the unique qualities of special traditional recipes, using local ingredients and prepared with characteristic flair and verve form the foundation of most cultures. It takes a Virtuoso Chef who has surrendered his ego long enough to absorb the depth and complexities of traditional ethnic cuisine to prepare a feast worthy of celebration by an entire culture.

Of course, some Virtuoso Chefs choose to strike out in new directions that combine ingredients and techniques from a variety of different traditions to develop *nouvelle cuisine*. Following their own intuition, they delicately blend flavors, textures and appearances of familiar foods into unique combinations that reveal a wealth of hidden complexities. These unique dishes can then form the basis for a new generation of classic cuisine.

The Virtuoso Manager

Successful managers at the Journeyman or Expert level have already demonstrated their competence in handling most any situation they are likely to find at their position. They fully understand the intricacies of the various jobs in their departments, and can motivate and guide the people they are managing. They have streamlined the workflow to meet advancing requirements for ever-greater departmental efficiency. These Pros have also figured out what key parameters need to be met to satisfy the demands of upper management. They know the ropes well enough to extract a high level of performance from their group, even under trying circumstances. You could scarcely ask for more.

Yet some professionals are able to go above and beyond by becoming *leaders*, as well as managers. The act of stepping up as a leader marks the shift into the Virtuoso level for any manager (or professional in any area for that matter.)

Often this transformation occurs in response to a crisis situation in the Pro's personal or professional life. She confronts difficult circumstances brought on by drastic changes in her life, and responds to those changes in a way that galvanizes her into bold new actions. These bold actions set an example for others to follow, and suddenly people begin to look to her for leadership.

In a manner totally consistent with the act of *losing yourself* in the depths of your practice, or following your *intuition,* or immersing yourself in the *flow* of the game, **leadership** emerges from within, directing you to act with an enhanced sense of spontaneity, power and purpose.

Facing tough problems that might devastate lesser people, the **leader** suddenly develops the **vision** to see beyond the current difficulties to a brighter set of possibilities that light the way to constructive change for herself and those around her. Armed with this inspiring vision, she seizes the opportunity and acts with **courage** to effect the changes that need to be made. Her vision shines so brightly in her mind that she is able to disregard the possibility of failure and **detach** from the opinions of others who stand in the way of the fulfillment of her vision. She *surrenders* herself to the demands of her new *intuitive* revelation, and dives into the *flow* of activities that mark the way forward.

Her bold actions, aimed at creating a brighter future, forge a new pathway for others to follow. Buoyed by the demonstration of her courage in service to a worthy cause, others in a similar situation see new hope from her example. As additional people begin to follow in her footsteps, the new **leader** is propelled into a position as spokesperson for the new movement.

Please note the internal nature of leadership. Despite the existence of dozens of books devoted to teaching the art of leadership, this is not another set of skills to be added to your repertoire. Leadership emerges in response to your recognition of a higher purpose, and your willingness to act upon that purpose.

Your ability to lead must be built upon a foundation of professionalism developed at the earlier levels of Mastery. When facing a crisis, you must have the Pro's depth of understanding of the issues in order to fully understand the ramifications of any action you may choose to undertake. The wisdom you can call upon in this demanding situation comes as a result of years of experience dealing with similar events. Likewise, those years of experience have taught you the value of the principles (like honesty, courage, compassion and integrity) you have already used successfully in your profession and your life.

When a higher purpose calls to you, you can then respond with the depth of character that you've been building all along. Thus leadership is the act of an inspired professional. The leader must step out from the herd and blaze a path for others to follow. Only when your colleagues see value in the example you set will they choose to follow your lead. In that sense, the leadership position is thrust upon the leader by the actions of her followers, not by being installed in an office and given a title by those higher up in the organization. While an advance in position brings broader authority and greater responsibility, your leadership abilities are not tied to your place in the organization. Leadership is earned, not bestowed.

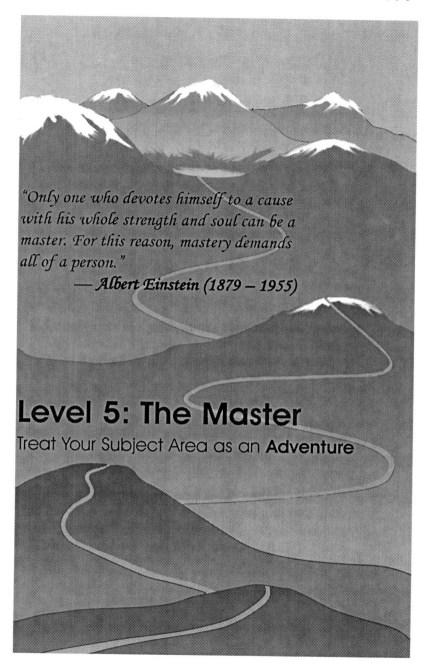

"Only one who devotes himself to a cause with his whole strength and soul can be a master. For this reason, mastery demands all of a person."
— Albert Einstein (1879 – 1955)

Level 5: The Master
Treat Your Subject Area as an **Adventure**

Level 5: The Master
TREAT YOUR SUBJECT AREA AS AN **ADVENTURE**

Objective: To advance your field to a new higher level, while simultaneously exploring the outer reaches of your own potenial as a human being.

Process: Concentrate your efforts into a tight focus, integrating your thoughts and actions in a single coordinated effort. Surrender further to the process of *losing yourself.* Follow your intuitive guidance into a sense of *anticipatory awareness.* Use this awareness to lead you to and through the unknown, into unexpectedly high levels of achievement. Focus on *being receptive to your intuition,* using it *to serve* your highest purpose.

Expected Results: A daring new discovery, creation or performance that expands the limits of what's possible. A **masterpiece** that unites a wealth of wisdom, beauty, elegance and effectiveness in a single peak effort.

Action Steps: Explore the limits of possibility within your field. Practice coming close to those limits, while remaining in the *flow.* Begin to incorporate the *flow* consciousness into everything you do. Look for connections that integrate all information, ideas and efforts into your purpose. Draw on these additional forces to assist you.

Keys to Success: Tighten your *focus* and refine and sharpen your *purpose.* Eat, drink and breathe your purpose, yet remember to be *playful.* Recognize and appreciate the source of your enhanced capabilities by being *grateful.*

Words of Praise/Encouragement: Awesome! Magnificent! Extraordinary! (Give in to the awe and wonder of it all.)

How you can help others: Blaze a new path to greatness that others can follow. Your masterpiece is your gift to all.

Chapter 11

Level 5: The Master
TREAT YOUR SUBJECT AREA AS AN **ADVENTURE**

Blazing a new trail up the mountain proved to be much more rewarding than she had ever imagined. By relaxing into her own unhurried hiking rhythm, and allowing the trail to open up before her, the mastery traveler smoothly and quickly climbed the steep wooded slopes. The strength and stamina she was able to summon surprised her. And even when the terrain looked most formidable, she found that she could read the subtleties of the ground as well as the elk, sheep and mountain goats. Picking the path of least resistance that the animals used was deceptively easy.

Before long her invisible path opened up into a lush meadow, bursting with bright wildflowers and tufts of short grasses, mixed with patches of rust-colored rocks. The trees surrounding the meadow were gradually thinning out as she neared timberline.

Ahead lay a small mountain lake, tucked into the bowl formed by a ring of snow-capped peaks. The smooth glassy surface of the water shimmered in a deep teal green reflection of the mountains rising before her. The sun shone brilliantly, lighting the landscape with a vibrant swash of deep, rich hues, contrasting strongly in the stark relief of long afternoon shadows.

Stunned by the sheer beauty of it all, she stopped abruptly to breathe in the majesty of the scene. In between the light gusts of thin air, the silence was deafening. Never before had such a profound peacefulness washed over her. A deep sense of fulfillment spread slowly through her entire being, quenching a thirst she never knew she had. She was home at last.

Over the next few years she made excursions back and forth to civilization for supplies and assistance in building a home by the lake. The simple path she had carved along the mountainside long ago had now grown into a well-worn road. By living and working in her element, she created a richly rewarding life for herself.

Then one summer day, as she was relaxing on the deck, enjoying the spectacular view, an old urge stirred within her. The rugged peaks that surrounded her cabin were calling her! "Climb me," they whispered. How could she have forgotten? There was still much more to explore. How high could she go? What amazing new views unfold beyond the tallest mountain? What new adventures lie ahead?

She had to find out. So, gathering her gear once more, she set off for the ragged edge of the unknown, to explore the very summit of her own capabilities...

At the pinnacle of the Pro level, the Expert has managed to expand the depth and breadth of his or her knowledge and skills to an amazing degree. For all intents and purposes, the Expert "knows everything there is to know" about his or her field, and can perform with technically flawless perfection. The Expert's command of the field is impressive, indeed. Clearly, Experts are sought after for the superior *expertise* that they can bring to any situation. For explaining new developments, solving intricate problems, and performing with consistent wide-ranging excellence, the Expert is the person to call upon. Hard to top, isn't it?

Yet, in the last chapter the Virtuoso introduced a whole new level of excellence that goes way beyond the technical perfection of the Pro. By becoming completely immersed in the *flow* of performing, the Virtuoso infuses his or her passion and personal expression into the midst of every action. Virtuosos stamp their own personality and creative vision onto each performance, carving out a new niche in the field, and leaving behind unique artistic contributions that move and inspire others. To go beyond mere excellence, and reach the level of inspired, brilliant, mesmerizing achievements, you'll need to become a Virtuoso.

So, given these extraordinary capabilities, coupled with the advanced level of consciousness utilized so effectively by the Virtuoso, what further heights of expression could possibly exist above this "level of the stars?"

Good question. Although some characteristics of true Masters are well known, others are more obscure. Since Masters operate at the very frontiers of our human capabilities, more is unknown than is known about the workings of Masters' minds, bodies and spirits.

Part of the difficulty in understanding what separates the Master from the Virtuoso lies in the tightly integrated nature of the Master's unique combination of talents. Prying these characteristics apart from their whole, complete expression inevitably misses much of the magic of the Master's extraordinary abilities. This is clearly a case where the whole adds up to much more than the sum of the parts.

So, in the description that follows, keep in mind that the only way to begin to understand what makes Masters tick is to think and feel in terms of *wholes,* and not parts. All aspects of the Master's highly developed capabilities work together to move them above and beyond the limitations of others.

Perhaps the most obvious characteristic of Masters is their amazing ability to *focus.* Spend some time around a Master and you cannot fail to notice this exceptional trait. When a Master looks at you, you can immediately feel the startling depth and intensity of his or her penetrating gaze. This has an unnerving effect on most people.

The depth of the Master's gaze provokes a riot of feelings within. It's as though the Master can see right into your very soul. Sensations of awe, wonder and power vie with feelings of pain, half-remembered fears, inadequacy and shame. Most folks shy away from such provocative encounters, without understanding the significance of their own reaction.

Few can handle the Master's intensity, for beneath that sharp focused look lies a challenge. That single brief stare stirs up long neglected feelings, and commands us to *deal with them* and move beyond the limitations they represent. In this sense, the Master's ever-present job is to act as a catalyst, stirring up evolution within us, provoking us to realize the glorious heights of our own capabilities. The Master's gaze issues a challenge to reach inside ourselves and pull up the courage, vision and determination needed to sweep away our petty fears and go on about the business of exploring the breadth and depth of all we can be. That one look says: *Why are you letting yourself down? What are you waiting for?*

While that single gaze has thrown your mind into a whirl of uncomfortable self-examination, imagine what that same level of intensity brings to the Master's work!

When you shine light upon any subject (or object), more and more of the *truth* of that subject is revealed. The shadows of the unknown melt away as the light uncovers additional detail and subtlety. The truth "comes to light." Imagine what happens when you shine a **laser** on that same subject! With such concentrated focused brilliance, the truth stands no chance of remaining hidden. The universe *must* give up its secrets to the penetrating gaze of the Master.

This is how Masters can so easily accomplish what appears to most people to be the impossible. Their laser-like focus reveals all, making new discoveries, inventions and advances in their fields seem routine. Marie Curie, Stephen Hawking, Albert Einstein, Neils Bohr, Nicola Tesla, Sir Isaac Newton, Buckminster Fuller and the other giants of science, medicine and technology all brought their incredible powers of focus to bear on the problems they were investigating, and the results revolutionized their fields.

Another manifestation of the power of focus is revealed in the depth of *purpose* displayed by Masters of any field.

Most of us can come up with some idea of the purpose behind our actions when asked why we do what we do. Yet many people would have to pause and search their minds for a while when asked what they hope to accomplish in their professions. Why are you involved in your profession at all? On a minute-to-minute basis, can you point to the purpose of each of your normal daily activities?

Didn't think so.

Much of our normal time is spent in a thick fog of self-doubt and indecision, as we weigh the merits of even the smallest actions. *What clothes shall I wear? Should I wash the dishes now or later? What do I want to eat? Which task on my "to-do" list should I do next? Can I really accomplish the goals I've set for myself?*

And these are all examples of the relatively few times when we bother to stop and think of our own actions and how we might proceed with them. Even more time is wasted on worry and gossip and complaining about things, events and people over which we have no control in the first place. If we had some type of "mental meter" that recorded the amount of time spent in different types of thought, it would be shocking to see how much of our time and energy is frittered away with these useless and/or destructive patterns of thinking and behavior.

The Master, however, operates in a totally different manner. Through years of concentration on his specialty—exploring and digging and unearthing the hidden secrets of his field—the Master gradually refines his purpose to an astonishing degree. All the grinding and polishing of years of practice produces a razor-sharp clarity of purpose that shines brightly in his mind, and cuts through the fog of mundane thinking like a sword slicing through gauze.

In this sense and others, Masters are not at all like regular people. At times, they don't even seem human. A breed apart, Masters do not concern themselves with the everyday trials and tribulations that plague the rest of the human race. They simply can't be bothered with such insignificant things. The full power of their intense focus constantly shines on their purpose, and blazes a path of thought and action directly through any self-doubt and indecision.

The Master's concentration is total. Nothing short of an earthquake can dislodge their thoughts and efforts from the task at hand. It is this single-minded, distraction-proof focus that so easily distinguishes Masters from lesser practitioners.

Spend some time around masters from any field and you'll quickly see that though their personalities vary as much as any group of people, they share several other common characteristics.

Masters are totally comfortable being themselves. Though they are often in the limelight, and sometimes appear quite eccentric, true Masters are never self-conscious or unsure of themselves. You can see it in their confident, upright stance, the depth and clarity of their eyes, the intensity of their gaze and the sure and deft way that they express themselves when in their element. Masters are *in command*. They have truly begun to tap the seemingly infinite well of their extraordinary powers as human beings. It shows.

Such clarity and confidence automatically demands attention, without any particular effort to do so. Crowds will gather around a Master, even when the group is unaware of the accomplishments of that particular Master. The Master's mere presence acts as a unifying and *cohesive* force. People easily sense the clarity and power that radiates from the Master. They are drawn to it like moths to a flame.

The Master derives much of her power from the harmony and unity of all her efforts. Shining the full light of her being in a tight focus on a clear purpose brings a potent coordinated effort to bear on every aspect of what she does. At least while engaging in her field, the Master never wastes time or energy. Each thought and motion is guided by a crystal-clear purpose that harmonizes and maximizes the effects of every effort. The cohesiveness of her thoughts and actions amplifies her power, and attracts others to her at the same time.

The efforts of a Master are like an ocean-going yacht, whose sharp prow and rounded bottom cuts through the waves and pounds them into a flat, smooth wake that easily draws smaller craft in behind it. Her unified and compelling actions pull others into the wake of her efforts, further synchronizing, integrating and intensifying the results she creates.

This combination of focus, clarity and power enables Masters to radiate a type of *fierceness* that is formidable. Sometimes the Master's power is so palpable, so intense, that it can frighten people away for reasons that they may barely understand. This fierceness is akin to the fierceness displayed by eagles, sharks, lions, cobras and wolves.

The ferocity of these animals stems from their extraordinary concentration, their unwavering purpose, and their exacting skills, coupled with their powerfully honed bodies. This level of clarity and power strikes fear into the hearts of their prey, leaving them helpless before the onslaught of their attackers.

With Masters, you can easily get the sense that **nothing** will stand in the way of their fierce intent. Former heavyweight boxing champion Mohammed Ali's ability to stare his opponent down, while lightly dancing from one foot to another, then striking hard and fast with a quick and powerful knockout punch was eerily reminiscent of the attack of the cobra as it sways hypnotically before striking its foe with lightning speed.

Thomas Edison's stubborn persistence in trying everything possible as a filament to his new light bulb invention exhibits a similar singularity of purpose. Like a pack of wolves, he attacked his problem again and again, until it finally yielded a solution.

The daringly swift, seemingly suicidal dive of the eagle to snatch the tiny field mouse from the ground could easily be likened to Michael Schumacher's extraordinary ability to extract every last ounce of speed from his Formula 1 Ferrari racer, while making daring passes of lesser drivers in his quest for victory.

Five-time Tour de France winner Bernard Hinault was known as "The Badger" for his ferocious attacks up steep mountain passes that demolished the opposition. With sudden and overwhelming acceleration, he would blaze past other competitors, leaving them gasping and demoralized.

Master researchers and scientists bring their single-minded focus to bear on their experiments and analyses to develop breakthrough discoveries in biology, psychology, medicine, physics, engineering, computer technology and many other fields. Their results vie for Nobel Prizes. Master artists, musicians and entertainers of every stripe hold their audiences spellbound by their awesome performances and incredibly creative masterpieces. Master lawyers, doctors, tradesmen and women, entrepreneurs,

CEOs, counselors, teachers, and other professionals push the frontiers of their fields by developing new cutting-edge methods and techniques, and leading their organizations to greatness. Master athletes and martial artists compete against one another at the highest levels, winning championships and setting records in the process.

At the peak of each field, only a handful of the top performers might possibly be considered Masters. You will know the true Masters by their intense focus, their unwavering purpose, their sharp clarity of intelligence and wisdom, the coherence of their efforts, the sheer power of their thinking and actions, and by the fierceness of their will.

To further understand their extraordinary capabilities, let's take another viewpoint and examine Masters from a different angle, using the perspective of *flow* consciousness as a way of understanding the unique awareness that Masters can employ.

In the previous chapter the shift into utilizing the special qualities of *flow* consciousness was presented as a sense of *losing yourself.* This shift into *losing yourself* could be described as a **magical** state of consciousness.

As an Adept or Pro you may have fleeting encounters with this magical awareness and the way that it can enhance your performance. At this point, in terms of your mastery of *flow,* you are operating as a **Novice magician,** struggling to understand and make use of the capabilities of your expanded consciousness.

You break into the Virtuoso ranks as you are able to sustain this state throughout your performance. The flavor and quality of your performances undergoes a complete transformation as a new, more artistic interpretation of your knowledge and skills takes hold. By the time you enter the Virtuoso level, you have become an **Adept magician,** capable of putting together complete performances that exhibit these enhanced qualities.

In traversing the Virtuoso level you advance from an Adept magician to a **Journeyman magician,** who can regularly and deliberately enter the *flow* state and remain there as long as necessary to complete the performance. Consistently captivating performances are the results.

At the Master level, you have progressed to the point where you become an ***Expert magician.*** Through the continued practice of your discipline while in the advanced state of consciousness that the Virtuoso enjoys, the Master develops considerable expertise in performing while in the *flow* state. So much so, that he is able to dip deeper into that well of awareness that is known as *intuition* and ***begin to anticipate what happens next.***

Hockey great Wayne Gretzky was interviewed late in his career and asked a simple question that reveals his expertise in utilizing the *flow* state. After setting scoring records for years in the NHL, and leading his teams to numerous championships, Gretzky had outstripped all who came before him to become the almost universally acknowledged "greatest hockey player who ever lived."

The reporter began by saying, "Wayne, at six feet tall and 180 pounds, you are not the biggest guy on the ice. Many other hockey players are faster and stronger than you are. What's your secret? How can you consistently outplay all those other great hockey stars?"

Gretzky replied, "Well, most players skate to where the puck is. I skate to where the puck is *going to be."*

Clearly, Gretzky utilized his anticipatory awareness well. Once you have a palpable sense of knowing what will happen next, even just a split second before it unfolds, an entirely new world of possibilities opens up. Like knowing tomorrow's stock market reports today, you can invest your efforts with increasing certainty of the outcome. The breadth and depth of rewards you can garner from this subtle advantage become rich indeed as you begin to utilize these expanded powers.

This successful anticipation of events brings with it a measure of control over any situation the Master encounters. That split second advantage may not seem like much, at first. But as you gain more confidence in your abilities to tune in to that anticipatory awareness, you will literally be (like Gretzky) "ahead of the game."

Your development as a Master proceeds as you learn to bring this bonanza under your control.

This developing sense of control that you now have over the *flow* state of consciousness enables you to be a step ahead of your opponent, a step ahead of your clients, competitors or the market that you deal with, and a step ahead of your colleagues in researching, inventing, creating or expressing yourself. As a Master, you seem to defy the laws of physics, and the rules and principles that govern your field. With that subtle, but powerful advantage in consciousness, you'll be a step ahead in any area you choose.

So you can see that the term **Master** is not used lightly here. A true Master in this sense not only has a comprehensive knowledge of the field, exceptional skill in any area of performance, and unquestioned superiority of capability over most others, but also possesses that extra quality of consciousness that enables extraordinary performances, breakthrough discoveries and masterpiece creations.

Masters typically comprise less than one percent of all the participants in any field. They are the *crème de la crème,* advancing their fields as they reach new heights of personal development.

Some examples of Masters in action:

In his best moments, former NBA basketball star Michael Jordan could drive to the basket, leap up for the shot, and hang an unnaturally long time in the air, as though he was imitating a puppet dangling on invisible strings. While in the air he would encounter several swarming defenders, twist his body through them like a knife through butter, alter his shot a couple of times, and still launch a delicately soft layup that slipped through the net without even rippling the cords. When the chips were down, he could single-handedly take control of the game and bend it to his will, and that resulted in a string of NBA championships.

Examples of masterful moments in athletics abound. Consider those memorable gold-medal performances of Olympic figure-skaters, downhill skiers, gymnasts, swimmers, divers, runners, and the US Olympic hockey team's amazing 1980 victory.

Take Greg LeMond's exceptional 1989 Tour de France win as another example. Still recovering from a near-fatal accidental shotgun wound that had sidelined him two years earlier, he gradually rode himself into top shape at the beginning of the Tour. Entering the last leg of the race with a 50 second deficit, LeMond's extraordinary final stage time-trial win stole 58 seconds from Tour leader Laurent Fignon in just 15.2 miles to snatch overall victory by a mere 8 seconds, after 3 weeks and over 2000 miles of racing. LeMond averaged over 34 mph for those 15 miles (the fastest time-trial in Tour history) to take the closest Tour victory ever.

We stand in awe of such devastating performances. These Masters rise above not only their competitors, but also the boundaries of what was previously thought possible by mere mortals. In every field, each time a Master sets a new standard, *the entire human race* is advanced to another level.

In fact, entry to the Master level comes when you create your first **masterpiece.** This masterpiece can take the form of a product, performance, discovery, invention, artistic expression, or any accomplishment that raises the bar in some area of human achievement. In creating a masterpiece, the *genius* of the Master becomes self-evident.

What allows a masterpiece performance to stand above the efforts of so many others? How does it differ from the "merely" brilliant performances of the Virtuoso? What makes it so special?

The secret lies beyond the breath-taking excellence of the results, beyond the Herculean efforts that the Master employed, beyond even the new standards that it sets. This secret is both simple and deeply profound—*masterpieces are **daring.***

Woven into the fabric of every masterpiece is a far-reaching vision—a vision that rocks the world. To produce a masterpiece, the Master *dares to do what no one else has ever done.* Adopting the mission of the Enterprise in the old Star Trek TV series, the Master "boldly goes where no man has gone before."

To follow that intuitive voice and dare to attempt the impossible again and again takes guts. This bold effort exposes the Master to considerable scorn and ridicule, since only a fool or a genius would dare to do the impossible.

Ask Galileo, the famous Italian physicist and astronomer of the Middle Ages, who used his invention of the telescope to prove that the Earth revolved around the sun, and not the other way around. How was this breakthrough discovery rewarded? His revolutionary ideas were scorned by the philosophers of the time, which led to the burning of his books and his arrest for heresy. Galileo lived out his remaining days under house arrest.

The revolutionary nature of true genius is not always appreciated right away. And the glory that comes with creating a masterpiece is sometimes delivered posthumously.

Yet despite the risks involved, the Master sees far beyond the ordinary, and dares to ask the greatest question of all, *What If?*

What if we could make light without fire? *What if* we could speak to people in a distant city without leaving home? *What if* people afflicted with the dreaded disease smallpox could be cured? *What if* a man could run a mile in four minutes?

Thomas Edison, Alexander Graham Bell, Edward Jenner, and Roger Banister were bold enough to pose those provocative questions, daring enough to wrestle with the impossible challenges they faced, and determined enough to forge solutions that ultimately advanced the entire human race.

Right now there are Virtuosos and Masters all around the world asking similar provocative questions that will lead to daring masterpieces of their own. *What if* we could all travel in vehicles that didn't pollute? *What if* we could speak with dolphins and whales? *What if* there were cures for cancer and AIDS? *What if* a **woman** could run a mile in four minutes?

To become a Master, you must think BIG. To create a masterpiece, you must have the vision to reach beyond the concerns of personal ambition and touch all of humanity with the fulfillment of a much larger purpose than the ego gratification of a single human being.

Fortunately, this comes with the territory for Masters. By being so attuned to the *flow* state of awareness, most Masters recognize that the intuitive insights and anticipatory awareness that they have learned to employ flow from a source that is infinitely larger than their individual limited understanding can fathom. In this sense, the Master, even more than the Virtuoso, becomes an agent, vessel or loudspeaker for the intuitive intelligence that acts through them. Their extraordinary masterpieces reflect the gift of that higher awareness, and the broader purpose that it serves.

Masterpieces like the *Mona Lisa,* the *geodesic dome,* the *Taj Mahal,* the *general theory of relativity,* the *printing press,* the *Sistine Chapel, Hamlet, Citizen Kane, fiberoptic cable,* the *semiconductor*, and *War and Peace* speak to all humanity, enabling an expansion of our ability to understand ourselves and the world around us, while adding more blocks to the foundation that supports even greater human achievement.

Producing a masterpiece takes a unique combination of vision, focus, skill, energy and dedication. The process is so special that it is rare indeed to find Masters who are masterful all the time. Most often, the extraordinary periods that Masters utilize to create new inventions and discoveries, artistic masterpieces, and dramatic new heights of performance are once-in-a-lifetime efforts.

Bob Beamon's amazing Olympic leap into glory is a good example. Coming into the 1968 summer games, the world record for the long jump stood at 27 feet 4 3/4 inches. Beamon's personal best was just an inch or so short of that mark. Yet on his first attempt, Beamon sped down the ramp and launched a colossal leap that soared almost *two feet* past the existing record! He (along with everyone else) was so shocked by his feat that he collapsed to the ground and wept for several minutes. He never again came close to that record-shattering distance throughout the rest of his track career. His new world record stood for 23 years.

Most Masters enjoy short periods of time where they produce

results that advance their fields, and then retreat back to being "merely" Virtuosos. It's tough to be out in the wilderness of the unknown for too long. To make an assault on the peaks of your field, you must align all available forces to your purpose, at just the right time and place. Few masters have the clarity and power to do this more than once.

The few who do manage this feat more than once become household names, and heroes for the rest of us. Thomas Edison, Nicola Tesla, Michael Jordan, Steve Spitz, Eddy Merckx, Tiger Woods, Nissan CEO Carlos Ghosn, GE CEO Jack Welch, Leonardo da Vinci, Michelangelo, Beethoven, Mozart, The Beatles, and hundreds of others throughout history show that it is possible for Masters to dramatically advance their fields again and again.

At the upper end of the Master level, we find the ultimate expression of Mastery—the Master of Masters. What would such a person be like? Surely, some of the Masters mentioned above would easily qualify.

Perhaps this ideal model of Mastery finds its most complete overall expression in the martial arts. Here is an example of what the ultimate Master might look like. It might remind you of the character Kane in the old TV series, *Kung Fu.*

To begin with, the ultimate martial arts Master has developed a broad, wide-ranging and deeply sensitive awareness that enables him to detect danger arriving from any direction. He also has lightning-quick reflexes to deflect or avoid an attacker's blows, coupled with extraordinary flexibility in both body and mind. This flexibility, along with the "early-warning system" of his anticipatory awareness allows the Master to squirt himself away from dangerous situations and instantly detect weak points in the attacker's moves, attitude and fighting strategies.

With laser-like focus on his objective, the Master strikes at the precise moment in the exact place needed to disable the attacker's threat. In the process, this ultimate Master uses the minimum amount of force, disruption and upset to thwart the attacker, while simultaneously showing the attacker the futility of any further attempts to gain the upper hand.

All the while, the ultimate Master has as his ultimate objective *to serve.* Thus the Master is a peaceful warrior, never seeking to harm, but rather using his considerable control and skill to restore peace as quickly and easily as possible in any situation. His wisdom matches his skill.

This Master never gets upset, thus maintaining his over-riding intent to serve at all times. This intent to serve the highest good lends him a peaceful serenity that calms others in his presence. While unfailingly polite and respectful, he is playful and rarely does the expected thing, preferring to surprise and delight when appropriate, while otherwise remaining out of the limelight. Most of the time, he prefers to be invisible, blending silently into the background and drawing no attention to himself at all.

While thoroughly enjoying life and all the material aspects of it, he has no desire to accumulate possessions, and lives simply and requires little, while giving freely without being asked. With his extraordinary skills and simple lifestyle, he relies on the broad range of his abilities to handle any situation, rather than any attempt to insulate himself from others behind collections of material goods. He challenges himself regularly, though rarely challenges others. Being the rascal sage, he stimulates people to advance their own development at the level and rate they are ready to handle, in a firm yet playful manner.

To the Master, the world is truly his or her oyster. That's why the Master's world is treated as an *adventure.* Literally, the sky is the limit for Masters. Out on the fringes of what is known and what is possible in his or her field, the Master advances into the unknown at every step. Taming the wild unknown, and bringing it under his or her control is the subtext for this adventure. Breakthroughs in research and knowledge, new theories and realms of expression, the development of cutting edge companies, fresh inventions, masterpiece creations and world records are all within reach for the Master who seeks the ultimate adventure.

Anyone aspiring to become a Master would do well to adopt

some of the character traits of that "Master of Masters" described above. With all the emphasis on focus, purpose, intensity and even fierceness, it may be difficult to see how being *playful* would fit in with the consciousness of the Master.

Yet, in order for you to be daring enough to become a Master, you will also have to recognize the very real possibility of failure. It is bold indeed to attempt the impossible. Despite your very best efforts, it is entirely possible that you could end up with egg on your face. Your giant ambitions may amount to no more than a colossal flop.

If you are going to risk being a fool, it may just help to start out with a *playful* attitude. Lighten up. After all, you are attempting the impossible. Faced with overwhelming odds against you, it should be no surprise if you don't succeed. So in creating your Masterpiece, you will need to throw all caution to the wind and put every ounce of effort you can muster into your performance. You'll have to give it your all, holding nothing back.

And once you've done everything you can possibly do, then you can let go of the outcome entirely, and let the chips fall where they may. When you've dropped your attachment to the outcome, *anything* becomes possible. Being *playful* requires just this sense of letting go completely.

Practicing this ultimate *yang/yin* discipline of intense effort followed by a complete release of all your concerns about the results develops this "devil may care" attitude. Being able to laugh at yourself and celebrate the folly of bravely attempting something you've never done before is the essence of the *playful* approach to mastery. With so much hanging in the balance, you simply cannot take it seriously. The price would be too great.

So instead of becoming devastated by each unsuccessful attempt, learn to roll with the punches, dodge the slings and arrows, pick yourself up when you've fallen, sing the blues with gusto, and dance with destiny. **Rejoice!** Dare to have some fun! This attitude is what gives life its exquisite bittersweet flavor. Like fine quality dark chocolate, you can taste both the sweet and the bitter together in delicious harmony.

By loosening up and accepting whatever comes your way, you are developing the *yin* side of Mastery. This counterbalances the intensity of the *yang* characteristics that constitute the focused drive to greatness. You must have both to become a Master. A spontaneous *playful* attitude allows you to be "light on your feet," flexible and easily capable of deflecting the pressures that come with your bold attempts at tackling the impossible.

A *playful* attitude also opens the door to **gratefulness.** The receptivity inherent in a playful approach enables each experience to be accepted and celebrated, regardless of your assessment of its success. At whatever stage of Mastery you've been able to attain, you have much to be grateful for. *Look! See what you can do! Isn't it amazing?*

Remember the definition of **gratitude** from Chapter 1: *the quality or feeling of being warmly or deeply appreciative of kindness or benefits received.* If you come to see each experience (whether successful or not) as a **gift,** then being grateful welcomes ever more experiences that you can learn from.

Another way to appreciate *gratefulness* is to see it as *full of greatness.* In this sense, to be *grateful* is to feel calm, fulfilled, uplifted and fully connected with all that is. Surely, as a Master, it should be easy to see yourself as *full of greatness.* Actually, at any level of Mastery you are *already full of greatness.*

Each time you create something new, or perform at a higher level than before, you have just released a bit more of the greatness you hold within you. When you experience *gratefulness* there is a palpable feeling of overflowing with greatness—so full, so appreciative, so generous, so complete, so grateful.

Perhaps the single most important key to living a fulfilling life is to see each moment, each effort, each experience, and each result you create as a gift to be appreciated. By fully appreciating each moment and all it has to offer, you are truly honoring yourself and all of creation at the same time. Make *gratefulness* a spontaneous response to every moment and the richness of life unfolds before you like a flower opening its petals to the sun. *Gratefulness* is the secret that allows true Masters to be humble and gracious in both victory and defeat.

[For a much more complete approach to incorporating *gratefulness* into your life, see Brother David Steindl-Rast's website at www.gratefulness.org.]

What are the limits of our capabilities? How do we move beyond them? Where do we go from the Master level?

As mentioned at the beginning of the chapter, many of the secrets to further development at the Master level remain hidden. The process that the Master goes through lies at the very edge of what is known, so we don't have a very complete guide to this final stage of Mastery. The frontiers of Mastery are being developed and expanded *right now*, by dedicated enthusiasts who are bold enough to expand their capabilities beyond what anyone thought possible. In the process, they lead us all into an even greater range of possibilities of what it means to be human.

You could be one of the leaders of your field, too. Take the Master's challenge and dive into the juicy part of life. What are you waiting for? Why not take yourself to the next level and strive for Mastery? What could be more exciting? What could be more rewarding? What greater contribution could you make to the world? Your daringly bold masterpiece will advance all of humanity, and you'll celebrate new heights of your own personal development in the process.

THE MASTER OF ANY PROFESSION

Laser-like focus; supreme clarity of purpose; relentless determination; bold vision; fierce intent; daring, yet playful attitude; humble and gracious in both victory and defeat. These are the fundamental qualities of true Masters. When blended together in synergistic harmony, they fuse into a single force of *power* that is impossible for the world to ignore. With such power behind them, Masters cannot fail to burst through the current frontiers of their fields.

To develop their masterpieces, Masters employ a secret ingredient that virtually guarantees their success. This secret ingredient is not simply another vital quality like those mentioned above. Instead, the secret to success of their masterpieces derives from the tight integration of *all* the qualities that Masters have at their disposal. *Integrity* is the key.

Masters **must** have it all together. The creation of a masterpiece can tolerate no weaknesses in any area. So Masters take great pains to correct any flaws they may detect in their creations or performances. They simply cannot afford any lapse in integrity.

Most Masters employ mentors or coaches or the counsel of a group of esteemed colleagues in their field. They choose people who have the broad range of skill and experience it takes to detect the most minute imperfections in their performances. These independent advisors, with their additional points of view, become invaluable to the Master's success. After all, no one person can see and understand it all. The unique observations and counsel of a group of advisors serve to round out and complete the Master's grasp of all the components that contribute to the generation of his masterpiece.

The tighter the integration of all these elements, the stronger each effort becomes. When every thought, word and motion contributes to a single overriding purpose, the synergistic power that emerges becomes overwhelming. Any lack of integrity at this level quickly reveals itself as a chink in the armor of the Master.

Unfortunately, many would-be Masters have allowed gaps in their personal or professional integrity to undermine the success of otherwise outstanding efforts. When this happens, the aspiring Master not only lets himself down, but also dashes the hopes and dreams of thousands of others who look up to the example set by their hero.

That's why so many become discouraged when their favorite sports or entertainment star reveals some character flaw by doing something disreputable and undeserving of their loyalty. The fan feels cheated when such things occur. A lapse in performance is always understandable, but a lapse in judgment can be unforgivable.

So each Master, whether he likes it or not, is charged with great responsibility for his entire field. By leading his colleagues into new territory, the Master automatically assumes the mantle of spokesperson for all who participate in his profession, and becomes a role model for everyone who is even interested in that subject area. In the minds of many, his name quickly becomes synonymous with his field.

Who could think about golf without Tiger Woods' name on the tip of their tongue? Think comedy and Robin Williams will surely come to mind. Even those who don't like classical music can agree on the musical genius of Beethoven and Mozart.

The trend and record setters of every field come to define—both literally and figuratively—the standards of their field. These Masters are then held up as the personification of those standards. Their further exploits then pile glory—or scorn—on everyone associated with their profession.

Remember that with great power comes great responsibility. The higher you reach on the Mastery scale, the greater your influence in the world. So use your development of the ten character traits mentioned in Chapter 1 to assist you in gaining greater wisdom along with your other remarkable talents. The wisdom you display can not only help you reach the top of your game, but ensure that you stay there for a while, as well.

Take a look at the people at the top of your profession. *You* decide who are the Masters and who are the pretenders. Who sets the standards by which others are judged? Who serves as a viable spokesperson for the field? Whose example would you wish to emulate? Whose respect would you most like to earn?

> *If you think you can, you can. If you think you can't,*
> *you're right.* — *Henry Ford (1863 – 1947)*

Chapter 12:

Unpacking Your Repair Kit
HANDLING THE HAZARDS OF THE MASTERY ADVENTURE

What can go wrong on the road to mastery? Lots of things. You could pick the wrong route, get lost, or arrive at a dead end. Your vehicle could break down or run out of fuel. The roadway can be littered with potholes, debris, blind turns and ominous hitchhikers. You could encounter steep lung-busting climbs, slippery harrowing descents and hot desolate stretches of desert highway. You'll be exposed to all the elements of sun, wind, rain and snow. Anything could happen.

After all, you've taken on a huge challenge to discover just how far you can go in mastering your field. In a sense, you're inviting disaster. Every step you take on your journey plunges you into the unknown. Who knows how it will all turn out?

Yet, this is the nature of an adventure. If it was easy, and you knew what was going to happen, that would take all the fun out of it. As a true mastery traveler you expect the unexpected, relish the difficult challenges, laugh at the danger, and revel in the glory of stretching yourself to the limit and beyond. You are daring!

The most exciting video games, the most dramatic movies and the most rewarding real-life adventures all have the same thing in common. In each case, the hero at some point finds himself lost in uncharted territory, battling fearsome adversaries against overwhelming odds. He struggles mightily. Then somehow our hero digs in and finds new resources that he didn't know he had, emerging victorious in the end. Exhilarated, we cheer him on every step of the way.

Clearly, any mastery traveler must be willing to take risks. And, with all the climbing involved, getting to the top is never an easy task. Even something as simple as gathering a bouquet of roses exposes you to a thicket of thorns. Taking risks is the price of admission to the mastery game.

The difficulties are worth the effort, though, since the juiciest rewards come wrapped in the most elaborate risks. If you have to slay a terrible dragon to rescue and marry the fair princess, then that will make your climactic wedding union even sweeter. After all, *why not go out on a limb, isn't that where the fruit is?*

Yet, as bold and daring as a mastery traveler must be, the successful adventurer is never foolhardy. Jumping out of the plane without taking skydiving training or without strapping on the parachute can put an end to your mastery travels once and for all!

What will make your daring leap out of the plane successful is your diligent preparation of all the details of your landing. Smart mastery travelers do their homework and come prepared. They recognize that there will be problems, difficulties and hazards along the way, so they prepare as best they can by gathering all the resources and training they might need to handle an emergency.

That's where your **Repair Kit** comes into play. At each stage of the mastery journey different types of problems emerge to challenge the unwary. This chapter examines the nature of those problems and provides solutions that you can use to keep moving smoothly along the road to mastery.

Borrowing a term from the computer software engineering field, the suggested solutions are called **debugs.** When software engineers write complex computer code they sometimes make mistakes that can be difficult to uncover. These errors in programming are called **bugs.** As the flawed program runs, it may do strange or unexpected things and deliver incorrect solutions. Thus the debugging process involves careful examination of the program's intended functions, and then noting exactly what happens when it runs. From there it's a matter of pinpointing any incorrect actions and revising the code to repair the flaws.

In a similar manner, the rest of this chapter identifies each problem that the mastery traveler is likely to encounter, and then offers a few ways to get back on track.

Even before you begin the mastery journey, you may have some problems. Fortunately, most of these preliminary issues have been addressed in earlier chapters.

For example, if you are having difficulty choosing a career to pursue that really excites you and provides the sort of satisfaction you desire, then the exercises in Chapter 2 should assist you in finding your niche. Likewise, if you are in a quandary about whether to take a class, buy some instructional tapes or hire a tutor to teach you French, then Chapter 5 should help you sort through the possibilities and find an approach that fits your situation.

Getting started uses the power of your inspiration to set you in motion. Once you're underway on your mastery journey, generating and maintaining your motivation to continue may well prove to be the most persistent and pervasive problem of all. In fact, many of the problems examined in this chapter do their damage by sapping your motivation, leaving you floundering and demoralized. So, in addition to the debugs mentioned here, you may want to refer to Chapter 6 for additional hints on keeping your motivation flowing.

The problems and debugs that follow are grouped and presented in order from Novice to Master. These difficulties are not necessarily limited to the level where they are introduced. Some types of problems may pop up repeatedly at several stages along your mastery route. They are introduced here at the first level you are likely to encounter them. For that reason, there are more problems listed at the earlier levels than the later ones. By the time you've reached the higher levels of mastery you will have handled some of the earlier problems completely, only to find new ones emerging to take their place.

PROBLEMS AT THE NOVICE LEVEL:

Feeling overwhelmed, confusion, struggle, discouragement, no fun, impatience and lack of focus.

Feeling overwhelmed: When you first take up a new discipline, the enormity of the task can be disorienting. So much to learn! As you dive into your new field there may be times when you feel that you are in over your head. It's all coming too fast. The waves of new information are washing over you before you can take the next breath, and panic sets in as you feel yourself drowning in a sea of new experiences. This panicky sense of being overwhelmed may be the first problem you encounter.

Debug: The first step in handling being this problem is to recognize that despite the panicky feeling that accompanies it, there is nothing life-threatening happening. When you feel that panic rise within you, *disengage.* Withdraw from the feeling instead of getting wrapped up in it. Let go, chill out, relax. Release the need to be in command of everything. Allow yourself to *not know.*

Once you've disengaged from the overwhelming event, take a few deep breaths and be patient with yourself and the process. Repeat the learning process you began. Take it slow. Break down each aspect of the event into smaller pieces. Study or practice each part by itself until you get it down. Then string the pieces together. This slower, more deliberate pace enhances understanding and eliminates the overload. There was nothing to panic about. You just bit off more than you could chew. Next time take smaller bites.

Confusion: Sometimes what you are learning just doesn't make sense. Confusion sets in when you cannot see how one piece of your learning connects to the others. You don't see *how* or *why* it works the way it does. You may find yourself reviewing the whole process over and over again in your mind, where it all seems fuzzy or jumbled. The internal sensation of confusion differs from the panicky feeling of overwhelm. When you are confused, you feel lost, dizzy or disoriented. In both cases the tendency is to stop the learning process until you can regain control.

Debug: Confusion arises from a lack of clarity. It's like being in a thick fog, not being able to see what's in front of you, and thus not knowing which way to go next. The solution is to restore clarity. Like before, relax, take it slow, and proceed cautiously one step at a time.

Ask questions. Questions slice through the fog of confusion. If you feel lost, you can ask the simple question, "How does this relate to my objective?" Reorienting your learning toward your objective can be like sighting the beacon of a lighthouse. Following the powerful beam of light home to its source can draw you back from the brink of confusion.

Have someone demonstrate or explain the confusing parts to you. Look for a new point of view. *Try it again.* Attempt to explain it to someone else. Keep at it until all the pieces of the puzzle fit together and make sense. As you begin to connect the dots, your confusion dissipates and the fog lifts.

Sometimes the sense of confusion can be so strong that you feel paralyzed with indecision. If only you could figure it out, then you'd know where to begin. In these cases, just *do something!* If you don't know where to begin, then one place is just as good as the next. You can't organize all the pieces of your puzzle when you don't yet know what they are. So begin by putting one piece together with the next, or one foot in front of the other. This will suggest the following step, and before you know it, the tangle of indecision will have unraveled right in front of you.

Another way to approach this scattered and confused state of mind is to journal. Sit down and simply write down all the random thoughts that come to you. Keep writing. Before long the random thoughts will sort themselves into coherent ideas and order will emerge from the chaos.

Struggle: As you continue to practice your discipline you will find that some of your attempts are successful and others are not. The sense of struggle comes from repeated unsuccessful attempts, where nothing you do seems to bring about a successful result. You try harder and harder, yet nothing changes. The internal sensation is like slogging through deep sand or mud. You are exerting a tremendous amount of effort to make little or no progress. The excessive efforts sap your strength, drain your enthusiasm and lower your morale.

Debug: If only you could create a successful result, then you would no longer be struggling. All you need is an example to follow. Find a Pro who can model the process for you, and you'll be on your way to reducing the struggle. Seeing the process done correctly will help reinforce your determination. If that person can do it, then sooner or later, so can you. Observe the demonstration closely, looking for any subtleties that may be different from your attempts. Ask questions, experiment, change viewpoints, and get some guidance to help you along. If you can't find a Pro, then look for a demo tape, or a different explanation or instructional approach from another source.

Sometimes, the sense of struggle can be amplified by a loss of perspective. If you get too involved with conquering a particular problem, you can blow the whole thing way out of proportion. Suddenly, what started out as a little bump in the road becomes a mountain of a problem. As before, it's time to disengage. Back up and see the bigger picture. By changing your perspective the difficulty shrinks to a more manageable size, and you can more clearly see alternatives to the way you've been approaching it. Often, solving an insurmountable problem takes only a simple tweak of some tiny detail that escaped your attention.

Discouragement: This is the feeling that comes when, despite your best efforts, it just doesn't work out. Your hopes are dashed. Discouragement can arrive gradually, as the accumulated result of too much struggle and too little success, or it can come in a single crushing blow, as one small glitch reduces your triumphant moment to dismal failure. Either way, it takes the wind out of your sails, leaving your spirits to sag like a deflated balloon.

When you are discouraged, you have literally *lost your courage.* Gone is your willingness to be brave and perform valiantly in the face of difficult challenges. For the moment, your bright, cheery confidence has given way to a gloomy sense of hopelessness. Inside, you hear yourself say, *What's the use?*

Debug: It's important to deal with discouragement as soon as you begin to feel it, since prolonged discouragement leads to despair, and you certainly don't want to go down that road. What has happened is that your attitude has taken a 180° turn, from confident and upbeat to doubtful and downtrodden. You are headed *down* the mastery road instead of *up* to greater heights. To turn yourself around, you'll need some *en-couragement*.

Unfortunately, the well-meaning "rah-rahs" and "attaboys" that you normally get from your friends are rarely enough to turn the tide. The encouragement needs to come from the inside out, not the other way around. At this point "positive thinking" and affirmations won't help any more than your friends' efforts, since they're just "more of the same." Besides, it feels particularly insincere to tell yourself something you don't currently believe.

To handle discouragement quickly and effectively, you'll need a method that can shift your thinking around in a hurry, before you get in too deep. As it turns out, the basic approach to changing discouragement into encouragement takes only three simple steps:

THE ATTITUDE REVERSAL METHOD (ARM)

1. **Hit the brakes: *Disengage.*** Stop putting energy into those discouraging thoughts and self-defeating behaviors that are dragging you downhill. Relax. Just let go...

2. **Turn around: *Change your point of view.*** Switch direction and reorient yourself back toward your objective. Ask yourself: *What have I already learned? What I can perform successfully? What is my objective in learning this?*

3. **Accelerate again: *Inspire yourself.*** Recall the event that inspired you to take up this discipline in the first place. Replay it again in your mind, including all the feelings and emotional impact you experienced before. Review and practice some of what you've accomplished so far. *Feel* the satisfaction that comes with successful accomplishment. Demonstrate to yourself that you *can* do it. You may be surprised to see how far you've come already.

By demonstrating your prowess to yourself, you renew your confidence and inspire yourself to continue up the road to the next level. This process should take little time and effort. In some cases, you could do all three steps over the course of a short walk around the neighborhood.

This process can be simplified even further and condensed down into just one or two steps. Depending on the circumstances and your state of mind, you may prefer to use one of the following alternative techniques:

THE PEANUT BUTTER METHOD

1. **Disengage.** Same as above. Relax. Just let go...
2. **Spread encouragement.** Immediately do three or more small acts that are directly and personally encouraging to others. Express your faith in others through encouraging comments, a hug or pat on the back, a letter or note, or any other gesture of kindness, gratitude, appreciation, or encouragement. You may also choose to assist someone in an unobtrusive way without being asked.

This technique restores your faith in yourself and your abilities at the same time that it assists others. That one-two punch gives this method extra power while it leaves you feeling great. Encouragement benefits everyone; so spread it around like peanut butter.

The last method is the simplest of all, and works only with those who have already reached a fairly advanced state of personal development.

THE INSIGHT METHOD

1. **Reflect.** Ask yourself one or more of the following questions as soon as you notice yourself feeling discouraged: *What's funny about this event? What's the lesson I need to learn here? How does this event apply to other aspects of my life? How can what I've learned here assist others?*

By reflecting on these questions you escape the cramped confines of discouraging thoughts and open up to a broader view of yourself and your place in the world. This method stimulates your mind to include more of your true capabilities.

You'll know that it's working when you burst out laughing or have an "Aha!" moment. In either case your discouragement will vanish and you'll find yourself renewed and refreshed. After a bit of practice, your response will come instantly, before you can even ask the question. Being able to laugh at your own foibles and learn from any situation are hallmarks of advanced mastery travelers. The insights and realizations you receive will open up new possibilities for you and provide additional inspiration.

Experiment with these techniques and use them when you feel discouraged. With practice, your response to discouragement should begin to come smoothly and automatically. Ideally, by practicing these methods you'll be able avoid the effects of discouragement altogether. Just think of how much wasted time, effort and heartache could be saved if you were *never* discouraged.

Since discouragement implies a complete lack of motivation, it may helpful to review Chapter 6, which deals extensively with the topic of developing motivation.

No Fun: Learning at the Novice level requires lots of study and practice. The slow pace, repetition and limited achievement found here can easily translate into practice sessions that seem to drag on and on. After a while you may find yourself losing interest in your field, simply because you're not having fun anymore. Whenever this happens, it's time to spice up the process.

Debug: The prescription here is very simple and obvious. If you aren't having fun, then go make some! Make sure that the fun you create involves your discipline. After all, you want to insert some fun *into* your field, not escape from it.

Reserve some time between learning sessions (or right in the middle of them) to *play* with the new material and skills you are learning. Make it a policy that during your "goofing around" time, there will be no mention of evaluation, comparison or achievement. After all, to ask "did I *play* better than I did last time?" is a meaningless question that misses the point of play.

With all the hard work that you put into your study and practice, you deserve some playtime. Remember that play knows no rules or boundaries, so be spontaneous and goofy. Make a game of it. By indulging in a bit of play from time to time you can actually build your creativity and broaden your imagination.

For example, if you're a writer, try making up your own words and writing a little story about them. (What's a Gringold Splunderbust?) In basketball, this is the time to shoot your half court hook shots, along with the game of shooting from behind the backboard, where you get extra points for hitting as many supports as you can before sinking the shot. In the business world you could make up the most elaborate position titles, or the most robust and engaging busywork, or speeches that really tell it like it is, but hide it in double-speak. The possibilities are endless. Laughter truly is the best medicine, and it works especially well when you are struggling or discouraged.

Impatience and Lack of Focus: These problems are gradually conquered by building *patience* and *mindfulness,* as described in Chapter 7.

PROBLEMS AT THE ADEPT LEVEL:

Clumsiness, frustration, performance dip, lack of discipline, lack of confidence

Clumsiness: At the Adept level you are learning how it all fits together. As you tentatively merge your small skills into larger techniques, the initial fit can feel awkward. You may know exactly where to place your feet for each dance step you've learned, but when it's time to put them all together with the music, you can fall all over yourself. Moving your body smoothly and harmoniously with your partner while keeping time to the music takes considerable practice. The result can be a series of ankle bruises for your partner, and the indelible feeling that you are a complete klutz.

Likewise, if you are studying economics, it may be difficult to see how all the economic principles you've studied could be combined into an *economic system.* Linking all those ideas together can prove to be cumbersome at best. You may feel awkward or embarrassed when called upon in class, or when presenting your marketing ideas at a business meeting. Your explanation or report may ramble on, or leave out key points that link the ideas together.

Debug: The real problem with clumsiness is not clumsiness *per se.* Clumsiness by itself is no big deal. Feeling klutzy can actually be a lot of fun when viewed in the correct light. The trouble comes when you are *caught in the act* of being clumsy.

In the examples above, everyone on the dance floor and in the class or meeting can instantly see what a doofus you are. Clearly, screwing up can be very embarrassing. So clumsiness really breaks down into three different problems: the *awkwardness of new efforts;* the *fear of making mistakes;* and the even greater *fear of embarrassment.*

There is really no way around the awkward feeling. It's the natural consequence of trying something new. The best you can do to mitigate the problem is to slow down and *feel* your way through each step, paying particular attention to the internal sensations involved. When you finally get it right, you'll want to have a clear memory of those sensations so they can be used as a guide for doing it correctly the next time. Be patient with yourself and the process. It just takes time and practice for your thoughts and actions to come together smoothly.

The *fear of making mistakes* and the *fear of embarrassment* both require the development of *detachment* and *courage.* Refer to Chapter 10 for details on handling these fears.

Frustration: Discouragement and frustration are related feelings. In both cases, your repeated efforts fail to yield the results you had in mind. You've worked your tail off, but the problem still will not budge. In this situation your reaction can take two very different directions.

One response might be to become discouraged, which has the internal feeling of defeat. You've exhausted all the possibilities you're aware of, and you simply don't know how to make it work. When left to fester, this discouraging feeling slides down the energy scale toward despair and depression.

Frustration drives you in the other direction. You know exactly how it's supposed to work. You've seen others do it successfully, and you've even had some experience doing it correctly yourself. But *this time,* nothing you try seems to resolve the situation. Your frustration feels like a battle between you and some other unseen force. As you increase your efforts, the unseen force counters with even greater resistance, battling you to a standstill, resulting in no progress once again. All that pent-up energy seeks a release as your frustration builds.

Frustration, like discouragement, needs to be handled as soon as possible, because all that built up energy soon leads to anger and rage. As the frustration bubbles up within, you can almost literally "blow your cork."

Interestingly, it's the twin feelings of discouragement and frustration that can do the most damage to your mastery journey and your life. Each of these problems eats away at your psyche, sapping motivation and souring relationships. As your efforts fail to achieve the results you desire, there is a tendency to blame someone or something for that failure.

With discouragement, the blame turns inward. *I'll never get it. I'm so stupid. I haven't learned anything all this time. What a loser. I'm terrible at this.* Yadda, yadda, yadda. With this type of self-flagellation, you are damaging yourself by systematically destroying your own confidence and motivation. Keep at it, and you *will* become a depressed loser, just as you told yourself.

Frustration turns the locus of blame outward. That unseen force you seem to be battling becomes personified by someone or something. When you are frustrated, you respond by blaming the equipment you're using, the instructor, the program, the other people involved, the circumstances, the weather, *something, anything... But not you!*

Frustrated people carry chips on their shoulders. They know exactly how it's supposed to be done, but there's some sort of conspiracy going on that is cunningly designed to prevent them from ever succeeding in doing it themselves. The entire world plots against them. This feeling creates a bitter, angry, spiteful personality that's nearly impossible for others to deal with. Of course, for the frustrated person it's no piece of cake, either.

Both the discouraged and the frustrated feel miserable. They just take it out on different people. The discouraged blame themselves, while the frustrated blame everyone else. But it doesn't have to be this way. You can nip those nasty feelings in the bud.

Debug: Handling frustration is a bit trickier than dealing with discouragement, because the situation is more volatile. The pressure of all that extra energy needs to be released before anything more constructive can take place. The discouraged person tends to withdraw and concentrate on beating herself up for her perceived failures. The frustrated person is more likely to discharge his venom on anyone who happens to be nearby.

All three of the methods recommended for handling discouragement **(The ARM, Peanut Butter and Insight methods)** can be used successfully to restore peace and motivation to the frustrated. But here, extra emphasis must be placed on the first step **(Disengage)** to insure that all of the bottled frustration is released before proceeding to the next step. Sometimes an extra decompression step is required to cool off a bit before being able to disengage.

Frustration and anger arise when strong efforts produce no clear changes in the situation. It seems as though the world is not listening, even when you shout! That's why it feels so satisfying to break something when you are angry. When you throw a plate against the wall, or slam a door loudly, the unspoken message that you tell yourself is: *At last the world is responding as it should. See, I really can make things happen! Finally, my power is restored. Now the world must listen to me.* It's this core feeling of powerlessness that drives frustration deeper into anger.

If you're all worked up over the situation, then take that extra step of decompression before continuing with the other steps. *Take a walk or go for a run. Head to the gym for a workout. Punch a punching bag. Kick the soccer ball around.* The key features of the DECOMPRESSION STEP are to make sure that you:

1. Do something physically strenuous. Work those muscles. Spend your extra energy on physical exertion, letting off steam.

2. Do something where you can easily see the results. Walking or running moves you from here to there. Punching the bag or kicking the ball moves the bag or ball in response to your efforts. Punching pillows is not very satisfying because the pillow absorbs almost all of the blow, and shows no signs of change. You'll want to use something like the bag or ball that puts up some resistance, but ultimately is overcome by your efforts.

3. Don't hurt anyone, including yourself. Ideally, you want to let off your steam where no one will be influenced by it but you. Develop some strategies that will take you out of the charged situation so you can work it off, before someone else suffers due to your frustration.

In some cases it might work best to shift some of the excess energy from your frustration directly into greater determination to continue your practice and conquer the problem you face. For this, just use a variation of the **Attitude Reversal Method** (ARM) where you substitute *Determination* for *Inspiration* in the last step. Since both produce the motivation you seek, either will work well.

THE ATTITUDE REVERSAL METHOD 2 (ARM2)

1. **Hit the brakes!** *Disengage.* Stop putting energy into those frustrating thoughts and self-defeating behaviors that are dragging you downhill. Relax. Just let go...

2. **Turn around.** *Change your point of view.* Switch direction and reorient yourself back toward your objective. Ask yourself: *What have I already learned? What I can perform successfully? What is my objective in learning this?*

3. **Accelerate again.** *Renew your Determination.* Focus on your overall objective in taking up this discipline. See the result you'd like to create clearly in your mind. Use affirmations like these to renew your determination: *That little setback was nothing. I'm NOT afraid of mistakes. I'll just make another small change and try again. I KNOW that I can do it. I WILL reach my objective.* Begin your practice again a step or two back from where you left off, going slowly and deliberately. *Feel* the satisfaction that comes with successful accomplishment. Demonstrate to

yourself that you *can* do it. Don't give up!

Another skill that will assist you throughout your mastery travels is the development of ***discernment.*** This can help you to avoid struggle and frustration, too. *Discernment* is the ability to distinguish between fine shades of various characteristics.

For instance, interior designers need to be able to discern the sometimes-subtle differences between similar shades of color, and distinguish between the distinctive textures of different grades of fabrics. Chefs must be able to sift through the intricate flavors of various spices, so they will know exactly how much to add to a given recipe. Some highly refined violinists have developed their discernment to such an exacting degree that they can distinguish between the instruments made by different violin makers just by listening to each violin as it's played.

When you can notice ever-finer distinctions, you can slip right past many problems. For example, frustration builds when you make multiple attempts without generating a noticeable difference in the outcome. By developing greater discernment, you can notice finer details in both the changes that you introduce with each attempt, and the results that you generate. Then you can more easily tell when your efforts have moved the results closer to your desired outcome.

You can become more discerning by expanding and deepening your *attention,* while following the guidance of a good instructor or coach. By placing more attention on what you are doing, you'll be able to pick up more information, and notice more details. With the guidance of someone who has learned to make those finer distinctions, you too can see deeper into each effort, and avoid becoming frustrated. For some additional tips on developing your attention, see the section on **mindfulness** in Chapter 7, or use THE REALITY ENHANCEMENT SHIFT (Hi-RES) exercise described in Chapter 9.

Performance Dip: Sometimes you may notice a significant drop in your performance level for no apparent reason. You'll be working along, practicing your routine like you've been doing for a while now, and suddenly everything you do seems to become more difficult, and your results start to sag.

You run slower than normal, or stumble playing the chords of a song you've played 50 times, or flub a series of easy layups that should be automatic by now, or you notice that the perspective in your last few paintings is somewhat skewed, or someone comments that your most successful dish tastes a little flat, or your department falls behind last quarter's performance levels, even though no crisis is evident in your group.

At first you may be alarmed by the difficulties, so you increase your efforts, trying harder to correct the problems and make up the deficit. Yet the extra effort does little good, and nothing seems to change. As you struggle with this mystifying problem, you can easily become frustrated or discouraged by this reversal of your progress. You may even start to doubt your memory of the more successful moments.

Debug: Despite the recent disappointments you've been through, the symptoms you've experienced are a sign that better times are ahead. Hang in there; you are about to have a breakthrough. Soon your performance will leap forward, accompanied by new realizations, fresh insights and extra energy that you didn't know was available. You are in the midst of a strange, but wonderful phenomenon. Runners call it ***second wind.***

When you first begin a run, you typically start off at an easy pace, getting into the rhythm of the running process. Once you've warmed up, you then increase your speed to your normal running pace for the distance you are planning to run. Everything is fine for a while, then gradually your speed slows and you struggle a bit with your breathing. Your performance dips.

At the biological level, your body begins the run by burning the glucose that is currently in your bloodstream for energy to power your muscles. As your supply begins to diminish, the muscles grow weaker, and your breathing becomes more labored as you attempt to compensate. You are literally running out of gas!

If you persevere for a little while longer, running at an even pace without panicking, you'll be rewarded with a *second wind.* The *second wind* comes as your body responds to the increased demand for fuel by switching systems and shifting to the process of burning fat for fuel instead of the more immediate glucose supply.

As your fat-burning systems come online, you get a surge of energy that feels smooth, strong and long lasting. This is your *second wind,* and it comes as a welcome relief.

Oddly enough, this *second wind* phenomenon is not unique to the world of running. It shows up in a lot of different areas, and exhibits similar characteristics in each case.

Bill Williams, author of *Trading Chaos,* calls this signal for a change in direction a *squat.* When you prepare to jump high in the air to touch the basketball rim, you can't do it without first bending down into a *squat,* gathering energy, and then launching your jump up into the air.

In trading the stock or futures markets, the *squat* effect occurs when there is a struggle between the bulls and the bears in a given time period. An increase in the volume of trading occurs, but the price changes very little as the buying pressure of the bulls is matched by the selling pressure of the bears. When the struggle is over, a winner emerges and the market trends in a new direction.

You may recognize this *second wind,* or *squat* idea in the familiar phrase "two steps forward, one step back." As your learning starts to slide back a notch, be ready for a big change in direction as you take the next two steps forward.

Here's how it works. You practice diligently, and gradually put together the steps needed to successfully perform a new technique. Hurray! You've done it. Two steps forward!

Now you continue to practice the new technique, but then, just when you think you've got it down, it stops working. So you increase your efforts, to no avail. One step back!

You're sure that you've learned how to do it, since you've performed it correctly at least once. But that first round of success was a bit of a fluke. It was more luck than skill. What may not be clear is exactly which aspects of your performance contributed to the success of your efforts, and which did not. You haven't yet figured out what the truly important parts are.

When your performance breaks down, it's a sign that there is still more to learn. This is exciting news! When the new realization comes, it will not only solve the problem of your sagging performance, it will point the way to still more improvements and a broader understanding of your entire field. Here's the formula:

THE BREAKTHROUGH FORMULA

1. **You notice a decline in your performance.** *Oh no!* For no apparent reason, your results start to slide.
2. **Step up your efforts.** *Compensate for any deficiencies.* Test your efforts and results. Repeat the technique a few times, making sure that you are using sufficient energy and are doing everything the way you first learned it.
3. **Relax.** *Don't panic.* This mysterious performance dip is the sign that a breakthrough it about to arrive.
4. **Increase your awareness.** *Pay attention!* Be extra alert to pick up any important details of the process that you might have missed before. *Feel* your way through it.
5. **Slow down and review.** *Pick the entire process apart.* Re-examine every aspect of your performance, noting which parts produce what results.
6. **Continue to practice.** *Persevere.* Use smooth, consistent effort levels to avoid frustration. Keep at it, until...
7. **You get a Breakthrough!** *Eureka!* Suddenly something clicks into place in your mind, and a new insight into your situation appears. You notice some important factor that restores your performance or improves it. *Why didn't I realize that before?*
8. **Implement your Breakthrough.** *Practice the improved technique.* Put your realization and broader understanding into play. Use the HABIT IMPROVEMENT METHOD (see HIM, described on page 221) to cement the insights you've discovered into your repertoire.

The Breakthrough Formula codifies the process that people

use to make discoveries of every kind, both large and small. It even echoes the folk expression; "It's always darkest just before dawn."

Lack of Discipline and Lack of Confidence: See Chapter 8 for hints on how to develop the discipline and confidence you'll need to continue on your path.

PROBLEMS AT THE PRO LEVEL:

Narrow-mindedness, inconsistency, arrogance, complacency, compulsiveness

Narrow-mindedness: It may well be a waste of time to write about this problem. That's because no one really *is* narrow-minded. If you don't believe that's true, just ask any person you suspect might be narrow-minded, "Are you being narrow-minded here?" Inevitably, the answer will be, "Of course not, I'm just right!"

Well, of course! Silly me.

At the Adept level you must be able to see the "big picture" in order to assemble all you've learned into a successful result. Broadening your attention and understanding to see how all the parts add up to the whole is a key feature of the process. Later on at the Rookie level you will need to adapt what you've learned to fit your new circumstances. Again, a wider view of the possibilities is necessary. Likewise, to move up to the Expert level you'll need to incorporate many different approaches to your discipline, and that will require you to sample a variety of viewpoints.

Narrow-mindedness interferes with these more expansive perspectives by insisting that there is one and only one way to do things: *my way.* When pressed, the narrow-minded individual may admit that there is indeed another view: *my way* or *the highway!* This fixed outlook can lend a sense of rigidity to your thinking that hinders your development and frustrates the learning process.

Lest you think that you are immune to narrow-mindedness, consider that every time you voice an opinion that you are not willing to back down from, you are being narrow-minded. *So in every argument you've ever had, you've been narrow-minded, regardless of whether you think you've won or lost.*

This kind of limited thinking can be even more pervasive than you may realize. In any given situation, if you can think of only one or two alternatives, that is narrow-mindedness! You've narrowed the wide range of possibilties to just a couple.

Our common thinking patterns are rife with examples of this type of two-valued, bipolar logic: *Win or lose, success or failure, easy or hard, simple or complicated, I-can-do-it or I-can't-do-it, and so on...* We snap back and forth between the two mutually exclusive conclusions without even noticing their all-or-nothing character.

To make matters worse, those conclusions are often linked together, leading to a drastic shift in attitude. Thus, when you are learning a new computer software program, or a new swimming stroke, it may start out simple and easy, so you conclude, *" I can do this." Success looks assured, so you start to feel like a winner.* Then you may stumble performing the next step, and your thinking can instantly switch to: *"Oh no, this is really complicated. It's too hard for me. I can't do it. I'm failing again. I must be a loser."* This sort of bipolar thinking can play havoc with your progress, reducing the once smooth learning process to a melodramatic nightmare as you lurch back and forth from one extreme to the other.

Debug: In each of the common bipolar examples mentioned above, there are actually wide ranges of possibilities both within those extremes, and outside of them. When examined closely, there are always degrees of success achieved by any attempt you make. You may have succeeded in some aspects and not in others.

Even in something as clear-cut as a sporting contest like tennis, where you either win or lose the match, you can achieve varying levels of success along the way. You could have improved your serve and aced your opponent seven times, while still losing the match. Disappointed with the outcome, and fixed in a narrow-minded view, you could leave the match sulking about your defeat. Yet that would fail to acknowledge the success you achieved.

It's easy to lose sight of the progress you've made in such situations. Viewed from a more expansive perspective, the gains you've made have significantly improved your overall game, despite losing the match. The truth of the matter is often much bigger than our simplistic conclusions about it.

Of course, an even broader view might come from another perspective entirely. Outside of the range of success and failure of your performance lies an infinite number of other ways to view the tennis match. You could view it as an opportunity to work on your serve, or to try out your new racquet, or to spend some quality time with a friend, or just to be outside and enjoy the fresh air. Not everything needs to be evaluated along some continuum of success and failure. By viewing the match in one of these alternative ways you allow for a greater degree of spontaneity and fun to enter the picture. You may even learn more in the process.

A broad-minded view that envisions many alternatives and incorporates multiple points of view naturally provides a more accurate picture of any situation. It even uses a larger percentage of your brain by linking together additional perceptions, ideas and experiences you've had. This brings more of your personal resources to bear on your problem. Any conclusions you reach will be *more intelligent,* and include more of the available information.

To snap out of narrow-minded thinking, use this variation on the familiar approach used in many of the debugs so far:

THE EXPANSIVE THINKING METHOD (THE ET METHOD)

1. **Hit the brakes!** *Disengage.* Stop putting energy into your rigidly held belief or point of view. Relax. Just let go of it...
2. **Scan the horizon.** *Look for new viewpoints.* Ask yourself questions like these: *What lies between the two possibilities I've identified? What factors could be varied that would enable me to see a variety of possibilities in this range? What other factors are involved? What if I varied them? What's funny about this situation? What would E.T., the extraterrestrial, think about this problem? What if this were not MY problem?*
3. **Take a different route.** *Re-examine your problem from a new viewpoint.* What new conclusions could you now reach

that add a different complexion to the problem?

Many different questions could be used for the second step of the ET method. The idea is to shake up your current restricted view of things and pose some additional possibilities. Using humor is a great way to bounce right past many problems and provide new perspectives. The far-out view of an extraterrestrial provides the guiding theme for this exercise.

OLD JEWISH PROVERB: *Faced with two alternatives, take the third!*

Inconsistency: One of the fundamental tasks facing the Pro is to refine your ability to consistently produce quality results. By painstakingly examining every detail of your work and comparing your results with the theoretical ideal, you can iron out the wrinkles in your performances. This is the basis of the ***refinement*** process described in Chapter 9.

Yet, even though you may have improved the quality of your work, inconsistency can still creep into your performances. The difficulty comes from a conflict between some of the habits that you've learned.

At first you learned a particular technique that produced a successful result. You practiced this technique until you integrated it into your repertoire of successful methods. Then you find some flaws in your original technique and make some subtle changes that produce an even better result. You practice this new modified technique and attempt to integrate it, as well.

But now you have two somewhat different ways to do the same thing. When you attempt to perform smoothly and quickly without thinking about the subtleties involved, the two automatic responses can compete with one another and generate erratic results. Your normal routine has now become a confusing mess.

Debug: To become consistent you'll need to completely extinguish the old habits that you've learned, and replace them with the new improved versions. The more time you've spent practicing the old technique, the more difficult it will be to make the switch.

Handling this problem is similar to performing maintenance

on a hiking trail. If one section of the trail becomes damaged by erosion, and you'd like hikers to take an alternate route around this section to avoid further damage, you have to do three things:

First, examine the trail erosion thoroughly, and devise an alternate route around the damaged section of the trail. Second, block the entrance to the damaged section and put up a sign telling hikers to detour along the new route. Third, wear in the new section so there will be no doubt in hiker's minds that this new trail is the one they should be using. When you're done, hikers will naturally take the alternate route without any fuss.

THE HABIT IMPROVEMENT METHOD (HIM)

1. **Devise new technique.** *Experiment and optimize.* Detect the flaws in your existing methods through careful observation of every detail. Experiment with new ways to produce better results by modifying your techniques or adopting fresh ones from other sources. Develop a revised approach that improves results.

2. **Block old technique.** *Set up a mental detour.* Sharpen the distinction between the new and old methods by concentrating on their differences. Note the first point where the two techniques diverge. Notice the differences in internal sensations when using the different techniques. The differences will become your inner detour signs.

3. **Practice new technique until integrated.** *Firmly establish the new method in your repertoire.* Practice the entire revised technique, beginning a couple of steps before the changes are introduced. As you approach the revised portion of your technique, feel the new sensations as you begin the altered method. Integrate the new technique into your repertoire by repeating it over and over until it becomes automatic.

Old habits never die; they just fade away. In the hiking trail analogy, if you don't tread on the old portion of the trail anymore, it will eventually return to its wild overgrown state. In a similar manner, by never performing in the "old" way again, you can gradually extinguish that outdated habit. Using only the new improved technique insures your consistency.

Arrogance and Complacency: These two attitudes don't seem to have much in common at first glance. Yet they are really two sides of the same coin. Arrogance and complacency are the twin responses to laziness. Let's take a look at how this works.

Most people who are going through the Novice and Adept levels remain pretty humble. They realize that they have a lot to learn, and they are usually more than willing to defer to more experienced and knowledgeable practitioners.

Yet things can start to change as you move farther up the mastery scale. As soon as you begin to perform successfully on a regular basis, you can start to feel invincible. Knowing that they can easily do whatever is required, some people will want to lord it over others as a way to demonstrate their superiority. This sort of arrogant behavior does nothing to endear such a person to their colleagues. It really doesn't do much for the arrogant person, either.

Complacency is the other response that can appear as you develop your competence. Once you can perform well without a lot of effort, you may find that you begin to just "go through the motions." After a while your effort will drop even further, as you explore just how little you can get away with doing.

Both arrogance and complacency are signs that you've stopped learning. The arrogant know-it-all thinks he has already learned everything he needs to know, and now devotes his time and effort toward convincing others of the superiority of his knowledge and skills. The complacent person has also stopped learning, and now she wants to do the least amount possible. Because her performance is adequate for her immediate needs, she sees no need to go any further.

With arrogance or complacency, either way you're in trouble. Soon people will begin to notice that you don't really know as much as you think you do, and the results will start to show. Continuing with your complacency or arrogance could easily get you fired from your job, or dropped from the team.

Debug: Treat the appearance of either of these attitudes as a warning sign. At the first hint of either arrogance or complacency, take a break from your discipline. You could just be tired from all the sustained efforts you've made to develop the competency you now enjoy. Relax a bit. Go someplace new and do something different. Come back to your work refreshed, renewed and inspired to continue. Usually an uplifting vacation is enough to shake out the cobwebs that are filled with stale thoughts and repetitive actions that may have lead to your condition.

If this doesn't do the trick, then stronger medicine may be in order. You may need to be both humbled and inspired at the same time. Go see a Virtuoso or Master in your field perform. Take an advanced class in your subject area, or a personal development seminar or workshop. In any of these cases you will likely be exposed to people whose skills and ideas are more advanced than yours. Realizing that there is still plenty more to learn may renew your incentive to continue on your mastery journey.

If all else fails, revisit Chapter 6 to find more motivation, or see the sections of this chapter that deal with discouragement, frustration and inconsistency. If you can find no resolution after using these methods, consider switching to another line of work.

Compulsiveness: Whereas arrogance and complacency are responses to laziness, compulsiveness can be a response that moves you in the other direction. Compulsive behavior demonstrates an obsession with, or an addiction to, some of the feedback that you get by participating in your field. The lazy person reduces his or her participation and effort as much as possible, while the compulsive person increases that participation and effort to unhealthy levels.

How can you tell the difference between normal dedicated participation and compulsive or addictive behavior? Sometimes the two may look alike to the person involved. To the musician obsessed with playing his instrument above all else, or the compulsive runner who can't seem to stop, despite her nagging injuries, or the workaholic who has no time for family or friends, it may all seem like they are simply doing what is needed to become successful.

The telltale signs that your dedicated efforts have become compulsive are an increase in efforts accompanied by a drop in enthusiasm. The compulsive person does more and enjoys it less.

Despite the increased effort, compulsive behavior usually leads to lowered performance. A robotic sameness enters into the performance that may be obvious to an outsider, but is often undetectable by the compulsive person himself. The dull repetitive quality of the performance reduces its effectiveness and fails to stimulate either the audience/boss/coach or the performer.

Compulsive behavior often begins in response to stress. Something has gone wrong somewhere, and the compulsive person's response to the problem is to throw himself into his work (or hobby) in an effort to escape the stress of the nagging problem. It feels comforting to do something he knows so well, something that provides a reliable source of satisfaction and results.

Under the illusion that "more is better," the compulsive person slogs through his work, putting in additional hours and becoming fatigued from the extra effort and struggle involved. Much of the fatigue comes from resisting and worrying about the problem (consciously or unconsciously) while he's busy doing something else. Since he's not really thinking about what he's doing, he may not realize how compulsive he's become. Hours and weeks pass, health problems and injuries appear, and important events in other areas of life go by unnoticed.

Debug: Here's another problem that you'll want to handle as soon as you can, since prolonged compulsive behavior can lead to serious psychological and physical damage. Such problems are well beyond the scope of this book. If you suspect that your compulsions have begun to damage you, please seek some professional assistance.

Compulsive behavior indicates a fixed pattern of thinking that is ultimately detrimental to the individual involved. Breaking this pattern of thinking calls for a shift to a new point of view. Shaking up the old routine can help snap you out of the trance you've been in, and shed new light on your situation.

The first step you might want to explore is to take a break from your routine. Relax. Go someplace new and do something different. Take enough time on this break to release your cares and allow yourself to enjoy the new surroundings and activities. Talk with someone you trust about your problems and explore new approaches to dealing with them. Sometimes all it takes is to "get it off your chest."

Armed with new insights, return to your situation and put those new insights into play. Pay close attention to your old routines, seeing them anew from a detached perspective. Be careful to avoid the old patterns that lead to your compulsions. Monitor your behavior and see how it goes. Don't hesitate to call on a professional if your problems persist.

PROBLEMS AT THE VIRTUOSO LEVEL:

Overconfidence, feeling trapped, lingering fears

Overconfidence: You've got the talent. You've spent years immersed in your field, learning everything you could. You've taken on some of the biggest challenges around, and you've come out on top. You kicked butt!

After all that time paying your dues, the accolades are now starting to accumulate. It's not just your friends and colleagues who sing your praises. Some of your competitors, and even a few of your harshest critics now admit that you have indeed accomplished a lot. You're good and you know it. The evidence is plentiful.

Here comes the tricky part, the point where quiet solid confidence balloons into bravado, cockiness and overconfidence. You've tasted victory, and it's sweet indeed. In fact, the taste is so sweet, so exotic, so thrilling that you soon become intoxicated. You play your winning events over and over again in your memory, swelling with pride each time.

Drunk with success and hungry for more, your mind starts to play tricks on you. You begin to exaggerate your victory and the talents you used to get you this far. You start to feel invincible. Soon no challenge is too great, no competitor too formidable, no objective unreachable. As drunks often do, you loudly announce your superiority over any and all. Before you know it, bravado, cockiness and overconfidence have taken over.

This brash, swaggering attitude of invulnerability can take over your thinking just as easily as it's counterpart—the timid, self-doubting sense that you are never good enough. Straddling the balance point between underconfidence and overconfidence seems so precarious. For most people, a pattern develops where they take one side or the other of that balance point.

Oddly enough, both overconfidence and underconfidence stem from insecurity. Those who lack confidence are not sure that they are ready to tackle the next challenge, so they shrink in fear from the limits they've set for themselves. Overconfident people are also insecure, but they overcompensate for their fear by attempting to convince themselves and anyone who will listen that they are fearless! Such proclamations form a smokescreen that hides their self-doubts. After all, when you are truly confident in your abilities, there is no need to convince yourself, or anyone else.

Debug: So, how do you build your confidence without letting your ego get out of hand? The key lies in a realistic assessment of the effectiveness of each effort, along with some faith in your ability to exceed your current limitations.

Every attempt you make results in some kind of outcome. By noting both the successful and unsuccessful aspects of each effort you can build a comprehensive understanding of your capabilities. You'll come to know both your strengths and your weaknesses, and be able to predict with reasonable accuracy where and when you can excel. With this sort of balanced assessment, there will be no need for excessive vanity or crippling self-doubt. You can let your results speak for themselves.

For further tips on this process, refer to the section on building *confidence* in Chapter 8.

Feeling Trapped: This problem can occur anywhere from the Journeyman stage on up, and it particularly affects those who choose to specialize in some narrow area within their field.

As you broaden and deepen your skills, you may find yourself gravitating toward some small subset of your field through your own interests or the needs of your situation. As you dig deeper into your niche and build your repertoire of skills around this area, you will begin to be recognized for your unique contributions. Your rewards, both personal and professional, grow in tandem with your expertise. Soon you may find that you are "indispensable" to the success of your organization, or have built a "name" for yourself in your field as a leader in your area. You are rewarded handsomely, and widely admired for your valuable skills and accomplishments.

At first your success is terrific. But after a while, doing what you do so well becomes routine, and you begin to long for something new, different and more interesting. This is the point where you can begin to feel trapped by your own success.

Your expertise has generated a comfortable and rewarding lifestyle that pays great dividends for you. To withdraw from your cozy little niche and pursue some other area of expertise, even within your own field, you'll have to abandon the recognition, pay and privileges that you've earned, and start all over again at a lower level. It's tough to reject the warmth and comfort of your own success for the uncertain lure of another interest.

Some people spend the majority of their careers in this predicament. Though they are outwardly pleased with the trappings of their success, secretly they resent the prison that they've created for themselves. Yet, as the walls close in around them, they feel powerless to change their situation.

Debug: Sometimes it takes something drastic to change the balance between the comfort of a secure lifestyle and the growing desire for change. As long as your security feels more powerful than your desire for growth and expansion, nothing will change in your situation.

When you are unwilling to act on your own behalf, sometimes the universe seems to sense your discontent and acts for you. As a result, you may suffer a heart attack, or get an ulcer, or break a leg while skiing, or develop some other type of health condition and not be able to perform the way you once could. Your job could be eliminated, or you might get laid off or fired. The market tastes could shift and your brand of expertise may no longer be in fashion.

In all of these cases, change may seem to be thrust upon you. You didn't really plan it this way, but now the balance has shifted and doing something different begins to look much more attractive. You could always wait for the universe to act for you, and then move with the flow of those changes and escape from your self-made prison.

Or, if you choose to be more proactive, you will still need to upset the current balance between your comfortable security and your desire to explore something new. This process of career change can be quite traumatic, or equally exhilarating.

If the field you're in continues to excite you, the best way to escape from your trap is to expand your niche. Instead of being confined to a small area of expertise, seek opportunities to explore neighboring subject areas where you can broaden your knowledge and skills to create a synthesis between the new subject and your existing expertise. That way you won't have to abandon your well-developed talents, and your additional explorations may prove to open up even more valuable opportunities.

If you have your heart set on pursuing another field altogether, then you'll need a different approach. Many people attempt to make the change gradually by getting a part-time position in the new field while they are still working in the old field, or by going to night school to get their new education while still working the old job. Some folks manage to make the transition successfully, while others never feel quite comfortable with one foot in each of the two worlds. The debug for this situation is perhaps best illustrated by the following story:

Once there was a chef named Jim, who worked at one of the better restaurants in town. Jim had spent many years learning his profession, developing into a talented chef with considerable skill. Yet after so many years in the kitchen, and all the long hours involved, Jim tired of the chef's life. He longed to explore his other artistic talents, which he had let languish when he took up culinary arts as a profession.

Jim loved to draw and had a gift for design, so he naturally gravitated to the graphic design field. He studied the dramatic ads in magazines and admired the creativity and exacting technique that went into creating some of the more striking billboards, posters and CD covers. The life of a graphic designer seemed so much more creative, glamorous and rewarding.

But alas, Jim couldn't figure out how to move from his career as a chef to his new calling in graphic design. Night school didn't seem to fit, since he ran the kitchen during the dinner shift at the restaurant. He knew he had the talent, but lacked the knowledge and skills needed to strike out on his own in this new field. He needed more training. Besides, as a rookie graphic designer he would only make about half as much as he was making at the restaurant. Jim had bills to pay. What was he going to do?

Feeling desperate, Jim decided to confide in a wise and trusted friend named Ole. Ole was a fierce old man known for his ruthless honesty and piercing insight. He seldom gave advice, for few had the courage to follow it, and Ole had no patience for fools. So it was with some trepidation that Jim approached Ole with his dilemma.

After hearing Jim's story, Ole asked just one question, "If you are really sincere about your desire to become a graphic designer, you must follow my advice to the letter, without any questions. Are you willing to do that?"

Jim hesitated, not knowing if he was ready to go through with this. At last he said, "Yes."

Ole replied, "Here's what you do. Go back to the restaurant and throw yourself into your work. Become the best chef you can possibly be. Work your butt off. Once you've done all you can do each day at the restaurant, if there is any time left over, then and only then can you spend any time on graphic design. Your work as a chef must come first. Do you understand?"

What Ole had said didn't make the least bit of sense to Jim, but he didn't know what else to do, so he said, "Yes."

Ole looked Jim straight in the eye and said, "Then go to it," and turned away.

Feeling bewildered, but determined, Jim began following Ole's advice. He studied the cookbooks of famous chefs and began dining at other restaurants to see what the competition was up to. He experimented with various recipes and preparation techniques, letting his own tastes and artistic sense guide him into new avenues of cuisine. Gradually, when he thought that the new dishes were of sufficient quality, he began introducing them as "specials" to the menu. Before long, diners at the restaurant began to take notice, and the specials became the most popular meals. The buzz spread quickly as Jim's restaurant became a hot spot for the cognoscenti.

One evening a new party of diners arrived at the restaurant and ordered some of the specials they had heard so much about. When the food arrived, they were excited to find that the buzz was true. Their dinner was magnificent. One of the diners was so impressed that he asked the waiter to bring out the chef so he could congratulate him for preparing such terrific meals.

When Jim arrived at the table, the man introduced himself and the others in his party and praised Jim for his efforts. Jim expressed his thanks, and his ears perked up when he heard that Barry, the man who had called for him, was the owner of a prominent local advertising agency. Eagerly, Jim told Barry of his interest in graphic design and mentioned that he had designed the new menus for the restaurant. After some polite conversation, Barry offered Jim his card and suggested that they have lunch together the next day at a neighboring restaurant.

At lunch the following day, Barry asked Jim what he should order. He was surprised to find that Jim knew the menu well, and suggested a particularly tasty meal. Without hesitation Barry immediately offered Jim a job at his agency.

Jim was taken aback. "Obviously, I'm flattered by your offer," he said, "but why choose me? I don't have much experience, and no formal training at all. You must have plenty of people applying for positions who are much more qualified than I am."

"That's true. And those menus you designed could use some work, too. But I'd be a fool not to offer you a chance. If you put as much talent and effort into your design work as you put into your culinary creations, you'll be the best designer on my staff in no time. I can't pay you much to start, but that will change as you learn the ropes."

Though excited by the possibilities, Jim reacted cautiously. "It sounds like a great opportunity, but I can't afford to take a cut in pay with all the financial obligations that I have."

Barry thought about it for a minute. "Why not set up a catering company and make some money on the side? We entertain clients all the time, and somebody has to provide the food. Besides, it would be a shame to throw all your culinary talents away. Our current caterer is not all that great. I'm sure you could do better."

Before long Jim was living his dream as a successful graphic designer. It even turned out that his catering company made him more money than the restaurant job ever did. When he heard the news, Ole just smiled...

What's the moral of the story? EXCELLENCE OPENS THE DOORS TO OPPORTUNITY.

Lingering Fears: The key to entering the Virtuoso level is to fully immerse yourself in your work and surrender to the *flow* state of consciousness. If you allow yourself to indulge in any of the more common fears that surround the learning process, your access to the *flow* state will be blocked. The fear of failure, the fear of success, the fear of embarrassment, the fear of not-being-good-enough, the fear of exposing your flaws, and the simple fear of making a mistake cannot co-exist along with a smooth uninhibited *flow* of thoughts and actions. To *lose yourself* in your work you'll need to let go of your fears completely.

Debug: In Carlos Castaneda's books known as *The Teachings of Don Juan* series, Don Juan describes four barriers to becoming a fully realized Yaqui sorcerer. The four barriers are Fear, Clarity, Power and Old Age. They must be addressed in order, one at a time.

For most of us, fear is our constant companion, seeking to protect us, yet holding us back from experiencing the most exciting possibilities. In the book, Castaneda gradually opens up to the world of the sorcerer when he learns to put his trepidations behind him. In later episodes he becomes a fearless sorcerer, who must then learn to handle the awesome clarity and power that is now available to him. Only the most revered sorcerers manage to avoid the seductive allure of Clarity and Power. And even they eventually succumb to Old Age, just like the rest of us.

These four barriers apply to the achievement of Mastery as well. At the Virtuoso level you deal with the last of your lingering fears, eventually banishing those inhibitions from your life completely as you develop the full measure of your artistry and move up to the Master level. Becoming fearless takes both *courage* and *detachment.* Refer to Chapter 10 for hints on the development of those valuable traits. Handling Clarity and Power is the province of the Master.

PROBLEMS AT THE MASTER LEVEL:

Selfishness, lack of wisdom, misuse of power

Selfishness, lack of wisdom and misuse of power: Since the master's special abilities stem from the tight integration of his or her extraordinary talents, the problems facing the master likewise tend to come bundled together as inseparable components of a single, larger malady. So it might be instructive to look at these three problems as symptoms of a "fall from grace" that can creep up on those who are dramatically successful.

Masters do seem to lead charmed lives. Their tremendous skills demand respect from all. When a Master sets his mind to accomplishing a goal, he is able to marshal more forces to his cause than most people can even begin to tap. With a tight purpose, keen focus, fierce will and boundless energy, success seems inevitable. Armed with tremendous control over the *flow* state of consciousness, the Master can even sense the outcome of his efforts before they are complete. With so much on his side, the Master can come to *expect* his every effort to yield extraordinary results. Using only a relatively small amount of energy, the Master can accomplish what others can only dream about. This level of excellence, coupled with the increased sense of awareness that accompanies the *flow* state, brings with it a heady sense of clarity and power.

Add all this to the adulation that most Masters enjoy from the public and it's not hard to see how they can get a little "full of themselves." If you had the "Midas touch," where it seemed that everything you attempted was wildly successful and "turned to gold," and those around you hung on your every word, could you see it all going to *your* head?

Well, that's what can lead to an egotistic selfish attitude, thoughtless irresponsible behavior and damaging misuses of the personal power you've worked so hard to generate.

Debug: The Master's "easy" successes brew a dangerous and potent cocktail of temptation that few can resist. The corrupting influences can be so strong that they can lead to all manner of excesses, ranging from the merely eccentric to the megalomanical.

It's easy to lose sight of the real source of the clarity and power that you enjoy. Despite your wealth of personal accomplishments, it's not you and your ego, but your ability to tap into the ultimate *flow* that has showered you with success. When you can control it so easily, it can be difficult to see that the inexhaustible *flow* encompasses far more than you could ever imagine. Like wielding a garden hose, you may be able to direct the flow of water in a thousand marvelous ways, yet the source of the water lies far beyond your "ownership," and has arrived at your faucet in an altogether mysterious manner.

When you are truly grateful for this bonanza of intuitive *flow*, and hold as your highest purpose to serve the best interests of those you influence, then you are working in harmony with these powerful forces. You serve your intuition, not the other way around. The *flow* moves through you only when this sense of harmony is maintained.

When you have strayed away from this smooth, easy, spontaneous *flow,* the remedy lies in simply returning to the warm and wise embrace of your own intuition.

The simplest way to accomplish this is to practice being grateful. Being grateful gives full recognition to the notion that your ego is not the source of your greatness, merely the benefactor. You cannot help but be humble when you're actions are guided by gratefulness. At the same time you are reminded that it is your privilege to perform so beautifully, so that others may enjoy the power and grace at your command. And when you have the best interests of those around you at heart, you needn't worry about acting imprudently or damaging others with your power. Your intuition will guide you flawlessly through these minefields.

Refer to Chapter 11 and www.gratefulness.org for assistance in developing a deeper sense of gratitude that can help guide you to the highest levels of your own potential.

> *A man may fulfill the object of his existence by asking a question he cannot answer, and attempting a task he cannot achieve.*
>
> — *Oliver Wendell Holmes (1809 – 1894)*

Chapter 13:

Beyond the Summit

THE NEVER-ENDING JOURNEY

Reading through all the chapters on the various levels of mastery may leave you thinking that you display qualities of several of them. This conclusion could easily be correct. Depending on which area of interest you choose to look at, you may describe yourself as an Adept in one subject area and a Pro in another. Even within a single discipline you may feel like an Expert most of the time, yet still find yourself making the occasional Rookie mistake.

Though you may be a practicing professional, every time you learn some new theory or technique you'll have to go all the way back to the beginning and become a Novice, then an Adept and a Rookie with regard to the new stuff before you can include it in your repertoire of knowledge and skills. As a result, you may be progressing well in many areas, yet feel clumsy and awkward when it comes to the newer additions to your arsenal.

Don't forget that as you rise to higher levels in any given area, you also have available all the skills and processes that you used at the earlier levels. The big advantage that you enjoy as a veteran of the mastery process is to be able to expand your repertoire much faster and more easily than you could when you were first starting out. Since you've been practicing for years, you've built an almost instinctive feel for your discipline. So adding something new at this point becomes a piece of cake.

It's a good thing that it works that way, since learning new things is a process that never ends. Even Masters are subject to learning more about their area of mastery. In fact, without exhibiting this kind of boundless curiosity, the Master would never have gotten as far as she did. Albert Einstein addressed this when he said, "the more I learn, the more I realize that there is more to learn."

Now that you have a solid background in the mastery process from the point of view of the student, let's examine the role of the teacher, and how the teacher impacts the student's mastery process.

First, please note that just like in other professions, the teacher goes through the same mastery process as anyone else, starting at the beginning as a Novice and progressively rising through the levels of mastery. Yet the teacher is actually working on two aspects of the mastery process at the same time, and each of them affects the outcome of the teaching/learning process.

The first factor is the teacher's own level of mastery of the material to be taught. The second factor is the teacher's level of mastery as a facilitator of the learning process. These two aspects of teaching are quite different, and both affect the students' progress profoundly. The first factor deals with the teacher knowing his or her stuff. The second factor involves the teacher's skill at transmitting the knowledge and techniques to the student.

It's quite possible to encounter a Master teacher who doesn't know much about some new subject matter, or an Expert in his or her field who doesn't know the first thing about teaching.

To get to the point where you really have something to teach that is worth learning, you'll need to advance to the Journeyman level or above in your subject area. Once you arrive at the Journeyman level, you've demonstrated your competence with the material by being able to consistently produce quality results. You "know how it's done." At any of the earlier levels you really don't have a handle on the material yet.

The Novice knows little or nothing about the subject, and thus is not in a position to teach. You can't teach what you don't know, after all. However, Novices can assist each other by not assuming that they know too much, and simply encouraging each other as they explore the new material together. This co-learner approach works very well, and often results in both participants learning much faster than they would on their own.

The Adept knows "just enough to be dangerous." Adepts may mistakenly think that they have the skills to teach, but that's where the danger lies. Having just recently "put it all together" themselves, Adepts don't necessarily have the depth of understanding needed to teach others. Adepts can "do it" pretty well, but they don't yet know *how* or *why* their results became successful. If something goes wrong in the instruction process, or the student poses a difficult question, the Adept will likely stumble, and not be able to resolve the situation. Or worse, in an effort to "save face," the Adept may make up a bogus explanation, instead of simply admitting: "I don't know."

The ideal role for the Adept is to assist the instructor. Help out with demonstrations and assist in guiding the new student through difficult steps. With the role of *assistant,* you don't have to know all the answers, and can defer to the instructor for any aspects of the learning process that you can't readily demonstrate or explain. The bonus is that you will learn those details for yourself, while performing a valuable personal service for both the beginner and the instructor.

Rookies are under a great deal of pressure to learn quickly and become productive as soon as possible, so they don't really have the time or inclination to participate in the teaching process at all. Like Novices, they can best serve each other by learning together and helping one another to cope with their new, more demanding circumstances. By working together, merging your strengths and mitigating your weaknesses, you can both progress faster.

Journeymen and Experts make ideal teachers. Their knowledge and skills are plentiful, and more than adequate for teaching students at the lower skill levels. The easy confidence that they have in their own ability to perform helps put the student at ease, and enables the student to concentrate on the material to be learned instead of second-guessing the instructor.

Seasoned Pros like these have acquired the depth of knowledge and skills to provide most all the information and perform all the demonstrations that a Novice or Adept might need for their development. The additional versatility and wide-ranging experience of the Expert contributes even more to the learning process for the student. Since the Expert possesses a wider range of theories, techniques and approaches to the subject matter, the student can benefit by learning the material from multiple perspectives.

Finding an Expert in the subject matter to teach Novices and Adepts is often difficult because Experts are in demand for other purposes. Their expertise in performing under duress and solving problems in the field usually make them too valuable to their organizations to spare for teaching the newcomers. So that task is invariably left to the Journeymen.

Likewise, you won't find many Virtuosos or Masters teaching the new students. Instead, they sometimes take on the role of the mentor. As a mentor they can guide and advise the seasoned Pro through the more demanding challenges they may face as they strike out on their own in some fashion. The extra fluidity and finely honed experience that Virtuosos and Masters possess can be very valuable to the Pro, while that additional level of subtlety might be lost on Novices and Adepts.

Usually, the Virtuosos are busy developing their own niche, striking out on their own, or leading their organizations, and have little time available to teach others. The dynamic nature of their activities serves well as an inspiration to others, though. The artistry and passion of the Virtuoso draws a loyal following, and the leadership position that the Virtuoso develops carries the added responsibility to encourage and support all those who look up to the new "star." So in that sense, the Virtuoso teaches by setting an example.

Since new students are looking up to the Virtuosos, those "stars" are also called upon to maintain their integrity, so they can remain worthy of the admiration of their fans, and inspire the loyalty of those they lead. Virtuosos serve a much wider section of their field than the typical instructor, so they are held to higher standards, as well.

Masters operate on a still higher plane. Since the Master leads the entire field by virtue of his breakthrough efforts, his responsibility covers the reputation and future of the entire field and all those who participate in it.

In professional cycling, when one cyclist ascends to the level of *campionissimo* or "champion of champions" by dominating the competition in important events like the Tour de France and the World Championships, he is often considered to be the "patron" of the peloton (the entire pack of racers.) The other competitors defer to the champion's judgment and follow his leadership in matters related to racing. The Master is truly *in command.* Even when no formal relationship exists to exercise that sort of leadership, the Master rises (or is pushed!) into that position.

Since Masters advance their field in new directions, they *must* become leaders. Like a scout for an expedition, they are the first to discover the new lands, and the first to report on what they have found. The others count on the Masters' recommendations, since they are the only ones armed with the newest information and experiences. The scouts *must* guide the others. Thus Masters teach everyone else in their field by *showing them the way* into new discoveries and inventions, new heights of creative expression and new expanded levels of performance.

The second factor that affects teaching effectiveness is the instructor's level of mastery as a facilitator of the learning process. As in other professions, new teachers start at the bottom and work their way up. For the student, here's where it gets dicey.

In most formal learning situations like our traditional American K-12 education system, teachers are trained in college before they take on responsibility for an entire classroom. K-12 teachers go through considerable training, including extensive student teaching experiences, all designed to take them through the

Novice and Adept levels of the art of teaching before they graduate.

Likewise, most corporate trainers go through a similar training experience that often includes college courses in curriculum design, teaching/learning techniques and adult learning psychology. Usually they are guided through their initial teaching experiences by senior trainers, where the apprentice/master relationship is utilized.

In other learning situations, including many colleges, technical institutes, and the training involved in various trades, little or no guidance is provided in the art of teaching for new instructors. Thus new instructors are often starting at the Novice level as teachers, and don't know much about the process of facilitating learning.

To their credit, most such instructors were selected to teach the newcomers based on their excellent credentials as Journeymen or better in the subject area to be taught. The difficulty comes when they realize that even though they may know the material backwards and forwards, teaching that to others is a whole new ball game.

Most people who are thrust into that situation are professionals in their field, and work diligently to get up to speed quickly with their new teaching responsibilities, and do the best they can in the circumstances. But the results can be trying for both the new instructor and the student trying to learn the material.

For obvious reasons, as a student you will want to find instructors who are at the Journeyman level in both their field of study and the art of teaching. In selecting an instructor, look for years of experience, both in performing in the selected field and in teaching it to others. Don't be shy about asking former students about their experiences with a particular instructor. Keep in mind the personality of the person you are talking to, and how his or her attitudes and efforts may have contributed to the results they obtained. Sometimes the teacher/student relationship will be strained by personality clashes that affect the outcomes for both.

The most delightful and rewarding learning experiences often come at the hand of the instructor who has advanced to the Expert or Virtuoso levels in their fields, **or** in the teaching process. Most people can remember some particularly exciting classes they took from special instructors who took them farther into the learning process than they expected. Here the additional depth of material and the challenging, yet satisfying manner of learning it combined to make a significant impact on the learner. This is the type of learning experience that both students and teachers love to see.

Problems sometimes occur when arguably more talented individuals are taught by Journeymen instructors. The cocky young Virtuoso-in-the-making complains to the Pro that she has nothing to teach him because the Pro has less raw talent and may never have been the sort of star that the young student is itching to become.

While the Pro may have less raw talent and less mastery of *flow*, that does not mean that there is nothing for the student to learn from her. What the Pro knows quite well is how to *apply* that talent toward getting the results that the student is looking for.

The Expert is the perfect person to train the precocious student, since he or she will be able to introduce ideas and techniques that the student probably has never imagined, and that greater versatility will enable the Expert to garner the respect that will be needed for the association of the two to bear fruit.

What neither person may realize is that the special attributes that the Virtuoso and Master display over the Pro are not additional theories, ideas, skills or techniques. The fundamental differences derive from their superior mental or physical gifts, and their enhanced abilities to *lose themselves* in their performances. Neither of these types of differences can be taught!

You can't learn to be more talented, any more than you can learn to be taller. But you *can* learn to utilize the talents you have to greater effect. You simply must work with what you've been given. Pros have spent a great deal of time doing just that, and their experience with the difficulties involved help them to guide the student past the thornier problems they may encounter.

Losing yourself in the *flow* likewise cannot be taught, as such.

While many Virtuosos and Masters have attempted to pass on their special abilities to others, the process is inherently different than the normal teaching process. Advancing to new levels of consciousness requires guidance in the sensitivity and discernment of your own internal processes, rather than learning new theories and techniques. Shifting your consciousness changes your entire internal experience of events, even though the outside world hasn't changed at all.

The difference is difficult to describe. Perhaps an analogy with swimming comes closest. You could read books about swimming written by Master swimmers, and take swimming lessons from Experts who could teach you all the theory you could ever want, and present every technique they know. All this will never fully register with you until you actually enter the water. Likewise, if you've never experienced *flow*, most of the two chapters on the Virtuoso and Master levels will not make much sense to you.

Once you are in the water, the techniques you learned about swimming take on a new depth of meaning and relevance. If you learn to swim in a pool, then the shift to swimming in a fast moving river or swimming in the sea will be a whole new experience. Even though the motions you go through are largely the same in each case, the internal experience of swimming in those three different environments produces subtle, but powerful changes in the way you regard the act of swimming.

Shifting consciousness doesn't necessarily change the things you do, but your appreciation of the process and the results you obtain change dramatically. In most cases, the extra abilities that Virtuosos and Masters display will not be of value to the newcomer. If you are already a Pro, then you might be able to follow the advanced example of the Virtuoso or Master, and utilize any guidance in the subtleties of shifting consciousness that they may be able to offer.

In any case, a deceptively simple policy to adopt is to *always begin right where you're at.* You can't learn calculus without first knowing something about algebra. You can't run without first learning to walk. The mastery journey must be completed by taking every step along the path. And, you have to take each step yourself. No one else can do it for you. If you attempt a shortcut along the path, then you face additional difficulties that may not be obvious.

Using the mountain metaphor, if the path crisscrosses along the face of the slope, you can always choose to ignore that path and go straight up the face of the mountain. Of course, there is a price to pay. You will find that on the new shorter route the angle of the slope rises dramatically, making progress much slower and more arduous. Since you are now off the beaten path, there are also additional risks that come in the form of slippery leaves, loose rocks, hidden potholes, streams and brush to block your way.

After a while most people realize that the path exists for a reason. Usually, the existing path is the ***path of least resistance.*** It winds its way up the slope in a manner that allows you to make maximum progress with a minimum of time and effort. This is why it is usually wise to follow an existing path of instruction at the early levels of mastery. You can make the most progress that way.

At the Expert level you begin to explore a variety of paths that all lead to the same destination. After you've familiarized yourself with a range of possible routes as an Expert, then you will be well equipped to strike out on your own as a Virtuoso. If you venture off on your own before attaining sufficient expertise in your field, you run the risk of getting lost or worse.

One secret that most Virtuosos and Masters have discovered is what Bill Williams, Master stock and futures trader and author of the book *Trading Chaos,* describes as *"making **winning** the path of least resistance."* Williams emphasizes that to become a successful trader, you need to develop habits, tools, and most of all, an advanced awareness that will allow you to be ***in tune*** with the markets you are trading, so your *instinctive* moves will generate profits and not losses.

The effect is like dancing with a skilled partner, and moving fluidly and harmoniously with each step your partner takes. Dance with the markets and you can skim some of the cream off the top.

Attempt to buck the trend, and the market will eat you alive. Just *go with the flow.*

As Williams suggests in *Trading Chaos,* the tools for self-development are the same tools you've been using all along in your quest for mastery of your chosen subject area. In challenging yourself to excel in your study of architecture, the harmonica, geology, sales, beach volleyball, or any other subject, you will set goals, strive to meet them, and overcome your limitations in the process. This is the essence of self-development.

If you look back through the five levels of Mastery, you'll find that as the knowledge and skills of each level are learned, an interesting thing happens. Once you have learned what you needed to learn at each level, your attention naturally shifts to the *next higher purpose.*

At each successive level, the purpose behind the activities becomes broader and deeper. There is a natural progression from self-centered absorption to a profound sense of service to others.

At the **Novice** level, the purpose behind the activities is to *internalize the fundamental knowledge and skills* being learned. This couldn't be any more self-centered. It's all about you! At this early stage you are literally *absorbing* all the new information, *soaking up* the concepts and principles, and *drinking in* all you can about your new field. This self-absorbed approach is natural and necessary to the learning process. After all, you have to "take it in" before you can do anything with it.

Once you've drunk your fill of new knowledge at the Novice level, you sit back and digest it all at the **Adept** level. The Adept digests what (s)he has learned in a manner similar to the digestion of food. In your body's digestive process, food is transformed into energy and the building blocks for repair and growth of new cells.

In the mastery process, newly acquired knowledge and skills are transformed into new capabilities in the learner. The purpose of activities at the Adept level is to *cultivate your potential,* building competence and confidence by making sense of what you've learned and developing the know-how needed to create successful results. This broader purpose is still centered on you, but now the transformation has begun, and your attention is beginning to turn outward toward the possibilities your new knowledge and skills can produce.

Only after you've acquired the ability to perform competently can you then put that capability to work. The **Pro** level deals with the learning involved in putting your potential into practice. The internal purpose behind the activities of Pros is to *accomplish something.*

The Pro's purpose of accomplishment moves the locus of attention from the internal to the external. When the fruits of your labors are successful and valuable to others, then the work *stands on its own.* It's an independent entity that fulfills the intention of its creator. It's useful.

And being *useful* carries its own reward. Pros are *paid* for their work because they produce consistent, high-quality, *useful* results. There is immense satisfaction to be found in successful accomplishment. That may be why so many people spend so much time at this level. The hunger for accomplishment can be so captivating that you may never escape its pull.

Oddly enough, this hunger for personal accomplishment sometimes drives people into the **Virtuoso** level. Following the urge to surpass your last accomplishment with something even better, you put more of who you really are into the results you create. As a Virtuoso, you find that by adding your artistic flair, your unique perspective, your moving message or your effervescent emotions, you can then create something truly memorable.

Thus the Virtuoso's purpose of making a mark on the world, or *making a unique contribution* often begins as a selfish expression of his or her "ultimate" personal accomplishment. But along the way, most Virtuosos begin to realize that their highest achievements come from the process of *going with the flow* and surrendering control of their creation to a deeper inner force that they cannot claim to own or direct. Their special personal accomplishment transforms into a unique contribution—**a gift!** It is indeed a humbling experience to realize that the heart of your most perfect and deeply personal creation isn't really yours at all...

The **Master** in you emerges as you discover that the only way to move forward is to merge your own personal purpose with the higher purpose of that inner force that moves you. *You begin to see that you are not wise enough to ignore your intuition, not smart enough to trick your own mind, and not skilled enough nor strong enough to disregard the forces of nature.* As you learn to work with these mysterious forces, you can gradually begin to direct them, in the same moment as they are guiding you, as long as you remember that your purpose is *to serve.*

As Master, whom do you serve? You serve your own inner voice of intuition. By doing so, you are being *true to yourself* in the most fundamental sense. Following this inner voice leads you through uncharted territory. You will be called upon to undertake lofty challenges, make personal sacrifices, and in the process, develop greater contributions than you might ever have imagined.

Oddly enough, by serving your intuition you will soon find yourself serving just about everyone else. As a Master, you are now playing a much bigger game than the one you started out learning. Just as your skills and capabilities have grown far beyond those of most people, your influence and responsibilities have also grown beyond your own personal goals and aspirations. You now answer to all those you touch with your talents and gifts.

Just as the world becomes your oyster, you wisely decide that the little mollusk really belongs back in the sea...

Paradoxically, to lead you must follow the example of those who have gone before you. To become a master, you must serve others. To succeed, you must be willing to fail. To discover something new, you must review what is already known (otherwise, how would you know if it were new?) To become more serious about your discipline, you must first learn to play with it. To become powerful, you must empower others. Aren't paradoxes wonderful?

Whatever you want most, you must first give it away. Want more love? Give it to others... Want more energy? Use you mind and body vigorously... Want to be respected? Try being respectful of others... Want to be wealthy? Start by being generous...

This paradoxical process involves a mental discipline that makes *winning* the path of least resistance. You may have learned about this discipline as it relates to **Have, Do,** and **Be.**

The general belief that most of us have internalized looks something like this: *I need to **Have** the time, money, skills and resources to **Do** what it takes to **Be** successful in my field.*

With this belief firmly entrenched, becoming successful then becomes entirely dependent upon the existence of the required amounts of time, money, skills and resources, and the willingness to do what it takes. Then and only then can you be successful. That's a lot of conditions to put on your success! It's no wonder that few people consider themselves to be successful. All those conditions create a lot of inertia to overcome.

So the tendency is to put the whole process off *indefinitely,* since you may *never* have enough time, money, skills and resources to feel comfortable enough to put yourself out and risk gaining some success.

Actually, to become successful in any realm, it is necessary to invert this commonly held notion of how the world works. Change it to **Be, Do,** and **Have.**

So, as a Novice, you must **Be** an Adept, and visualize yourself succeeding at the level of an Adept. Then **Do,** which means to practice using the knowledge and skills that lead up to the next level that you have already visualized. See yourself accomplishing the results you have envisioned, and then do the work to get there.

Along the way, by doing the study and practice you will demonstrate that you are giving away the very thing that you hope to gain. In your visualization, you already **are** the person who has the necessary knowledge, skills and capabilities. You practice **(do)** to generate the results you have already foreseen. Once you have done all that, you will reap the rewards, and **have** the results you desire.

This paradoxical process works like priming a pump. To get a water pump to begin pumping water through the lines, you have to siphon off the air in the lines to get the water moving in the right direction. Once you've primed the pump, it will continue to pump the water smoothly through the pipelines as long as it has power.

By giving away what you desire, you are priming the universe to pump more of what you desire *through you* into the world. So if you want more love in your life, you can prime the pump by **being** more loving to those people you encounter. The universe responds by pumping more love *to you,* and *through you* into the world. Instantly, you **have** more love in your life.

As you continue to prime the pump for a while, it will suddenly dawn on you. *Hey, I really am a loving person!* The evidence will be all around you. As you demonstrate more love to others, more loving people will be attracted to you, and their loving actions will wash over you and add to the love you experience. You are now both giving and receiving more love, which is just what you felt you needed in your life. Keep the pump primed, and it will faithfully reward you with more of what you desire.

A Peek Over the Summit

As mentioned way back in Chapter 1 of this book, the road to mastery offers a path to self-mastery as well. And one of the keys to self-development involves the cultivation of your own consciousness. The mastery process helps you every step of the way, culminating in the amazing self-control of the Master.

If you look at *your own* big picture, your self-development involves the expansion and refinement of who you are. As you move forward along the road to mastery you discover more of your limiting beliefs, along with the boundaries of your experience. With each advance you make, those boundaries fall, to be replaced by new limits that represent the extent of your current capabilities.

Amazingly, as you burst through each new limitation, *an even larger world of possibilities reveals itself.* As you expand the bubble of your experiences and capabilities, you become a *bigger person*: smarter, more skilled, with sharper reflexes, broader and deeper understanding, and greater wisdom. You will find yourself standing straighter and taller, smiling more often, with clear eyes, a steady gaze and a rosy glow. You can even become better looking!

Your confidence in yourself grows as you become secure in the knowledge that you can do more than you thought you could. With practice, you'll find yourself including that capability among the others you possess. *Exceeding your own capabilities becomes one of your capabilities!*

How do you know that you can exceed your own limits? Because you've already done it many times! You've been growing your capabilities since you were a baby.

Just follow the advice of *Yoda* in the *Star Wars* movies, and "trust the force." How could you ever go beyond your limits if there were no intelligence guiding you as you step into the unknown again and again? It is this larger, higher intelligence that mysteriously calls to you and draws you forward into your own personal mastery journey.

As you advance further along the road to mastery, you'll also be advancing the rest of civilization. Your personal mastery process not only inspires you, it lights the way for all of us. By moving up a stage in your mastery of whatever you choose to learn, your purpose grows to include more of who you are, and influences a broader group of people. Your consciousness also expands, reaching new heights of awareness, and new depths of compassion and service to others.

Our world urgently needs more evolved beings **like you** to lead and guide our way forward, out of the narrow-minded self-interest, greed and vengeance that seems to be so prevalent. Use this book as a compass to guide you in the direction that calls to you. If you have some doubts, or feel lost, then just like a compass, bring out this book, turn to the appropriate section and realign yourself to your personal *true north.*

As this book comes to an end, I invite you to share in a vision of your own expanded possibilities. Instead of putting this book away on a shelf somewhere to gather dust, try something different. When you close this book, let it open a door to a new depth of involvement in your own personal development. Begin a new expanded life with this simple exercise. Practice it often.

1. *Set the book aside, and sit in a comfortable, relaxed, upright position, with your eyes closed.*

2. *Relax your body slowly and easily, and slip into a contemplative or meditative state, where your internal dialog subsides.*

3. *Now think of the skill or subject area you would most like to master. In your imagination, see and feel yourself experiencing the very pinnacle of this mastery. Imagine putting the finishing touches on your masterpiece, or performing superbly, or presenting your greatest work to the world. Picture it in vivid detail. Feel all the emotions that accompany your triumphant event.*

4. *Continue with your vision. Replay it again. Allow the scene to evolve in your imagination, including results that are **even better** than the way you originally pictured it. Crank up your emotional involvement in the unfolding scene. Enjoy every moment of it. Take as long as you like.*

5. *When you are ready, return to the here and now. Bask in the glow of your achievement. Then go out and take the next step on your Road to Mastery. Your vision is calling you...*

Our deepest fear is not that we are inadequate.

Our deepest fear is that we are powerful beyond measure.

It is our light, not our darkness, that frightens us.

We ask ourselves, who am I to be brilliant, gorgeous, talented and fabulous?

Actually, who are you not to be?

You are a child of God.

Your playing small does not serve the world.

There's nothing enlightened about shrinking so that other people won't feel insecure around you.

We were born to make manifest the glory of God that is within us.

It's not just in some of us, it's in everyone.

And as we let our own light shine, we unconsciously give others permission to do the same.

As we are liberated from our own fears, our presence automatically liberates others.

— from Nelson Mandela's Inaugural Speech, 1994
Author Unknown

Index of Exercises

References to other works

"For me there is only the traveling on paths that have heart, on any path that may have heart. There I travel, and the only worthwhile challenge is to traverse its full length. And there I travel, looking, looking, breathlessly."

— *Don Juan*

(from Carlos Castaneda's book, **The Teachings of Don Juan**, above.)

Stages Chart:

Levels of Mastery	Music **Piano**	Athletics **Basketball**
Level 1: **NOVICE** Practice	Learn to play the individual notes and chords by heart. Study music notation and its translation to the piano keyboard. Play simple songs.	Learn the rules and theory of the game. Practice basic skills like dribbling, passing, shooting and man-to-man defense until it becomes automatic.
Level 2: **ADEPT** Craft	Put notes & chords together into songs. Play with both hands. Develop timing. Play moderately complex musical passages without errors.	Scrimmage. Learn position on the court, offensive & defensive plays, team tactics, and the overall flow of the game. Execute successful plays.
Level 3: **PRO** Science	Practice complete passages to be able to play them with perfect timing and timbre, eactly as written in the score, day in and day out.	Learn team strategies that lead to winning. Refine your skills and plays to produce consistent success. Optimize each player's strengths.
Level 4: **VIRTUOSO** Art	Lose yourself in the music, as your fingers dance over the ivories. Communicate the *soul* of the music as you develop your own unique style.	Get into the *flow* of the game, feeling each movement and play from the inside out. Smooth, easy efforts produce unstoppable results.
Level 5: **MASTER** Adventure	With tremendous dedication to your music, you pour all your efforts into a single magnificent performance that sets new standards.	Using your growing anticipatory awareness, you move with supernatural grace and power to take control of the game for your team.

Mastery of 5 Disciplines

Visual Arts **Drawing/Painting**	Trades **Culinary Arts**	Business **Management**
Learn to draw items that you see. Use gesture drawing, basic proportions, color & shading for true representations of real-life objects.	Learn basic food types, tastes and textures, knifework, cooking methods, measuring portions, following recipes, preparing dishes.	Learn the basic responsibilities of your group, the people, tasks, schedules, quality standards, documents, budget, procedures, reports.
Place objects into scenes. Learn to draw from various observer positions, use layering, light, perspective, shading, shadows, 3-D effects.	Combine color, flavor, texture & nutrition of various dishes to produce complete meals. Learn service, presentation, kitchen management.	Learn just how your group fits within the company & the limits of your influence. Develop techniques for handling various situations effectively.
Refine your drawing/painting techniques to quickly and easily create near photo-realistic scenes. Work on accuracy, detail and speed.	Put together a menu of complimentary meals with a theme. Refine recipes and procedures for consistency & quality of food and service.	Refine the workflow and polish your skills as a manager. Measure your group's progress in meeting company goals and standards. Optimize.
Express yourself! Use your skills to reveal new subtleties and emotion. Get into the *flow* of your artistic passions. Forge your own unique style.	Caress your tools into performing their magic, losing yourself in the process. Infuse your love of food into your dishes. Surprise and delight.	Use your intuition to guide you to new insights. Act on your inspirations with virve and conviction. Take the initiative and become a leader.
Your bold vision, intense focus, relentless dedication and playful attitude combine to forge a new masterpiece of artistic expression.	Using extraordinary skill and highly refined tastebuds, your intuitive guidance leads you to perfect an entirely whole new form of cuisine.	Refining your ability to communicate your vision and catalyze the people you lead, your organization sets new standards of accomplishment.

Process Chart:

Levels of Mastery	Objective	Process	Expected Results	
Level 1: **NOVICE** Practice	To learn the language, basic concepts and fundamental skills of the subject area by heart.	Study the rules, history, principles & terminology. Break activity into small component skills. Drill until it all becomes second nature.	Solid basic knowledge of your subject area and the ability to perform fundamental skills automatically.	
Level 2: **ADEPT** Craft	Develop deeper understanding of your field while combining your skills in ways that produce whole, complete, successful results.	Step back to see the big picture. Assemble ideas & information into understanding. Join skills into complete techniques.	To understand your field as a complete entity, and successfully craft a portfolio of quality products and/or techniques.	
Level 3: **PRO** Science	Integrate and refine your knowledge and skills to generate consistently excellent, winning results.	Practice effective techniques to build fluency. Expand repertoire and experiment to streamline your efforts. Combine theory & practice.	Comprehensive understanding of your field that incorporates success strategies. Ability to deliver reliable hi-quality performances.	
Level 4: **VIRTUOSO** Art	Develop your ability to *lose yourself* in your work. Move people with your vibrant passion.	Immerse yourself completely in your practice. Concentrate. Go with the *flow*, and allow intuition to guide you. Let go of fears.	Development of a uniquely artistic style that defines a niche in your field. Exquisite performance that inspires others. Leadership.	
Level 5: **MASTER** Adventure	To advance your field to a new higher level, while exploring your own ultimate potential.	Concentrate your efforts into a tight focus, honing in on your purpose. Follow your intuition into an anticipatory awareness. Use it.	A startling new discovery, creation or performance that constitutes a *masterpiece*.	

The Mastery Matrix

Action Steps	Problems	Debugs	Keys to Success
Immerse yourself in your new field. Build a solid base of core abilities. Study & practice diligently. Don't give up! Focus on content.	Overwhelmed by it all, confusion, lack of focus, struggle with unfamiliar tasks, impatience, little or no fun, discouragement.	Relax! Be curious & play with new material. Divide tasks into smaller steps. Keep at it. Seek assistance when needed. Build motivation.	Follow a proven approach to learning the basics. Cultivate mindfulness and patience. Join other Novices as co-learners.
Ask lots of "how" questions. Tinker with new combos of ideas or skills. Observe carefully. Discover what works. Use it. Focus on process.	Clumsiness, frustration, lack of discipline and confidence, decline in performance.	Slow down & feel each step. Be flexible. Back up & review. Surrender judgments. Investigate what others are doing, and borrow it.	Discuss the issues with others to forge relationships & understanding. Build discipline and confidence. Emulate Pros. Assist others.
Ask lots of "why" questions. Dissect your knowledge and skills to reconstruct better techniques and ideas. Focus on optimizing results.	Narrow-mindedness, arrogance, inconsistency, complacency, compulsiveness.	Remain open to new ideas & methods. Keep working hard. Renew your enthusiasm by exploring new related areas.	Practice strengths and shore up weaknesses. Build resource base. Devise winning strategies. Teach. Cultivate desire & perseverance.
Recognize and cultivate the feeling of *flow*. Practice it. Study the work of other Virtuosos and Masters. Develop your unique vision.	Overconfidence, feeling trapped, lingering fears.	Practice realistic assessments of every effort. Expand standards of excellence while broadening your horizons. Take chances.	Remove all distractions. Focus completely on the task at hand. Detach from the outcome and be courageous. Go for it! Lead, inspire.
Explore the limits of your field, peeking beyond, while in the *flow*. Look for links that unite info, ideas and efforts to your purpose.	Selfishness, lack of wisdom, misuse of power.	Recognize the source of your greatness by being grateful for your many gifts. Be spontaneous and playful.	Tighten your focus. Sharpen your purpose. Eat, drink and breathe your purpose, yet remain playful. Practice being grateful & daring.

Printed in the United States
84888LV00003B/262-294/A

9 781933 265315